Metric Conversion Table

	1/64	1/32	1/25	1/16	1/8	1/4	3/8	2/5	1/2	5/8	3/4	7/8	1	2	3	4	5	6	7	8	9	10	11	12	36	39.4
Inches (in.)	1/64	1/32	1/25	1/16	1/8	1/4	3/8	2/5	1/2	5/8	3/4	7/8	1	2	3	4	5	6	7	8	9	10	11	12	36	39.4
Feet (ft.)																								1	3	3¼†
Yards (yd.)																									1	1 1/10†
Millimeters* (mm)	0.40	0.79	1	1.59	3.18	6.35	9.53	10	12.7	15.9	19.1	22.2	25.4	50.8	76.2	101.6	127	152	178	203	229	254	279	305	914	1,000
Centimeters* (cm)							0.95	1	1.27	1.59	1.91	2.22	2.54	5.08	7.62	10.16	12.7	15.2	17.8	20.3	22.9	25.4	27.9	30.5	91.4	100
Meters* (m)																								.30	.91	1.00

To find the metric equivalent of quantities not in this table, add together the appropriate entries. For example, to convert 2⅝ inches to centimeters, add the figure given for the centimeter equivalent of 2 inches, 5.08, and the equivalent of ⅝ inch, 1.59, to obtain 6.67 centimeters.

* Metric values are rounded off.
†Approximate fractions.

Conversion Factors

To change:	Into:	Multiply by:
Inches	Millimeters	25.4
Inches	Centimeters	2.54
Feet	Meters	0.305
Yards	Meters	0.914
Miles	Kilometers	1.609
Square inches	Square centimeters	6.45
Square feet	Square meters	0.093
Square yards	Square meters	0.836
Cubic inches	Cubic centimeters	16.4
Cubic feet	Cubic meters	0.0283
Cubic yards	Cubic meters	0.765
Pints (U.S.)	Liters	0.473 (Imp. 0.568)
Quarts (U.S.)	Liters	0.946 (Imp. 1.136)
Gallons (U.S.)	Liters	3.785 (Imp. 4.546)
Ounces	Grams	28.4
Pounds	Kilograms	0.454
Tons	Metric tons	0.907

To change:	Into:	Multiply by:
Millimeters	Inches	0.039
Centimeters	Inches	0.394
Meters	Feet	3.28
Meters	Yards	1.09
Kilometers	Miles	0.621
Square centimeters	Square inches	0.155
Square meters	Square feet	10.8
Square meters	Square yards	1.2
Cubic centimeters	Cubic inches	0.061
Cubic meters	Cubic feet	35.3
Cubic meters	Cubic yards	1.31
Liters	Pints (U.S.)	2.114 (Imp. 1.76)
Liters	Quarts (U.S.)	1.057 (Imp. 0.88)
Liters	Gallons (U.S.)	0.264 (Imp. 0.22)
Grams	Ounces	0.035
Kilograms	Pounds	2.2
Metric tons	Tons	1.1

THE FAMILY
Handyman ®

Using Power Tools

THE FAMILY
Handyman ®

Using
Power Tools

Techniques and Tips for Getting the Most Out of Your Power Tools

THE READER'S DIGEST ASSOCIATION, INC.
Pleasantville, New York/Montreal

A READER'S DIGEST BOOK

Produced by Roundtable Press, Inc.
Directors: Susan E. Meyer, Marsha Melnick
Editor: William L. Broecker
Assistant Editor: Abigail A. Anderson
Design: Sisco & Evans, New York
Editorial Production: Steven Rosen

For The Family Handyman
Editor: Gary Havens
Executive Editor: Ken Collier
TFH Books Editor: Spike Carlsen

Library of Congress Cataloging in Publication Data
   The family handyman using power tools: techniques
and tips for getting the most out of your power tools.
                p.   cm.
      Includes index.
      ISBN 0-89577-982-X
      1. Power tools—Amateurs' manuals. 2. Power tools—Maintenance
and repair—Amateurs' manuals. I. Reader's Digest Association.
      II. Family handyman.
   TT153.5.F36   1997
   684'.083—dc21   97-3673
Reader's Digest and the Pegasus logo are registered trademarks of
The Reader's Digest Association, Inc.
The Family Handyman is a registered trademark of RD Publications, Inc.
Printed in the United States of America.

A Note from the Editor

Okay: you've got a headful of ideas and a basement full of construction materials, but neither will do you a bit of good until you have the tools and the skills to put them together. That's what this book is about: power tools and the best way of using them. Here you'll see how to get the most out of basic tools like circular saws, power drills, and belt sanders. You'll also learn how to use more specialized tools like hammer drills, biscuit joiners, radial arm saws, and lathes. Some are tools you may rent to complete a project. With this book you'll know how to make them work for you.

Here is bread-and-butter information, and dozens of time-saving tips, solutions to difficult problems, and tricks of the trade that pros have learned over the years. Want to make a $10 jig that will allow you to cut like you had a $1,000 table saw? Check out page 37. Want to turn everyday boards into classy moldings? Turn to page 94. On other pages you'll learn how to keep saw blades clean (use oven cleaner), sharpen chisels fast (use a belt sander), and turn your wet/dry vacuum into a dust collector.

Because we believe safe work is also good work, that is the focus of the first section; additional safety information is included throughout the book. And, just in case you need a few projects to hone your skills, we've included workbenches and sawhorses that will make your shop a better place to work.

All this information has been taken from the pages of *The Family Handyman Magazine,* which got its start right after World War II, just about the same time that mass-produced power tools became available to do-it-yourselfers. We've learned and grown with the market. This book is an additional way of passing on what we've learned to you.

Gary Havens
Editor
The Family Handyman

Using Power Tools

Shaping and Sanding

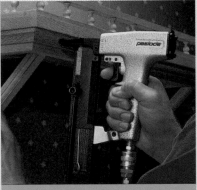

Fastening

Multipurpose Tools

Workplaces and Spaces

Introduction

Power tools are the delight of every home craftsman and do-it-your-selfer. This has been especially true in recent years, as power tools for home use have improved in quality, variety, and sophistication, at prices well within the budget of nonprofessionals and weekend workers. These modern tools make it easy to complete some of the most labor-intensive projects within the space of a weekend or two, and they put professional-level work within the grasp of those who have not devoted a lifetime to learning a craft.

You will find many familiar tools in this book: electric drills, jigsaws, circular saws among the smaller hand tools, table saws and drill presses among the larger ones. You will also find some less familiar tools, such as hammer drills and reciprocating saws, which most homeowners will never own but will have occasion to rent from time to time. Whether you rent or own them, you still need to know how to get the most out of every tool. That's what this book is all about.

Here you'll find a wealth of information about all these tools. You'll learn what features to look for when you're buying or renting a tool. You'll find plenty of advice about using large and small tools efficiently and safely. And, you'll learn a number of professional tricks of the trade for using and maintaining your tools.

This book also stresses how to use your power tools safely. The speed and force with which power tools operate can cause serious injury, if you are careless or use a tool improperly. The first section, Safety and Maintenance, shows you what you can do to protect your body when working with tools. The other sections contain specific safety precautions for each tool discussed. These, and especially the safety information in the tool manual or operating instructions, are extremely important. Follow them religiously. They make work easier as well as safer, and that in turn makes it fun to get excellent results.

Safety & Maintenance

Protect Your Eyesight

Flying debris, ricocheting nails, household chemicals—all these are potential hazards to your eyesight. Don't risk injury or blindness. Select the proper eyewear for your DIY work.

12

Protect Your Hearing

Power tools such as circular saws can be dangerously loud, and hearing damage is permanent. Choose the appropriate protection to prevent hearing loss as well as headaches.

14

Protect Your Breathing

The right mask or respirator will protect you from dust, vapors, and pollutants that can cause sore throats, coughing, headaches, and other sometimes lasting ailments.

16

Protect Your Body

Don't suffer needless back pain and sore knees, or contribute to carpal tunnel syndrome. Use the techniques and personal protective devices that professionals use to help minimize strain.

18

Using Extension Cords

When working with extension cords, choose the right one to make sure your equipment has enough power to run properly. The wrong cord might damage a tool or cause a fire.

20

Basic Repairs

Learn how to diagnose and treat a number of common tool troubles, like a damaged cord or a bad switch, without the hassle and expense of bringing the tool into the repair shop.

23

Protect Your Eyesight

Your eyes are a precious asset. Protect them every time you work, even on the simplest do-it-yourself project.

Nearly 1 million Americans are visually impaired or blinded due to eye injuries; 90 percent of these injuries could have been avoided with proper safety precautions and protective eyewear. The hazards fall into three broad categories.

▶ Saws, routers, shapers, and lathes throw sawdust and wood or metal chips into the air with great force and speed. Drills, power screwdrivers, sanders, and sharpening wheels throw off bits of material, grit, and sparks.

▶ Volatile liquids give off fumes whenever their containers are open and can spatter when being poured or applied. Adhesives give off fumes, too.

▶ Radiation hazards to eyesight are of two types. Extreme brightness can lead to momentary dazzling or partial blindness during which accidents can occur. And the intense infrared light emitted by welding and brazing operations can permanently damage the retina.

Kinds of Eye Protection

There are three basic kinds of vision-protecting devices: face shields, goggles, and safety glasses. All three kinds of protection must provide a physical barrier without impeding your vision. Acceptable protective lenses and frames will be stamped by the manufacturer to indicate they have passed safety tests. Frames will be stamped "Z 87.1." Most off-the-shelf safety goggles and glasses sold are polycarbonate, the most impact-resistant lens material.

Choose protective eyewear that's right for the job and comfortable to wear. (Unless it's comfortable, you'll be tempted to skip the protection—a dangerous trap.) Welding or brazing requires specially shaded eye protection rated for welding use to guard your eyes from the extreme brightness and infrared rays of these processes.

Selecting Protective Eyewear

To help you choose the eye protection that will best fit your needs, here's some information about the devices shown opposite.

Glasses

Ordinary eyeglasses do not offer adequate protection for most work. They are open at the top, bottom, and sides, and their lenses are not made of safety glass or plastic. In fact, everyday glasses can *cause* injury if shards from a broken lens fly into the eye. Only true safety glasses can offer working protection.

You can also get prescription safety glasses from eyewear stores. Those with polycarbonate lenses and side shields offer the best protection. The frames, available in plastic or metal, are more rugged than ordinary eyeglass frames.

Goggles

Goggles are close fitting and provide front, side, top, and bottom protection. Goggles with pliable sides are more comfortable to wear and provide a cushion against impact.

Full-face Shields

Face shields offer full-face protection and are ideal for blocking chips and shavings from lathes or routers. They have a brow band and one or two bands that pass over the top or around the back of the head.

Face shields don't offer good protection against heavy impact or objects that fly up or around their edges, so always wear safety glasses or goggles as well.

Glasses

Prescription safety glasses are ideal for those who need to wear glasses all the time. Side shields are essential.

Tinted lenses in safety glasses are especially good for outdoor work. Special tinting is required for welding or brazing.

Large slip-over frames like these permit wearing safety glasses over most styles of ordinary eyeglasses with large bows.

Goggles

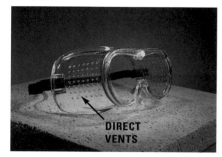

Direct vent goggles, which protect eyes from chips and large particles, provide air circulation through small holes.

Indirect vent goggles guard against liquid splashes and fine particles. Baffled vents provide air circulation.

Combined goggles and noise-reducing earmuffs provide two important types of protection in a single unit.

Full-face Shields

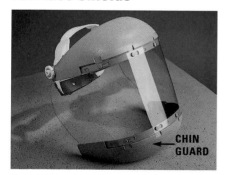

Face shields with a chin guard offer extra protection from flying debris.

Specially shaded lenses are a must for welding or brazing.

Wire mesh shields are well ventilated and good for outdoor work.

When to Wear Eye Protection

You should always wear eye protection when using power tools and whenever using hand tools in which force is involved: hammering, prying, splitting. Wear protection also when using household paints, especially when painting ceilings, and chemicals such as solvents, thinners, and cleansers. Wear indirect vent goggles when using, mixing, or pouring any chemical that emits fumes. And wear eye protection when cleaning up, whether you use a broom, a vacuum, or a damp rag. Eye protection is important during other jobs around the house, including these:

Lawn and garden work

Thousands of eye injuries occur when stones or sticks are hurled from mowers or when branches snap back during hedge trimming. Goggles offer the best eye protection for lawn and garden work. Always wear a face shield and glasses or goggles when using a chain saw.

Automotive work

Wear goggles to protect against a battery explosion when jump-starting a motor or working beneath a car, where grime can fall into your eyes. Also, protect your eyes when working with antifreeze, brake fluid, engine cleaners, and other volatile or caustic fluids.

Household paints and chemicals

Wear indirect vent goggles when using, mixing, or pouring oven cleaners, swimming pool chemicals, pesticides, and paint thinners.

Protect Your Hearing

Repeated exposure to noise from power tools can add up to hearing loss. By the time you notice it, the damage has been done. Here's how to protect yourself against noise hazards.

There are two basic types of hearing protectors: those worn in the ear, such as earplugs; and outside the ear, such as earmuffs. Choose a protector with a noise reduction rating (see table at right) that brings noise into the 85 decibel safe range. For example, a circular saw can scream at 110 db. So you need a hearing protector that will reduce it at least 25 db. Extremely loud situations may call for using both earmuffs and earplugs. Be sure to pick a hearing protector that is both comfortable and convenient, so you'll actually wear it.

When to Wear Protection

It's wise to wear hearing protection any time the noise level exceeds 85 db (see table). That's about the volume of an electric drill. Take special care to protect your hearing from the following noise sources:

Power tools. The high-pitched whine of a router or radial arm saw can be especially damaging. Cleaning up with some wet/dry vacuums can be painfully noisy.

Impact sounds. Hammering in a confined space, even with a small hammer, can be hazardous to your hearing. The crack and screech of pry bars during demolition can also be amazingly loud.

Outdoor equipment. Chain saws, lawn mowers, and string trimmers all call for

hearing protection. Hard hats with integral earmuffs and a face shield for eyesight protection are available for chain sawing and similar jobs.

Getting Used to Protection

At first, hearing protection may make you feel uncomfortable or out of touch with the sound of your tools. The whir and warning noises of your power tools will sound different, but after a while you'll relearn these sounds. In time, wearing hearing protection will become a habit and you will no more cut a board without your earmuffs on than drive your car without fastening your seat belt.

Use hearing protection even for short periods. Remember that hearing loss is cumulative; a lot of short working spurts without hearing protection can add up to hearing loss. Also remember to keep an extra set of earmuffs or plugs around for visitors or helpers.

Noise and Loudness

Noise is measured in decibels (db); the louder the noise, the higher the db rating. Most experts say 85 db is the safe maximum noise level for human ears. Devices for hearing protection are rated for their ability to block noise and reduce decibel levels. A device with a noise reduction rating (NRR) of 30 will reduce the noise reaching your ears by about 30 db.

Loudness levels	decibels	
Painfully loud	140 db	Gunshot at close range; jet engine
	130 db	Jackhammer
Extremely loud	120 db	Chain saw
	110 db	Circular saw; gas-powered mower
Very loud	100 db	Router; vacuum cleaner
	90 db	Drill press; truck traffic
Acceptable	80 db	Typewriter; electric razor
	60 db	Normal conversation

In-the-Ear Hearing Protectors

Plugs for in-the-ear use are inexpensive yet offer extremely good protection because they conform to the ear canal, blocking the sound path. Foam earplugs are twisted, then inserted in the ear, where they expand to block the ear canal. Flange plugs have two or more flanges that act as sound baffles. Be aware that both types block noise so well they can make conversation difficult.

Because these protectors go inside the ear, they pick up wax and oils and so are likely to attract dirt and sawdust when removed. They must be replaced or cleaned often. Also, some people simply don't like putting things inside their ears.

Foam earplugs are available with or without cords. Inexpensive and difficult to clean, they are considered disposable.

Flange earplugs are washable, reusable, and comfortable. They are available with or without cords.

Banded earplugs provide in-ear protection with the convenience of a headband. Pads swivel for comfort.

Outside-the-Ear Hearing Protectors

Earmuffs for outside-the-ear protection cost more than earplugs but last longer and are harder to misplace. Most earmuffs have a fixed level of sound blocking; noise-activated muffs—the most expensive type—increase their blocking or sound-canceling level as noise grows louder.

Almost all types of earmuffs permit conversation better than earplugs do. Because they are connected to a head-band, they can be looped down around the neck when not in use. Unlike earplugs, they do not risk carrying dirt into the ear canal, they block the infiltration of airborne sawdust and similar waste, and they physically protect the outer ear from flying debris.

Noise-activated earmuffs can be either battery operated or nonelectronic. They gradually increase the amount of hearing protection as noise levels rise, yet permit (or amplify) normal conversation.

Wrap-around earmuffs with a neck strap permit wearing a hard hat or helmet. Other versions have muffs that attach directly to protective headgear.

Foam ear caps are ideal for those who don't like using in-ear earplugs or larger muff-style hearing protection. Worn with a connecting band that passes under the chin, they are lightweight and easy to use.

Combination goggle-muffs combine hearing and sight protection in an easy-to-use unit.

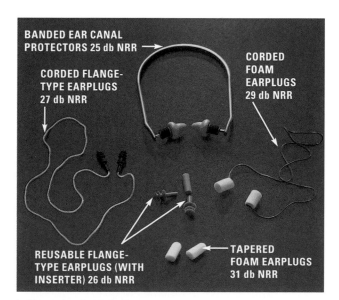

In-the-ear hearing protectors.

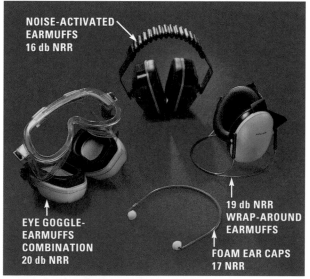

Outside-the-ear hearing protectors.

Protect Your Breathing

Dust, vapors, and mists may be invisible, but their effects on your nose, throat, and lungs can be very real. Use the proper protection to avoid potentially serious health problems.

Many do-it-yourself projects put you deep in clouds of dust, paint vapors, or other airborne pollutants. While this is rarely life threatening, you can easily inhale enough to cause throat irritations, headaches, coughing, and other temporary discomforts. Worse, repeated exposure can transform a minor reaction into a more serious condition. If you have allergies, you should be especially careful of what you breathe.

A workspace with good ventilation is the best defense against airborne pollutants. But you need a good second defense too—a mask or a respirator. There are various types of devices, each intended to protect against a specific pollutant. Following are some of the most common hazards and the protection available against them.

Pollutants and Protection

Most pollutants fall into one of three groups: (1) dusts and mists, (2) vapors and gases, (3) vapors and mists. Manufacturers make a variety of devices that give effective protection against each group. Here are their general uses.

Dusts and Mists

Small, solid, or liquid particles that float in the air can be easily trapped by a mesh filter mask. Pollutants of this sort include dust from sawing, sanding, working with insulation, and even using a leaf blower. A rising cloud of dust or mist is a sign you need this kind of mask, but often you can't see the smallest particles. You have to anticipate them and wear protection.

Vapors and Gases

Pollutants in this category are made up of particles that are too small to be trapped in a mesh. However, they can be absorbed by the chemical action of special charcoal filters called organic vapor filters.

Most harmful vapors and gases around the home come from solvents that evaporate from paints and strong cleaning agents like paint thinner. You can't see these pollutants, but you can usually smell them. If you do, immediately check the solvent container for a DANGER or other warning notice and read the instructions for proper handling. You must not breathe the vapors from any such substance. To avoid that, wear a special "organic vapor" respirator and maintain good ventilation in your work area.

Vapors and Mists

This category consists of pollutants made of both invisible vapors and a mist of liquid particles that may or may not be visible. The most common example is paint spray, whether from a power sprayer or a pressurized can. The proper respirator combines a mesh particle filter with an organic vapor filter.

You'll also need a combination mask to work with smoke from burning wood, leaves, paper, or tobacco. But no filter or cartridge will stop smoke's most dangerous component, carbon monoxide, so avoid smoke whenever possible.

Special canisters for this kind of filter are rated for use with pesticides, and others are rated for the toxic fumes from welding. Be sure to use the right kind.

Choosing and Buying a Respirator

The photos on the next page show some of the masks and respirators available. For assured safety, buy only a mask carrying the official test mark "NIOSH Approved" and a test number beginning with the letters TC. NIOSH stands for the National Institute for Occupational Safety and Health. The mask and filtration device will list the categories of pollutants for which it is approved: dusts, mists, vapors, fumes, gases, pesticides, paint mists, or others. This certifies that the mask or cartridge has been tested and meets official standards.

No matter how well the filter works, a respirator can do a good job only if it doesn't leak. Each time you put your mask on, make sure it seals tightly to your face.

Dust and Mist Masks

Simple, basic dust masks have a filter or mesh material to trap small particles of solid and liquid materials. All work well, but only if they fit well. They must seal tightly to your face and have two straps.

Mask 1 *(below left)* is the least expensive kind of disposable fabric mask. It is light, cool, and maintenance free. Mask 2 is also disposable, but it has a plastic frame with a fabric filter. It lasts longer, seals better, and is not affected by moisture. Silicone or rubber masks such as Mask 3 are more expensive. However, they use inexpensive replaceable filters, so they are a good investment. They seal best but are heavier and hotter than the other two types and need periodic cleaning.

Vapor and Gas Respirators

A mask with one or two chemical-action cartridges instead of a physical particle filter is called a respirator. The models shown *(below center)* have replaceable cartridges, which represent good value for long-term use. Extra organic vapor cartridges for the mask can be purchased.

When shopping for this kind of mask, be sure to choose one with a face piece made from rubber or silicone, which is able to conform to your face better than a molded plastic frame. Adjustable straps are also essential for getting a seal that is tight to your face. Do not settle for straps that are elastic but cannot also be easily and securely adjusted for length.

Vapor and Mist Respirators

This kind of breathing protector *(below right)* is a vapor and gas mask combined with an additional mist/dust filter. Like the best models of the other respirators, it has a silicone or rubber face piece and adjustable straps. The vapor canisters and the filters are replaceable. When used together, the canister and filter provide the only effective protection for applying paint by spraying.

With the proper canisters, you can also protect your respiratory system when working with pesticides or welding. For simpler jobs, you can use only the mist filter for dusty work, or only the organic vapor canister for protection from vapor and gas.

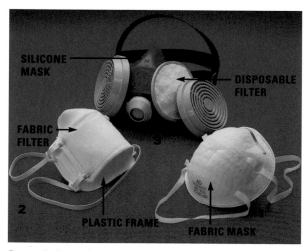

Dust and mist masks.

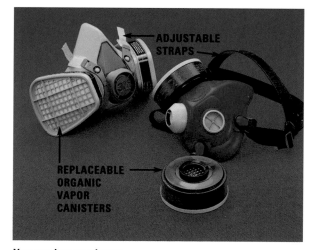

Vapor and gas respirators.

Vapor and mist respirators.

Protect Your Body

Heavy work and repetitive actions can take a toll on muscles, bones, and nerves. Use the proper devices to minimize the effects of physical stress.

There's no doubt about it: projects such as building a deck or shingling a roof can leave you exhausted and aching after a weekend of strenuous, repetitive work. But it doesn't have to be that way. There are simple protective devices that can minimize pain and potential injury and leave you feeling good at the end of a job.

First of all, it's important to stay fit and work smart. Exercise regularly and use proper body mechanics when lifting, carrying, climbing, or working with tools. Working hard can build muscle, but it can also lead to injury when done improperly or to excess. Work injuries and pains are often the result of "micro-injuries" that add up to cumulative trauma disorders (CTDs). Such injuries are caused by the sum total of thousands of hammer blows or hundreds of improper lifts. The personal protective devices discussed here can help prevent micro-injuries and CTDs by reducing the risk factors associated with repetition, stress, and vibration.

These devices are simple, but select and use them properly.

▶ Buy one that fits well. For example, antivibration gloves that are too small will cut off blood circulation; if they are too big, you will be forced to grip tools too tightly for comfort.

▶ Buy a device that is well designed. Materials should breathe or wick moisture away from the skin to lessen overheating and discomfort.

▶ Wear and use each device correctly. Common mistakes are wearing a back support too high, and wearing elbow supports *on* instead of *below* the elbow. Follow the directions given here and packaged with the device.

Back Supports

Ninety-five percent of all back injuries occur in the lower back. Back supports help prevent injuries in two ways: by stabilizing and supporting muscles in the lower back and by acting as a psychological reminder to use correct body mechanics while lifting.

Most support belts are secured in two stages. First, fasten the waistband snugly, with the upper edge about 1 inch below the navel. Then, just before you lift a heavy object, pull the outer elastic bands forward and tightly fasten them to lend added support. Loosen the outer bands when not lifting.

When selecting a back support, choose one made of breathable material to prevent overheating. Those that dip slightly in the back lend extra support. The suspenders found on many models don't add support but do help you quickly and correctly position the belt before tightening the outer bands and lifting.

Back supports promote proper body posture and lifting position while helping support the muscles of the back.

Elbow Bands

Whether it's the result of too much drilling, too much painting, or too much hammering, elbow pain is quite common during or after prolonged activity. The pain is usually located where the tendon connects the forearm muscle to the joint. The elbow is a small joint that absorbs a large amount of strain and movement.

Elbow bands apply pressure to the forearm muscle before the strain of your labor can reach the elbow. They fool the arm into thinking the connection point is at the elbow band rather than the joint. This takes strain off the elbow and, in many cases, instantly provides relief while you work.

The proper position for an elbow band is two to three finger widths below the elbow. Proper tightness is "comfortably snug"—not so tight as to reduce circulation, but tight enough to relieve tension at the elbow.

Elbow bands move the pressure point away from the elbow, farther down onto the forearm.

Wrist Supports

Wrist pain can plague everyone from meat cutters to computer operators to do-it-yourselfers. Failure to heed the early warning signs of numbness and pain can eventually lead to carpal tunnel syndrome. This serious injury is created when the nerve traveling through the carpal tunnel in the wrist becomes compressed, causing loss of feeling in parts of fingers or entire fingers. The nerve compression is often caused by repetitive wrist movements. Such movements need not be high impact; activities as seemingly tame as painting or pushing a sanding block rapidly back and forth can, as a result of thousands of small repetitive movements, damage the nerve. Wrist supports limit wrist movement and help hold it in a neutral position, thus lessening the chance of this kind of injury.

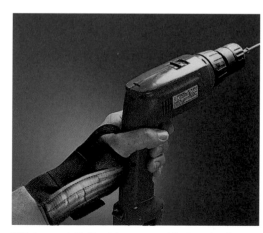

Wrist supports limit wrist movement that can lead to tendinitis, carpal tunnel syndrome, and other injuries.

Antivibration Gloves

Long-term or intense vibration can break down the small blood-carrying capillaries in the hand, resulting in tingling or numbness. Antivibration or impact gloves cushion hands against shock by absorbing vibration and turning it into a small amount of heat. Half-fingered gloves are adequate for light-duty tasks like hammering or lawn mowing. Use full-fingered gloves for tasks like chain-sawing or jack-hammering.

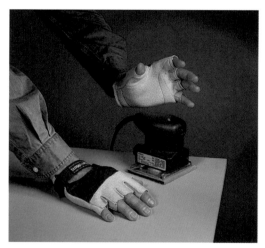

Antivibration and impact gloves convert harmful vibrations into heat. Use long-fingered gloves for heavy-duty work.

Knee Pads

Knee pads supply the cushion nature forgot, and reduce injuries and stress from contact with hard surfaces. They spread the pressure normally concentrated on a small area of the knee cap to a larger portion of the knee for protection and comfort when kneeling.

Using Extension Cords

It's senseless to spend hundreds of dollars on a good tool only to risk ruining it by using the wrong extension cord. Here's how to select and maintain the proper cord.

Whether you're working on a fence in the yard, repairing a dormer on the roof, building a deck, or working far from an outlet inside the house, you need your power tools, and you need them working at full efficiency.

But sometimes that's not what happens. Instead, your powerful circular saw strains and overheats, bogging down as if the blade could hardly cut balsa wood. Or your electric drill runs slower and slower as the hole gets deeper, grinding and growling in protest against the load.

Usually, the tools aren't the difficulty; they're simply not getting enough electricity, because the extension cord is too small or damaged.

The right size cord, in good repair, delivers enough electric current for your tool to run at full power. A cord that is too small or has partially broken wires resists the flow of electricity, delivering too little and generating a good deal of heat. It can create a fire hazard or even destroy a tool. Small, cheap extension cords are actually an expensive waste of money, not a bargain.

Types of Extension Cords

Extension cords are rated for indoor or indoor/outdoor use. Indoor/outdoor cords are heavier duty with better insulated wires, plugs, and receptacles. Their inner wires are individually insulated, then wrapped in an outer jacket. They are almost always round and bear the designation "W-A." Flat cords are rarely rated for outdoor use; that makes them less useful and a poorer investment.

Four cords with unique features are shown on the opposite page. Those with a built-in circuit breaker or with a GFCI (ground fault circuit interrupter) outlet provide maximum safety and protection. A retractable cord is often a great convenience where working space is limited. A triple-outlet cord avoids repeated plugging and unplugging when you need to switch among tools or are working with a helper. But you can't run two tools at the same time if their combined load exceeds the cord's capacity.

If your tool has a grounding plug—one with a round prong in addition to the two flat blades—the extension cord and wall outlet must also have matching connections. Never plug a three-prong adapter into a two-prong cord to run power to a tool.

Newer extension cords and tools are "polarized," with one plug blade wider than the other; connect them only to outlets with matching wide and narrow slots.

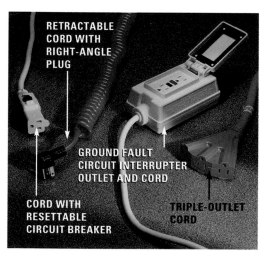

Four types of extension cords.

Selecting the Right Cord

Extension cords come in a variety of wire sizes called "gauges." The lower the gauge number, the larger the wire and its current-carrying capacity. Put another way, heavier-duty cords have larger—lower gauge number—wires. The most common are 18-, 16-, 14-, 12-, and 10-gauge.

To determine the right gauge extension cord, look on the metal plate on the tool for its electrical load factor, listed in either amps or watts. Then consult the table below to find what size wires a 25-, 50-, or 100-foot extension cord should have. Most tool instruction manuals also give guidelines. You can use a heavier-duty cord (lower gauge number) than the one listed, but not a lighter one. Invest in good, heavy-duty cords with three-prong plugs and receptacles. You'll pay a bit more, but they can be used in more situations and will help your tools perform as they should.

Using Extension Cords

Never use an extension cord for permanent wiring. It's illegal and a fire hazard to conceal one in a wall or ceiling, or nail it in place. Also:

▶ Unplug extension cords when not in use.
▶ Don't use a cord that is hot to the touch; it's a sign that the cord is overloaded.
▶ Don't use a cord with cracked insulation, plug, or receptacle. Make repairs as shown in the box on page 22.
▶ Always uncoil a cord fully before using it. A coiled cord generates heat.
▶ Don't let cords or connections sit in wet areas or outside for extended periods. Sunlight can make the outer jacket brittle; oil and grease can soften or degrade it.
▶ Use duct tape to cover and hold down a cord that crosses a foot traffic path so people can't trip on it.

Selecting Extension Cord Gauge

These are general use guidelines. To be sure, consult the tool's manual for recommended sizes and especially for limitations on cord length.

	Load Listed on Tool Nameplate in Amps (A) or Watts (W)				
	0–5A Up to 600W	5–8A Up to 960W	8–12A Up to 1440W	12–15A Up to 1800W	15–20A Up to 2400W
	Fan, Hedge trimmer	Wood trimmer, Small drill	Router, Circular saw	Drill press, Shop vacuum	Table saw, Air compressor
Proper Cord Gauge					
25- or 50-ft. Cord	18	16	14	12	10
100-ft. Cord	16	14	12	10	Not recommended

Repairing Extension Cords

A cord with broken insulation, plug, or receptacle, or one that has been accidentally cut must be repaired. Never splice an extension cord that has been damaged in the middle. Instead, cut it in two and create two shorter cords by installing a new plug or receptacle. You can purchase these fittings in different amperage ratings, with or without ground prongs. Always buy fittings that are compatible with your cord. Take it with you to the store to make sure. Then install fittings as follows, referring to the numbered pictures:

1. Loosen the assembly screws and separate the fitting into its two parts. Cut the cord end cleanly with a wire cutter. Use a sharp utility knife to remove a short section of the outer jacket. Use the "stripping gauge" molded into the new fitting or look in the instructions to determine how much of the jacket to remove.

2. Use a wire stripper and the stripping gauge to remove the insulation from the two or three wires inside the cord.

3. Slide the back portion of the fitting onto the cord, then slide the wires through the opening of the front portion. Connect the wires to the proper screws: black (hot) wire to brass screw, white (neutral) wire to silver screw, green (ground) wire to green screw.

Screw the two halves of the fitting together, then tighten the saddle clamp onto the cord. This clamp must grip the cord jacket tightly to reduce strain on the connections inside the new plug or receptacle.

1 JACKET AND WIRE STRIP GAUGE

2 WIRE STRIPPER

3 SADDLE CLAMP / CONNECTOR SCREW

Handling Cords

Connect tool and extension cords with a loose square knot or a cord connector *(top right)* to prevent accidental unplugging. Remember to always unplug tools and cords by pulling on the plug or receptacle, not on the cord itself.

Unroll new extension cords and let them "relax" for a while. When you coil them, give a half-twist with the fingers of one hand as you add each loop to the other hand *(bottom right)*. This will prevent tangles and make the cord easier to unroll later. Tie a small length of rope or a shoelace on one end and use that to secure a coiled cord.

Keep a long cord in a bucket for easy use and storage *(below),* but remember to uncoil it before plugging in. A coiled cord generates heat. Hang other cords where they won't get walked on or driven over. The legs of ladders and sawhorses, and the wheels of tools, vacuum cleaners, and heavy toys can weaken or break the wire strands in the cord.

Extension cord bucket.

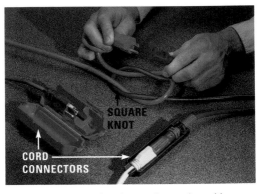

SQUARE KNOT / **CORD CONNECTORS**

Prevent cord pull-out by tying cords together with a loose square knot or by using a simple connector sold at most home centers.

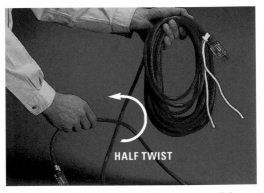

HALF TWIST

Give cords a half-twist with each loop as you coil them up to prevent tangles and "figure-eights." Short rope secures loops after coiling.

Basic Power Tool Repairs

When a power tool misbehaves or simply won't run, your big project screeches to a halt. Here are do-it-yourself tool repairs to get you going again—and save money as well.

Power tools may be powerful, but not invincible. Parts wear, switches break, motors run sluggishly, drill bits wobble—these problems are facts of do-it-yourself life. But there are DIY repairs you can make quickly and cheaply. Problem diagnosis and repair basics are covered on this page; specific fixes are explained on pages 24–25.

Diagnosing What's Wrong

Here are a few ways to determine what the cause of a tool problem may be:

The tool doesn't run. If the tool starts only when you wiggle the cord or hold it in just the right position, there's most likely a separated or broken wire; you'll have to replace the cord.

If the tool starts momentarily when you tap it with a rubber mallet with the trigger "On," the motor brushes probably need replacing.

The tool runs intermittently. This could be a bad cord. But if the tool starts for an instant then quits, or if it won't turn off, a bad switch is likely. If you see excessive sparking through the air vent holes, the brushes should be replaced, or dirt cleaned out of their holders.

The tool sounds or smells weird. A tool that "squeals" when it starts and stops probably has a bad bearing. A constant rough, "grinding" sound usually indicates a bad gear. A smell of burning rubber means the motor is seriously damaged. All of these problems should be repaired by pros.

Drill bits slip, wobble, or bore enlarged holes. The drill chuck needs replacing. This is a good excuse to change from a standard "keyed" chuck to a "keyless" chuck, which is both easier and more convenient to use.

Repair Basics

Always unplug a tool before opening it. Take an instant picture of the opened tool, make a sketch, or label all wires and parts, so you know where they go during reassembly. Failure to do so could be hazardous.

▶ Use replacement parts made specifically for the tool you're repairing. Get parts from the manufacturer's local service center (look in the Yellow Pages under "Tools, Electric, Repairs"). If the old cord has a ground wire, replace it with a similar, three-wire cord.

▶ When replacing parts with "stab-in" electrical connectors, first "tin"—stiffen—the ends of the stranded wires. Lay the bare wire end on a soldering gun or iron and touch solder to the heated wire. The solder will jell the strands into a single, solid wire that is easier to "stab" into the connector holes.

▶ Torx, hex, straight, and Phillips head screws are all used to hold tools together. Use the right tool—and penetrating oil as necessary—to remove stubborn screws.

▶ When replacing a screw, especially one that threads into the plastic housing of a tool, turn the screw to the left until it "drops" into place, then to the right to tighten it.

▶ A rule of thumb for motor brushes is to replace them when they're worn down to half their original length—if you know what that was. If not, take the old brushes to a service center to compare with new ones. Brushes come in hundreds of shapes, sizes, and compositions, and replacements must match exactly. Always replace brushes in pairs.

NEW BRUSH

WORN BRUSH

Replacing Motor Brushes

Brushes are carbon contacts that deliver electricity to the rotating part of the motor. They are pushed against the rotor by spiral or leaf springs, and eventually wear down too short to be useful *(left)*.

Brushes are sometimes accessed from outside the tool by removing a brush cap on each side *(below)*. But often you will have to open your tool by removing the screws that hold the two halves of the handle or casing together. When you have the brushes, your only tasks are finding exactly matching replacements and installing them.

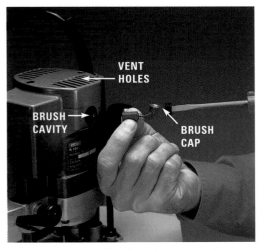

VENT HOLES

BRUSH CAVITY

BRUSH CAP

Brush caps on either side of a tool motor make it easy to change worn old brushes, which get too short to make good electrical contact. Install exact replacements or the tool won't work properly.

Replacing a Bad Switch

Open the tool as described for replacing a motor brush. Diagram the route wires take through the handle to the switch. Then lift the switch out so you can get at the wire connections; they may be made by small screws or by a clamp.

Remove all the wires connected to the switch. There will be two or at most three wires to a simple on-off switch, but more if the tool has variable speed or reverse features. When possible, move wires directly from the old switch to the new, as shown below.

Otherwise, label each wire with a letter or number so you know exactly which wire goes where when you install the new switch. Replace and secure the switch, routing the wires in the handle as before. Reassemble the tool case, making sure no wires are crimped or pinched.

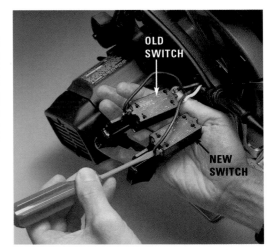

OLD SWITCH

NEW SWITCH

Connect new switch wires one at a time to avoid errors.

Replacing a Damaged Cord

Open the tool, diagram the path of the cord wires, and disconnect them from the switch.

To release wires secured with "stab-in" connectors, push a dart tip or paper clip into the opening the wire fits into *(below)*.

Before stabbing in the wire leads of the new cord, "tin" the stranded wire ends as described in Repair Basics, page 23, and shown in the bottom photo.

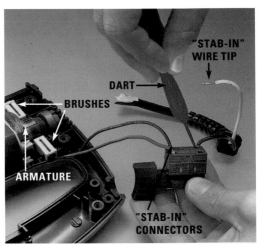

"STAB-IN" WIRE TIP

DART

BRUSHES

ARMATURE

"STAB-IN" CONNECTORS

Release wires from stab-in connectors by inserting a dart, thin nail, or straightened paper clip.

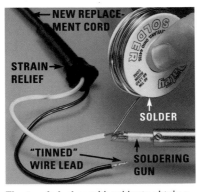

NEW REPLACE-MENT CORD

STRAIN RELIEF

SOLDER

"TINNED" WIRE LEAD

SOLDERING GUN

Tin stranded wires with solder to obtain a stiff end to insert into a stab-in connector.

Replacing a Drill Chuck

Open the jaws of the chuck fully and use a hex wrench or screwdriver to remove the screw at the bottom that secures the chuck to the drill *(Photo 1)*. The screw is "left hand" or reverse threaded, so you must turn the wrench or screwdriver clockwise to remove it, just the opposite of a usual screw.

Next, place the key in the chuck and give it a rap with a rubber mallet or ball peen hammer *(Photo 2)* so the chuck loosens and spins, this time in the usual counterclockwise unscrewing direction.

Screw the new chuck tightly onto the threaded shaft *(Photo 3)*. A keyless chuck is a great working convenience. When it is in place, insert the reverse-threaded screw and turn it counterclockwise (to the left) to tighten it.

Preventive Maintenance

Here are a few things to remember in the future to make sure your tool keeps running well now that you've fixed it:

▶ The best way to ensure a tool's longevity is to make sure it operates coolly. Use an air compressor or a wet/dry vacuum cleaner frequently to remove sawdust and dirt from the air vent holes. Use sharp saw blades, drill bits, and sanding belts so the tool isn't overworked and generating damaging heat.

▶ Avoid tying knots in power cords or raising and lowering tools by their cords when you're working in high places. Use a properly sized extension cord (see pages 20–22) to deliver full power to the tool, so it can operate without strain.

▶ Most power tools today require little or no internal lubrication. You can help drill chucks operate longer and smoother by spraying them with a nonsticky or Teflon-based lubricant. Teflon lubricant also makes it easier to adjust angle, depth, and other settings on circular saws, table and scroll saws, routers, and similar tools.

▶ When in doubt, take the tool to a factory-authorized service center or specialty repair shop where experienced people have the tools and know-how to correct difficult problems.

REPLACING A DRILL CHUCK

1

Remove the drill-chuck retaining screw. It has a reverse thread, so turn the wrench or screwdriver *clockwise* to remove it.

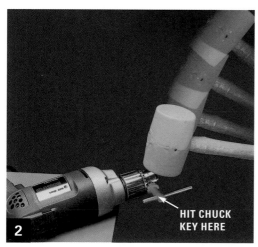

2

Hit the chuck key with a mallet to spin the chuck *counterclockwise* in order to loosen and unscrew it from the drill shaft.

3

Screw the new chuck, keyed or keyless, onto the shaft. When tight, replace the reverse-threaded screw that secures it.

Sawing

Jigsaws

Jigsaws are not just for curves; they also cut holes, compound angles, and straight lines through wood, metal, plastic, or tile. They're also good for those who shy away from circular saws.

28

Circular Saws

Circular saws are the workhorse tools that you can use to make smooth, accurate straight cuts. They're powerful and fast-cutting, so it's important to learn how to use them safely.

32

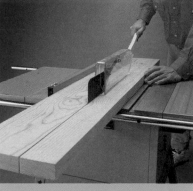

Table Saws

Table saws can do more than just rip and crosscut. Once you know how, you can use your table saw to cut tapers, raise panels, bevel edges, produce many identical pieces, and more.

45

Radial Arm Saws

Radial arm saws can cut like table saws, miter boxes, or circular saws, but can't do everything equally well. Get the best results by knowing the saw's strengths and weaknesses.

58

Power Miter Saws

Power miter saws are great for cutting trim, accurate miters, and precise square cutoffs. Use them right, and you'll get silky smooth cuts and perfect 90- and 45-degree angles.

61

Band Saws

Band saws are the best at cutting curves quickly and smoothly. You can also make thin slices of veneer, saw precise "dead end" cuts, and even produce tricky angled curves with ease.

64

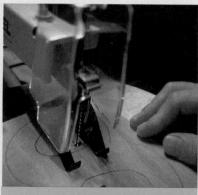

Scroll Saws

Scroll saws are fun to use even if you're not an experienced woodworker. They're fairly safe power tools to operate, and you can make toy parts, or cut molding decorations, with ease.

66

Reciprocating Saws

If you're doing renovation work, the reciprocating saw is a tool you'll want. This fast, maneuverable brute can cut almost anywhere, more quickly and safely than other power saws.

70

Jigsaws

Versatile, portable, and affordable—
a jigsaw is an indispensable tool
for the do-it-yourselfer.

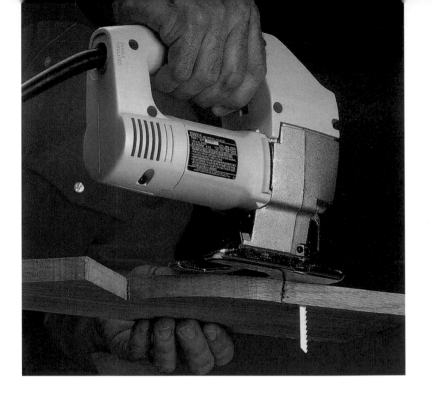

A hand-held jigsaw and an electric drill should be the first two power tools in every home toolkit. A jigsaw, also called a saber saw, not only excels at cutting curves but can cut holes, compound angles, and straight lines (using a guide). It can cut through wood, metal, plastic, ceramic tile, leather, and vinyl. It can handle a range of work, from intricate trim to coarse remodeling.

A jigsaw cuts slowly, but that's a bonus when it comes to safety and cleanup. For a small tool, it is amazingly useful; the longer you own one, the more uses you will discover for it.

Features and Accessories

Jigsaws range in price from $30 to more than $300. One big difference between a cheap saw and an expensive one is the accuracy and rigidity of the blade guide. That's a small roller or mechanism that helps support the blade near the base of the saw. A well-constructed guide will help keep your blade perpendicular to the workpiece, let it follow the line of your cut more accurately, and minimize blade breakage.

The following are some other jigsaw features to consider:

Stroke length. This refers to how far up and down the blade travels. A saw with a 1-inch stroke will cut faster and use more of the blade (giving you more for your blade dollar) than one with a 1/2-inch stroke.

Orbital action. This thrusts the blade forward at an angle as it moves up to cut into the material, and then slightly back, out of the cut on the downstroke. Orbital action greatly increases the speed of cutting and is ideal for rough cuts.

Variable speed. This usually ranges from about 500 to 3,000 strokes per minute. This feature is handy when working with different densities of wood and other materials.

Tilt base. This feature allows you to adjust the base shoe left and right for angle-cutting up to 45 degrees.

Blower. Many jigsaws have a blower tube that directs air from the motor across the blade to keep the cutting line free of sawdust.

Flush-cutting adapter. This blade-mounting accessory extends the blade so its cutting edge is at the very front of the shoe (instead of being set back an inch or so as in normal mounting). This lets you cut right up flush to a wall or a piece attached at right angles to the end of your workpiece. Often, a special flush-cutting blade is easier to use instead (see Other Kinds of Blades, page 30).

Cutting guides. Two accessories attach to the front of the shoe to help guide cuts. They can be mounted at an adjustable distance on either the left or right side. A *circle cutting guide* has a point that you place at the center of the circle to be cut *(below);* the saw is mounted on the attached guide bar, which pivots around the center point as the cut progresses.

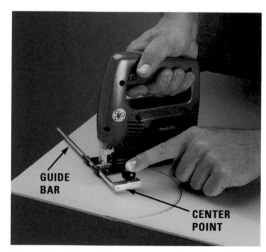

Cut perfect circles with an accessory circular guide. The center point digs into the work surface and acts as a pivot. The jigsaw can be secured along the guide bar to create different radiuses.

A *straight guide* has a "finger" at the end of the guide bar that hooks over the outside edge of the piece being cut. Keeping it tight against the edge of the workpiece guides the saw blade along a parallel line. However, it often is easier—and necessary with a wide piece or one without a straight outside edge—to clamp or tack a straightedge to the work and run the side of the jigsaw's shoe against it as you make the cut.

Blades for Your Jigsaw

Almost all jigsaws use blades of a universal design. The tang of the blade fits into a slot in the vertically traveling motor shaft and is secured with setscrews. Blades are interchangeable among most saws; however, Bosch and Porter-Cable jigsaws require specially designed blades.

A jigsaw will cut only as effectively as the blade that's in it. What gives a jigsaw its great versatility is the wide variety of blades available for different materials and kinds of jobs. Most blades have the teeth pointing upward, because cutting is normally done on the upstroke. However, blades with downward-pointing teeth *(right)* are available for cutting surfaces that might chip or splinter.

Most blade manufacturers label their blades according to "best use," so follow their guidelines.

Wood-Cutting Blades

Probably 90 percent of the work you do with a jigsaw will be with wood. When selecting a wood-cutting blade, keep in mind the following:

▶ The radius of the curve affects how wide the blade should be. Blades 3/16-inch wide can cut tighter circles than ones 3/8-inch wide, but they also break more easily.
▶ The smoothness and speed of the cut you need will determine how many teeth the blade should have. One with ten teeth per inch will produce a smoother, slower cut than a coarser-cutting blade with six teeth per inch.
▶ The thickness and hardness of the wood will influence your choice of blade. Cutting a curve in 1-1/2-inch-thick oak will require a thick, coarse blade.

Cut plastic laminate, vinyl, and veneer with a blade that has fine, downward-angled teeth *(detail, upper right).* The downstroke cutting action will produce the smoothest results. Upward-cutting blades are more efficient for other materials.

TOOL TIP

Jigsaw blades are not expensive. Replace them at the first sign of dulling or bending from rough use. For economy, buy blades in packs rather than individually. Get a couple of assorted packs, to have a variety of blades on hand, and two or three packs of the kind you use most, so you won't run out in the middle of a project.

Other Kinds of Blades

In addition to wood-cutting blades, a great many specialty blades are available.

Knife blades (sharp edged, with no teeth) can cut leather, rubber, cardboard, and other materials.

Metal-cutting blades can cut soft steel, aluminum and other metals, and pipe up to 1/4 inch thick.

Flush-cutting blades extend forward enough to cut right up to another surface. Their extra width limits them to only straight cuts.

A flush-cutting blade extends in front of the shoe and the body of the jigsaw. For strength it is thicker as well as wider than normal blades.

Carbide-grit blades can cut really hard materials: ceramic tile, slate, fiberglass, stainless steel, and even brick.

Remodeling-type blades are sturdy enough to cut through wood and nails.

A carbide-grit blade can cut curves and inside corners as well as straight lines in ceramic tile. Other specialty blades cut metals, laminates, plastics, and fiberglass.

Heavy-duty remodeling-type blades are specially designed to cut through nail-embedded wood, which you are sure to find when doing remodeling or demolition work.

Cutting Techniques

In addition to choosing the correct blade, you must use the proper cutting technique to get the best results with a jigsaw. Here are the basic techniques to follow:

▶ Always start with the shoe of the jigsaw resting firmly on the workpiece and the workpiece clamped or held firmly in place.

▶ Make sure you have plenty of clearance for your blade below the project.

▶ Make relief cuts *(below)* and complete your cutout in several small passes rather than one long, continuous cut. This will allow your blade to "corner" easier and let you approach the piece from different directions.

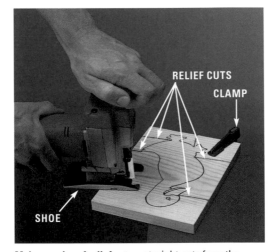

Make a series of relief cuts—straight cuts from the edges of the workpiece in to the outline of the shape to be cut. This makes it easier to negotiate sharp inside and outside curves and turns that might otherwise bind or break the blade.

► Because of the saw's up-and-down action, jigsaw blades tend to splinter thin veneer plywoods. Prevent this by using an antisplintering accessory (usually a clear plastic plate that's mounted on the shoe and closely hugs the blade) or by sandwiching your workpiece between two layers of scrap plywood.

► When precision is important, cut just to the outside of your mark, then sand to the line by hand or with a power sander. Even the finest blades leave a bit of a rough edge; leave yourself some room for sanding.

► Clamp or hold moldings firmly to make coped cuts *(below)*. Use a thin, fine-tooth blade and make relief cuts as needed.

► Make cuts in the center of boards by drilling a small starter hole or by making a plunge cut as shown below.

Jigsaw blades tend to wander. While you may be following your line on the surface, the blade below may be angling inward or outward. This is especially a problem when making turns in thick woods or when using the orbital action found on some saws. Minimize wander by using a blade stout enough for the job and making relief cuts so your blade can get back on track as necessary.

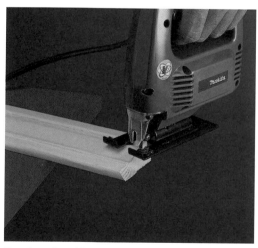

Coped cuts in moldings are fast and easy to make with a jigsaw. Use a thin, fine-tooth blade and make relief cuts to avoid sharp turns. Be sure to clamp or support the molding firmly as close to the cut as possible.

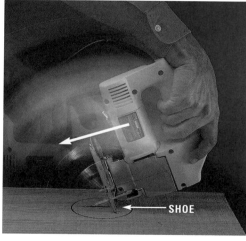

Make a plunge cut to start in the middle of a workpiece. Put the front of the shoe on the work as shown, start the saw, and lower the blade slowly and firmly into the wood.

Pro Working Tips

SHEET METAL

Cut Curves in Metal

Cut curves in metal with a jigsaw and a fine-tooth metal-cutting blade. Sheet metal will jump around a lot because of the action of the saw, so sandwich it between two pieces of scrap wood.

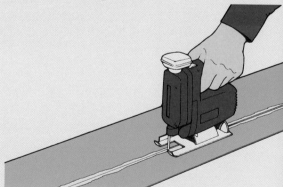

Make Straight-line Cuts in Aluminum

Make straight-line cuts in aluminum or other soft metal by laying down a line of light oil along the line of the cut. It will prevent the teeth from clogging, keep the blade cooler, and reduce vibration.

Circular Saws

For smooth, accurate cuts of both framing and finish lumber use a circular saw. Portability and a wide variety of blades make it a carpenter's workhorse.

You'll be impressed the first time you buzz through a 2 x 6 with a circular saw. It's as easy as cutting butter with a hot knife, and just about as fast, too. You'll be equally impressed when you see how easy it is to cut construction-grade lumber to size one moment and make precise, controlled cuts of finish panels and trim the next, often with the same blade.

What makes all this even better is that you can do these things where you are working. There's no need to carry lumber to the basement or garage, make measurements at the work site, go back to cut the pieces, and then carry them to the job. Instead you can do it all on the spot,

where it is easiest to measure twice before cutting once and to put each piece in place immediately. In addition to the convenience, having your saw at the job site can reduce project time by at least a third.

The next several pages show you how to use a circular saw for many different projects. They stress how to use the saw safely while exploiting its versatility. And they give you lots of tips and special techniques for getting the best results in all your work.

Choosing a Circular Saw

There are many different models of circular saws, from dozens of manufacturers, with a variety of features. Here's what you should look for and get.

Size. Saws are usually identified by the diameter of the blade they use. For do-it-yourselfers the smallest practical size is 5-1/2 or 6 inches. However, because blade size determines the maximum depth of cut, a saw that takes a 7-1/4-inch blade is far more useful and costs about the same. (Larger sizes—8-1/4, 10-1/4, and even 16 inches—are professional-grade saws necessary only for day-in and day-out construction or landscaping work.)

Motor position. In most circular saws the motor sits crosswise and the blade mounts directly on the motor shaft *(opposite page)*. Worm-drive saws (page 35) mount the motor body parallel to the cut. The blade is driven by a geared shaft. This design permits a slightly narrower body and a balance that is preferred by some. Either type is equally versatile and useful. In both types the blade is usually on the right side; however, some models have the blade on the left, providing right-handers better visibility when cutting (see page 35).

Blade guard. The blade protrudes down through a foot plate, or shoe, and is protected by a retractable blade guard; this is an essential safety feature. Buy a saw with a substantial spring that pulls the guard over the blade as it clears the workpiece. The shoe rests flat on the workpiece and slides over the surface as the saw is pushed forward to make a cut.

Depth and tilt adjustments. The depth of cut is set by raising or lowering the saw body to adjust how far the blade extends below the shoe. Make sure the adjustment lever or knob is large and easy to get at and has a positive locking action. Look for the same feature on the tilt control, which lets you tilt the body and blade left or right to make bevel cuts up to 45° or so. Positive stops of 45° and 90° are helpful in setting the blade at the most-used positions quickly and accurately. Be sure to use this feature. Trying to make bevel cuts by holding a saw up at an angle is definitely not a safe technique.

Braking. Electric or electromagnetic braking is a valuable safety feature. It stops the blade within seconds when you release the trigger switch. Even though there is a blade guard and the power is off, a freely spinning blade is a potential hazard in a saw without braking.

Blade lock. A feature variously called a motor, blade, spindle, or shaft lock is a convenience but not a necessity. It keeps the blade from turning as you undo its retaining bolt when you change blades. If the saw does not have one, you can dig the blade teeth into a piece of scrap wood or stick a large nail through a hole in the blade and turn it until the nail is against the shoe.

Getting Ready to Work

First, read the instruction manual supplied with your saw. The directions here apply to all circular saws, but there may be special procedures with your particular model.

Mount a Blade

With the saw unplugged, bolt on a sharp blade. Blades are discussed in detail on pages 42–44. In general, you can do most everything with just three blades:
▶ An 18–24 tooth combination blade for both ripping and cross cutting.
▶ A 36–40 tooth finish blade.
▶ A nail-cutting blade for floors or old wood where it's impossible to avoid hitting nails.

If you are changing blades, immobilize the blade with the built-in lock or by digging the teeth into soft wood *(below)*. Remove the blade-retaining bolt with the wrench supplied with the saw or another exactly fitting wrench. Do not use pliers or a wrench that is a bit too large; it will quickly round off the corners of the bolt head, making it useless. Turn the wrench counterclockwise, in the direction of the blade teeth, to undo the bolt.

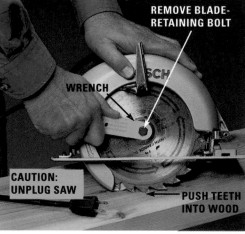

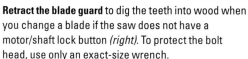

Retract the blade guard to dig the teeth into wood when you change a blade if the saw does not have a motor/shaft lock button *(right)*. To protect the bolt head, use only an exact-size wrench.

When the new blade is in place on the mounting shaft, be sure to replace the large washer that goes under the bolt head. A carborundum or other special-purpose blade may require an oversize stabilizing disk in place of or in addition to the regular washer. The disk is essential to keep a nonmetal blade running true and avoid the danger of cracking or breaking under stress. Do not operate without it. Turn the blade-retaining bolt clockwise and tighten it firmly.

Square the Blade

Every so often, and especially after tilting the blade repeatedly, check that the blade sits at a right angle to the foot plate.

Turn the unplugged saw upside down and hold the blade guard retracted *(below)*. A helper simplifies this task. Set an accurate square on the foot plate and align the blade to its vertical leg. Some saws have a separate adjustment screw for this purpose; others are aligned with the tilt-adjust control.

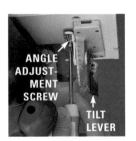

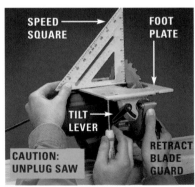

Use a square to align the blade at a precise right angle to the foot plate. You may need a helper. Use the adjustment screw if there is one, or the tilt-adjust control.

Set the Blade Depth

Do not simply set the blade for maximum depth for sawing all thicknesses of wood. Excess blade depth generates heat and increases the danger of kickback. Instead, with the saw unplugged, adjust the depth so the blade teeth will extend below the wood about 1/4 inch. With the proper blade, this will always keep three teeth within the thickness of the wood.

Set blade depth 1/4 in. below the wood thickness.

Secure the Work

Clamp your workpiece to a couple of sturdy sawhorses or a workbench to keep it rock steady. Although for some quick cuts you can steady the workpiece with one hand and operate the saw with the other, often you'll need to use both hands to guide the saw and won't be able to hold the workpiece. When cutting off a short end, make sure it can drop freely.

Clamp work securely so that you can work with both hands.

Mark Depth Settings

With the saw unplugged, retract the blade guard and adjust the blade to extend 1/4 in. below the thickness of a 2x4 (actually 1-1/2 in. thick). Lift the saw, release the guard, and mark a line labeled "2X" (for nominal 2 in. stock) at the underside of the saw's foot plate. Do the same with a piece of 1 in. stock (actually 3/4 in. thick), marking a "1X" line; it will serve for 3/4 in. plywood as well. Repeat with 1/2 in. plywood, marking a "1/2" line.

To quickly make a setting, raise the saw until the proper line is at the foot plate.

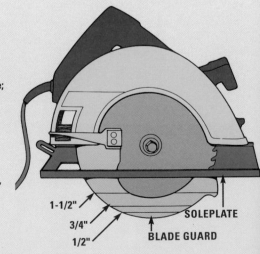

Making Freehand Cuts

There are really only two tricks to making circular saw cuts: 1) Get started on the line. 2) Guide the saw along the line with a light, steady pressure. But first get in the right position.

For a quick cut with hand-held work, stand off to one side, not directly behind the saw. Tilt the work up on a support so you can saw at a downward angle *(below)*. This keeps the wood from sliding away from the saw and allows the weight of the saw to push the blade through the wood.

When work is clamped in place, align the blade's teeth with a guideline drawn on the wood. There's a guide notch in the front edge of the saw foot plate, but it's more accurate to sight along the blade itself. However, with a right-mounted blade, when you stand so you're not directly behind the saw, to avoid kickback, it's very difficult to see from the left side *(Position A, right)*, and awkward—but

better—from the right *(Position B)*. It's much easier to see the blade and the line of cut with a left-mounted blade, as found in many worm-drive saws *(bottom)*.

No matter where the blade is mounted, practice makes perfect. As you use it, you'll quickly get the feel of the saw and figure out how to best sight down the blade. If a cut goes off the line, stop the saw, lift the blade out of the kerf, and start over. You can't twist a circular saw back on line the way you can a jigsaw.

Tilt wood at an angle against a solid surface when you can't clamp it. Don't push; let the weight of the saw push the blade. *Caution: Keep hands away from blade; do not stand behind blade.*

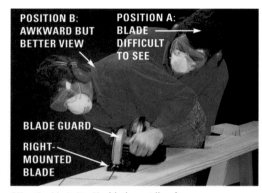

Align the blade itself with the cut line for accuracy. Experiment to find the position that seems best for you, but *do not stand directly behind the saw.*

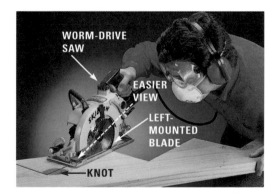

Use a saw with a left-mounted blade for best sighting if you are right-handed. A worm-drive saw is preferred by many. Go slowly through harder wood like knots.

Avoid Dangerous Kickbacks

Kickback occurs when your saw suddenly jerks backward in a saw cut. Here's why it happens: The leading edge of the saw blade cuts on the upstroke, essentially pulling the foot plate securely down against the wood as it cuts. However, the teeth on the rear part of the blade circle downward. If they catch the edge of the saw cut, they can pop the spinning blade up out of the kerf. You'll feel the saw buck upward and perhaps even run back toward you before you can release the switch.

Whenever you feel the saw start to kick back, stop and correct the problem. Look for any of these causes:

1. Binding board. Natural stresses in the wood cause the saw kerf to close, or the cut-off end doesn't fall free and pinches the blade.

2. Dull blade. Dull blades heat up and bind readily (see page 44).

3. Large panels. These are the exception to the free-fall rule. The cutoff section almost always binds as it falls away. The solution is to fully support plywood and cut it on the floor (see page 39).

4. Twisting the blade. Twisting in the kerf to keep the blade on the line always causes binding.

5. Back-sawing. Backing up the saw with the blade spinning guarantees kickback.

Even the most careful carpenters experience kickbacks and you will too. So make these safety practices a habit:

▶ Keep your hands well away from the blade.
▶ Stand to the side of the cut, never directly behind it.
▶ Insert shims or wedges in the kerf of a long cut to keep it open.

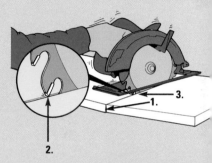

Kickback: (1) Sagging board pinches the blade, so (2) the rear teeth catch on the edge of the kerf, causing (3) the saw to jump up and back.

Solution: Insert a shim or wedge to keep the kerf open.

Guiding the Saw

When you need clean, straight cuts, there are several ways to guide the saw, as shown here and on page 37. They all are better and more precise than just sighting along the blade.

A simple method to use for cutting a "pretty straight" strip from a board is to use your fingers as a rip guide *(below)*. Position the saw at the end of the workpiece and grip the front edge of the foot plate with one hand touching the edge of the board, but with your fingers well away from the blade. As the saw moves forward, keep your "guide" fingers against the edge to maintain a constant width of cut.

The guide-finger technique is essentially the same as using a saw rip guide, which attaches at the front of the foot plate *(below)* and permits controlled cuts up to about 8 inches wide.

In both the above methods, the edge of the board must be straight in order to get a straight cut. That is often not the case, and the solution is to use a separate straightedge and keep either side of the saw's foot plate against it as you make the cut. You can hold the guide in place for short cuts *(right top)*, or clamp it to the workpiece for longer cuts *(right center)* or when you need to use both hands. For angled cuts, clamp a straightedge across the work at the required angle, or use an adjustable protractor guide *(right bottom)*; there are several types.

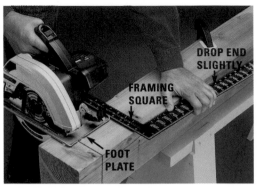

Hold a framing square flush against the side of the piece as a guide. Drop the far end to raise the short leg a bit against the foot plate.

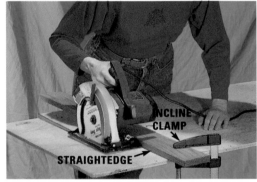

Clamp a straightedge or other guide in place on a wide workpiece. This lets you use both hands as required. Cut-off piece should drop free.

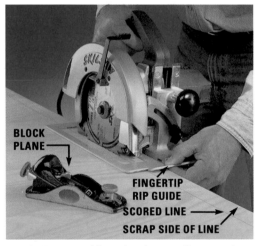

Grip the footplate with one hand so your finger can be a width gauge against the board edge. CAUTION: Keep your fingers well away from the blade.

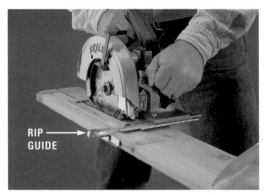

Fasten a rip guide to the front of the foot plate for cuts up to about 8 in. wide. Keep the guide against the board edge as you cut.

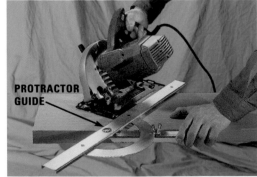

Make precise angle cuts by using an adjustable protractor guide. For a compound angle, tilt the saw too, as shown.

Making Saw Guides

For a combined straight and angle guide, cut the corner from a square edge of 1/2-inch plywood *(right)*. If you make the two short legs equal, say 12 inches as shown, the slanted side will form 45° corners. To get a 30° angle at one corner and a 60° angle at the other, cut sides 18 and 10-1/2 inches long. Clamp the guide flush with one edge of the workpiece *(far right)* to guide the saw at the desired angle.

Long cuts require a long, absolutely straight guide. It's not easy to keep a long board true and undamaged, if you can find one, or to position it at just the required offset from the intended line of cut. The cutting jig *(below)* solves both those problems and is especially useful when you have a number of large panels to cut, or long boards to rip. Simply mark the line of cut, place the outside edge of the jig along it, and cut away. Just remember which side of the mark you want to cut on.

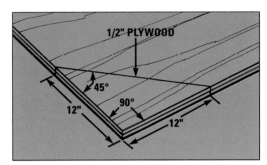

Cut off a plywood panel corner to make a useful straight and angle guide. The factory-cut corner should be a right angle, but check it with a framing square and trim before measuring and cutting the guide.

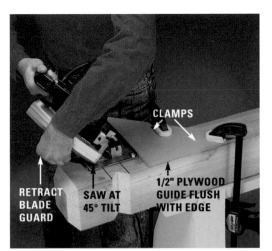

Clamp the guide with the appropriate side flush with one edge of the work, depending on whether you want a straight or an angled cut.

WORKING TIP

Circular saw teeth cut as they rotate upward, so turn the workpiece good side down to minimize splintering. If both faces are good, score the cut line on the upper side with a utility knife, and run two strips of masking tape along the foot plate of the saw to keep it from marring the surface.

MAKING A CIRCULAR SAW CUTTING JIG

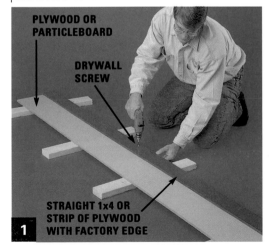

1 **Glue and screw** a perfectly straight 1x4 or strip of plywood with a factory edge to a 1-ft x 8-ft piece of plywood for a base.

2 **Run the foot plate** of your circular saw along the 1x4 strip, cutting the scrap width off the plywood base.

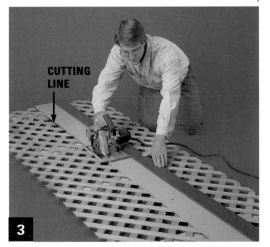

3 **Mark the cutting line** on the workpiece and line up the edge of the cutting jig base with it. Then run your saw along the jig.

A Cross-cut, Dado, and Miter Jig

This clever jig lets you use your circular saw much like a radial arm saw for cross-cutting and cutting dados. You can build it in just an hour or so, probably using left-over pieces of lumber. You can make a similar jig for fixed-angle miter cuts across boards.

First you need a base that has exactly parallel edges and is 1-1/2 inches thick, to give proper support to the other parts and to resist distortion with use. For a working width of at least 12 inches, glue and screw two pieces of 3/4-inch plywood together and trim one side parallel to the other. Make the base 4 to 5 feet long; you can provide extra support for the far end of really long boards when necessary.

Attach side pieces as shown to extend 1-5/8 inches above the base, just tall enough to clear the thickness of 2x stock. Make the fence side 2-1/2 feet long, and the opposite, rear side 18 inches long.

Cut two runners—colored blue in the pictures—to support the saw. Rout each runner so it has a lip to guide the edge of the saw's foot plate. Mount the runners at exactly 90° to the side pieces, with the lips spaced just wide enough for the foot plate.

Clamp or screw the base of the jig firmly to your bench when sawing, and rub a little wax on the runners to reduce friction with the saw's foot plate. For cross-cutting, set the blade depth to just cut through the work, about 1/16 inch into the jig base. For dados, raise the blade to get the desired depth and make repeated passes, sliding the workpiece a little bit each time. To cut dados in thicker stock, use the technique shown on page 39.

For an angle-cutting jig, make both side pieces 2-1/2 feet long and mount the parallel runners at exactly 30°, 45°, or 60° across their top edges.

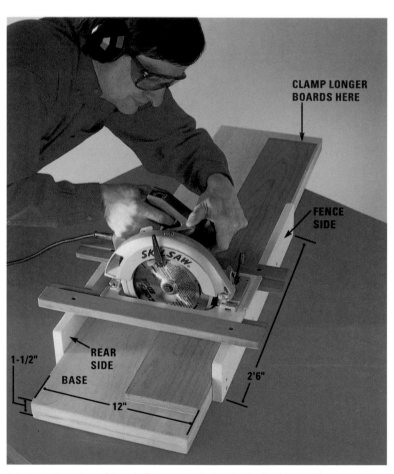

Adapt the dimensions shown to fit your saw, but make the jig at least 12 in. wide for various sizes of stock and extend the runners for full support before and after the cut.

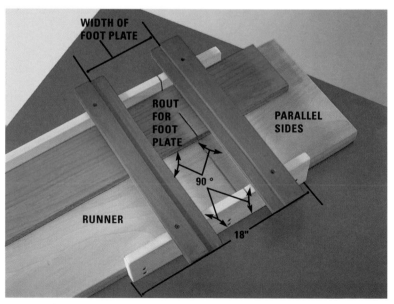

Be precise in getting the sides parallel and the runners at right angles to them, so cuts will be absolutely square. Make test cuts before finally fastening the runners.

Cutting Dados in Thick Stock

Here's what to do when you need to cut a notch or dado in a piece that is too big to fit into a jig or has to be cut in place—such as a railing post. Mark the notch or dado width and set the saw blade to the proper depth. Use a guide for accuracy. Cut a kerf along each marked side, then cut a series of kerfs between them at about 1/8-inch intervals. Switch off the saw and let the blade stop completely after each pass before lifting it up. Otherwise you'll tend to get kickback that can ruin the dado. Clean and smooth the notch with a chisel.

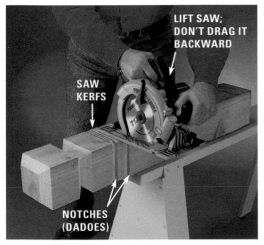

Make repeated cuts closely spaced to form a notch or dado. Clamp the guide on a vertical workpiece such as a post in place.

Cutting Large Panels

Wrestling a large panel onto a workbench or supporting it securely without sagging on sawhorses to avoid kick-back is not easy, especially if you don't have a helper. Here are some easy ways to cut a large panel.

On the Floor
Put down a waste panel of 1/2-in. plywood and lay the panel to be cut on top. Set the saw blade to just cut through the thickness of the upper panel and go to work. You can kneel on the workpiece to guide the saw, and can see the marked line easily all along the cut.

With a Guide
If you need to clamp a guide to the panel, you can still have the convenience of working at floor level. Simply lay the panel to be cut on 2x4s spaced every 2 ft. under the work, with or without a waste panel. Place the supports crosswise so the cut runs at right angles to them, to avoid sagging that could close the kerf and pinch the blade. If necessary, stack up two or three 2x4s so the clamps will clear the floor.

On the Ground
If you are working outside, you can quickly cut a panel on the ground. To keep the blade teeth out of the dirt and away from hidden stones, set the depth of the cut just a fraction less than the thickness of the panel. Make the cut, break the last little bit by hand, and sand or plane the rough edges. With care, you can also use this technique indoors when you don't have a waste panel or 2x4s to put under the workpiece.

On the floor

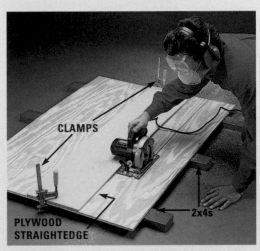

CLAMPS

PLYWOOD STRAIGHTEDGE

2x4s

With a guide

TINY BIT OF PLYWOOD LEFT AFTER CUTTING

On the ground

Making Difficult Cuts

Some projects require trimming a curved board, ripping a narrow piece of stock, or cutting an opening in the middle of a piece. The tips shown here make such difficult cuts easy.

Ripping Narrow Stock

A narrow board can't support the foot plate to keep the saw from wobbling. So add a wider support or "carrier" board of the same thickness. Use double-sided tape every 6 inches to temporarily hold the edges of the two boards together.

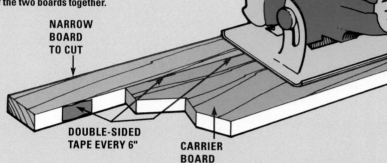

NARROW BOARD TO CUT

DOUBLE-SIDED TAPE EVERY 6"

CARRIER BOARD

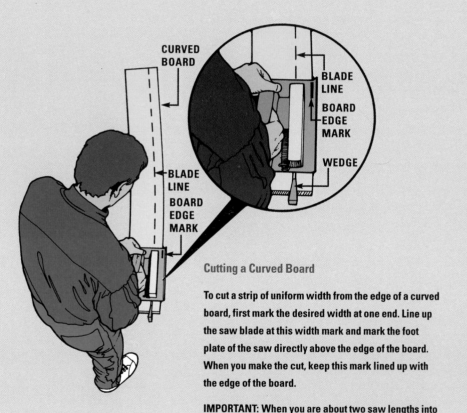

CURVED BOARD

BLADE LINE

BOARD EDGE MARK

WEDGE

BLADE LINE

BOARD EDGE MARK

Cutting a Curved Board

To cut a strip of uniform width from the edge of a curved board, first mark the desired width at one end. Line up the saw blade at this width mark and mark the foot plate of the saw directly above the edge of the board. When you make the cut, keep this mark lined up with the edge of the board.

IMPORTANT: When you are about two saw lengths into the cut, stop and tap a wedge into the kerf to keep it from closing up and causing kickback. For a long cut, you may need to shift the wedge once or twice.

Pocket Cut

To cut an opening in the middle of a workpiece, make a pocket or plunge cut. Do it this way to avoid kickback:
▶ Rest the front of the foot plate firmly on the work, with the rear raised. Retract the blade guard and align the blade directly over the marked cut line, in the center of the cut.
▶ Start the saw and lower the blade into the wood. When the foot plate is flat on the surface, move the saw forward to the end of your marked line. DO NOT MOVE THE SAW BACKWARD.
▶ Stop the saw, lift it clear, turn it around, and insert the blade in the kerf to complete the cut in the other direction.
▶ Repeat for each side of the opening. Complete the cuts in the corners with a hand saw.

FOOT PLATE

Cutting Hard Materials

Plastic laminate, metals, masonry, ceramics, and concrete all pose special cutting difficulties. Here's how to deal with them.

Plastic Laminate

As with all materials with a finished surface, turn the workpiece over so the best side faces down, as shown with the countertop below. To cut unmounted sheet laminate, sandwich it between two pieces of 1/4-inch plywood along the cut line. Use a fine-tooth carbide blade and a guide to keep the cut straight. Any wandering or twisting is almost sure to chip or crack the laminate.

Metals

To cut aluminum, use a 40-tooth carbide tip blade (see pages 42–44). For ferrous metals—thin steel, like corrugated roofing, chain link fence posts, steel studs—use an abrasive-grit or carborundum blade or a specially hardened steel blade. For thicker steel use an abrasive blade. Make sure the blade is specifically marked for use with metals, and mount it exactly as specified; some blades require reinforcing plates.

Wear eye and hearing protection, and be sure the saw has a metal, not plastic, blade housing.

When you cut ferrous metals there will be plenty of sparks *(below),* so work far away from sawdust piles, flammable liquids, and other fire hazards. And be careful: the freshly cut edges will be hot!

Masonry, Ceramics, and Concrete

Use an inexpensive composition masonry blade to cut both concrete slabs and concrete blocks and pavers *(below left)* or even large ceramic tiles (use a hand-operated cutter for small tiles). Slowly cut a groove 1/2 to 3/4 inch deep in concrete materials, then break the piece with a heavy hammer. If you need a very clean edge, however, you'll have to rent a concrete saw with a masonry blade *(below right).* The rate will be high, because it includes a charge for wear on the blade.

With either saw you absolutely must wear eye, hearing, and dust protection. There will be lots of dust, so if you're indoors, enclose your workspace completely and turn on a window fan.

Turn the work upside down when it has a laminated or veneered surface, to minimize chipping or splintering. A saw guide is essential.

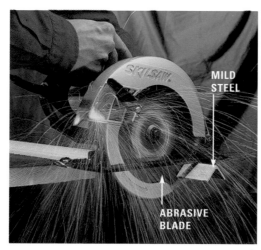

Cut ferrous metal with an abrasive blade. Keep well away from flammable materials; the shower of sparks can be dangerous.

Use a masonry abrasive blade to score concrete, then break the halves apart with a hammer. Cutting outdoors is best.

Rent a concrete saw and diamond-edge blade for clean-edged cuts and extensive work. They are too expensive to buy.

Circular Saw Blades

Buying a circular saw blade can be intimidating because there are so many to choose from. If you know what kind of material you are going to cut, consult the chart on the opposite page. But to get the maximum benefit from your saw, you need the following information.

There are two basic types of circular saw blades: those made of high-speed steel, and those with brazed-on teeth of tungsten carbide. A blade with carbide teeth will cost more, but it will stay sharp up to 50 times longer than a steel blade, so you may never have to resharpen it. Materials like plywood, particleboard, waferboard, and hardboard are made with abrasive glues that quickly dull steel blades. A steel blade, however, is the one to buy when you want the finest possible cut in veneered material or when you want a disposable blade for cutting through shingles or used wood with rocks and dirt embedded in it.

The major differences in carbide blade teeth are explained at the right. Blades have different numbers of teeth. The basic principle is that more teeth means a smoother, but slower cut. Fewer teeth means easier, faster cutting, but a rougher cut. Wood cuts vary differently depending on whether you are going across the grain (cross-cutting) or along the grain (ripping). Saw blades are discussed according to their best uses on pages 43–44. Specific recommendations as to type of blade and number of teeth for cutting various materials are provided in the chart on page 43.

Carbide Blade Teeth

Basic and very important differences in blade design are illustrated below. Combination and finish carbide blades generally have teeth with the same, or very similar, design. The major difference is the number of teeth—finish blades have two to four times more. Because the finish blade teeth are more closely spaced, they take smaller, more frequent bites out of the wood.

Nail-cutting blades for rough, heavy-duty work have far fewer teeth, set and angled to resist damage no matter what they encounter. They don't give pretty, smooth cuts, but like a brawny lumberjack they do their job vigorously and reliably.

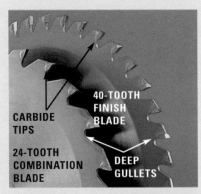

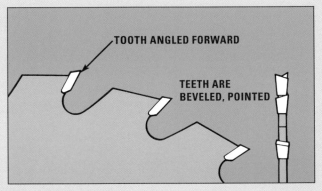

Combination blades and many finish blades have teeth angled forward, with carbide tips ground at an angle so they slice through the wood rapidly. Deep gullets carry the sawdust away to avoid clogging the cut.

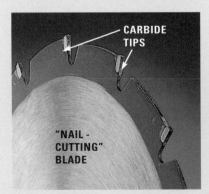

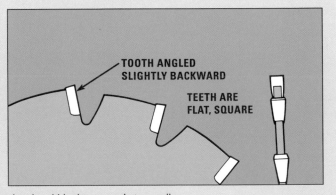

Nail-cutting blades have teeth angled backward and carbide tips ground at a smaller angle so they won't chip as easily or dull as rapidly as sharp-pointed teeth. These blades cut slower and rougher than other ones.

General Purpose Blades

The one blade you should not be without is one labeled either "combination" or "general purpose." It will do a good job of either ripping or cross-cutting, although with a slight loss of speed when ripping.

Combination blades are also good for miter cuts, which are essentially both a rip and a cross-cut. There are three variations of this blade:

A 16- to 20-tooth carbide blade is the best general purpose blade. It cuts smoothly and quickly across the grain of wood, with the grain, or at an angle, in softwood or hardwood, and can cut abrasive materials like particleboard.

A steel combination blade is also good for every direction of cut. It is less suitable for plywood and particleboard because it will dull quickly, but for cutting solid wood it is an old favorite.

A special-grind carbide blade produces a very smooth cut. Its specially ground teeth have either a hook shape or a "V" shape. Most often produced as a general purpose carbide blade, it does cut more smoothly but is no replacement for a blade with more teeth.

Ripping and Rough Cutting Blades

These uses require blades with fewer teeth. There are two major choices:

Carbide blades with 12 teeth or so are good when speed is more important than the smoothness of the cut. Examples are framing and outdoor construction. This blade is also good for landscape timbers and preservative-treated lumber, which

are often wet. If you are doing a lot of cutting with the grain of the wood (ripping), this blade is a good choice.

Steel rip blades are usually made with about 36 teeth. The teeth are specially shaped for easier cutting with the grain.

Smooth Cutting Blades

These blades have the greatest number of teeth, because more teeth means a smoother cut.

Carbide blades with 40 teeth or so are designed for smooth cuts. This is critical when cutting hardwood plywood or paneling. For splinter-free results, remember to always face the good side of the wood down when you are cutting.

Plywood/paneling blades are steel blades, particularly good for smooth cuts. Generally they have over 100 small teeth. Since the teeth are so small, these blades will burn and bind easily, so don't use them to cut solid wood.

Hollow-ground plywood blades, also called "thin rim" blades, have the blade ground thinner than the teeth to lessen binding and splintering. They give the best cut in plywood and paneling.

Planer blades are essentially hollow-ground steel combination blades. They are designed for smooth cuts in hardwoods and are equivalent in performance to 40-tooth carbide blades.

Choosing a Blade for Cutting

Material	Type of Blade	Comments
Clean, dry lumber	16- to 20-tooth carbide	General purpose
	12-tooth carbide	Ripping/rough cutting
	40-tooth carbide	Smooth cuts
	Steel combination	General purpose
	Steel ripping	Ripping/rough cutting
	Steel planer	Smooth cuts
Plywood, hardboard, paneling	16- to 20-tooth carbide	General purpose
	40-tooth carbide	Smooth cut
	Steel plywood/paneling	Smooth cut
	Hollow-ground carbide	Super smooth cut
Particleboard	12-tooth carbide	Fast cut
	16- to 20-tooth carbide	General purpose
	40-tooth carbide	Smooth cut
Damp lumber	12-tooth carbide	——
	Steel ripping	——
Wood with dirt or nails	Carbide nail-cutting	——
	Disposable steel	Inexpensive
Aluminum, copper	40-tooth carbide	——
Acrylic plastic	40-tooth carbide	——
Plastic laminate	40-tooth carbide	——
Iron or steel	Metal-cutting abrasive	——
Masonry	Masonry-cutting abrasive	——

Blades for Cutting Old Wood with Nails

If you need to cut wood with nails in it, buy a specialized blade for the job.

Nail-cutting blades have impact-resistant carbide teeth that slope backward (negative rake). You can use these blades to cut old flooring, used lumber, and concrete forms or other dirty lumber.

Metal and Masonry Blades

You can use your circular saw to cut metal and masonry if you have the right blade and the right saw. Your saw must have a metal guard, because the sparks and chips will ruin a plastic guard. Be sure to wear eye protection, and use light cuts.

Abrasive metal-cutting blades are made of abrasive particles like those in a grinding wheel, reinforced with fibers. These blades can be used for cutting downspouts, corrugated roofing, pipe, angle iron, or steel cable.

Abrasive masonry-cutting blades are made for cutting cinder and cement materials such as blocks and pavers, tile, and brick. Use them dry and cut slowly.

Dull Blades

A saw usually sends clear signals that the blade is going dull, as shown at right. You hear the motor slow and labor while cutting. You have to shove the saw through the wood, rather than feeling it glide through. You may smell smoke from the blade overheating and burning the wood. The blade will slow and stick—called "binding"—and become gunked up with sticky brown sap called "varnish." Binding blades are dangerous because they can cause kickback toward your body (see box, page 35). These signs mean the blade needs to be cleaned and perhaps sharpened as well. You can clean it yourself and even sharpen a steel blade, although it is tricky and tedious. Sharpening a carbide blade is definitely a job for a professional.

Cleaning Blades

Do not try to remove the scorched sap buildup on a saw blade with abrasives or steel wool. You will get nowhere fast, and will probably score the surface, leaving gouges that will only cause rougher cutting and more rapid varnish accumulation when you put the blade back in use. Instead soak the blade in kerosene, or use oven cleaner, as shown at the right. Then wash the blade in warm water. Wear rubber gloves, and if necessary go over the teeth and gullets with a nonmetallic scrub pad of the type that is safe for nonstick kitchen pans.

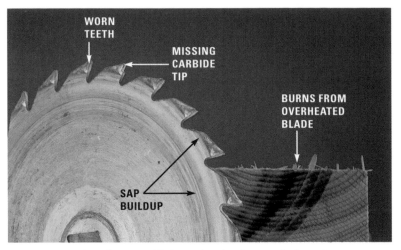

Be aware of the signs that a saw blade needs to be sharpened, cleaned, or thrown away: chipped or missing teeth, sap or varnish buildup, saw motor slowing and laboring, the smell of burning wood, or the blade binding in the cut.

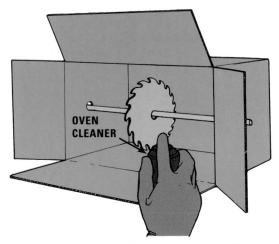

Clean resin and pitch from saw blades with spray oven cleaner. Suspend the saw blade from a dowel run through a cardboard box. Spray both sides of the blade, close the flaps for 10 to 20 minutes, then wash the blade clean in warm water. Be sure to wear rubber gloves.

Table Saws

At the heart of every well-equipped workshop is a table saw. It can cut in more ways, more precisely, than any portable saw, and it's safe and easy to use when you know the tricks professionals use.

Precision and versatility—no tool provides a greater share of both than a table saw. You may love the adaptability of a reciprocating or circular saw, but while both tools will get the job done, a table saw will do it with style: Perfect joints, tight miters, and accurate dadoes are the table saw's bread and butter. No craftsman could live without one.

Of course, the saw can't do it alone. You have to add two key ingredients: test and adjust your saw to be sure it will make precise, controlled cuts every time, and use the techniques and professional tricks that experienced workers use to make difficult tasks easier. The following pages illustrate and explain how to get the most out of this invaluable tool.

Testing Saw Alignment

Make sure you are familiar with the operation of your saw: If you are a beginner, read the instruction manual to find out:

▶ How to use the blade guard and other safety features

▶ How to adjust the height of the blade

▶ How to set the tilt of the blade

▶ How to cross-cut a board using the miter gauge, and how to cut at an angle

▶ How to rip a board using the rip guide

▶ How to change blades

▶ Where adjustment screws or bolts are located, and how to change their settings.

Make a Test Cut

As shown below, mark an "X" in the middle of a 1x3 or 1x4 and cut it through the center of the X. Use the miter gauge as a guide, set to "0" for a right-angle (90°) cut.

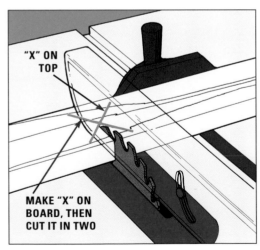

"X" ON TOP

MAKE "X" ON BOARD, THEN CUT IT IN TWO

Make a test cut through an X marked on a short length of wood. Use the miter gauge set at 0°, the setting for a right-angle cut.

Evaluate the Test

1. Turn over one half of the test board, butt the cut ends together, and look at the joint from the side. If you see a gap between the ends, the saw blade is not square to the table.

2. With the cut ends still butted together, lay a carpenter's square along their edges and look down from above. If you see a wedge-shaped gap between the wood and the square on either or both sides of the joint, the miter gauge is not square to the saw blade.

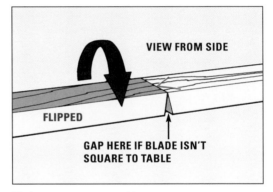

VIEW FROM SIDE

FLIPPED

GAP HERE IF BLADE ISN'T SQUARE TO TABLE

Blade not square to saw table.

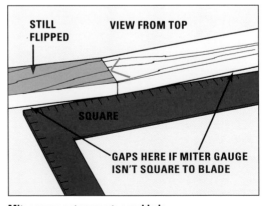

STILL FLIPPED

VIEW FROM TOP

SQUARE

GAPS HERE IF MITER GAUGE ISN'T SQUARE TO BLADE

Miter gauge not square to saw blade.

Adjusting Saw Alignment

If your sample cut did not pass the test, you can readjust the saw to correct these and other problems.

Before making those adjustments, however, check to make sure the blade is parallel to the miter gauge slots. It should be, unless your saw has been moved or banged around a lot. If the blade is not parallel, some of the other adjustments will be useless.

To begin, UNPLUG THE SAW and leave it unplugged through all the checks and adjustments you make.

Crank the blade to its full height. Measure from the front and rear of the blade straight over to one of the miter gauge slots. If the blade is parallel to the slots, the measurements will be identical. If they are not, loosen the bolts on the underside of the table that secure the blade carriage, slightly reposition it, and measure again. On saws with four bolts, loosen three of them and use the other as a pivot point. When the blade is parallel to the miter gauge slot, tighten the adjustment bolts. Consult your owner's manual for the specific steps.

Now, with the saw still unplugged, proceed with the adjustments shown and explained on the opposite page.

Blade Angle Adjustment

Set the blade angle (the "tilt" scale, usually on the front of the saw) to "0." With the blade raised to full height, rest one leg of a square on the table and the other 1/16 inch away from the blade. Sight between the square and the body of the blade. If you see a wedge rather than a straight line of daylight between blade and square, adjust the screw that stops the blade in the perpendicular position. On some saws this is a little hex screw on the table top. When the blade is perpendicular, readjust the arrow on the blade angle scale to 0 degrees. There may be a lock screw to loosen; otherwise simply bend the pointer to correct its setting.

Check blade angle with a square.

Miter Gauge Squaring

Place one leg of a carpenter's square against the saw blade. Loosen the locking handle of the miter gauge and align the gauge against the other leg of the square. If the arrow on the gauge doesn't point to "0" on the scale, loosen the setting screw and reset the pointer to the "0."

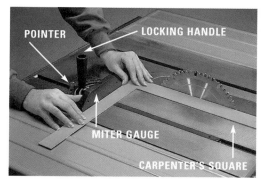

Adjust the miter gauge with a carpenter's square.

Miter Gauge Wobble

If the gauge is loose in its slot, remove it and dimple one edge with a center punch in a zigzag pattern. Deepen each dimple until the gauge fits snugly in the slot. If it is too tight a fit, file dimples until the gauge slides freely.

Dimple the miter gauge to eliminate wobble.

Rip Fence Alignment

Position the rip fence next to one of the miter gauge slots and lock it in position. If it doesn't align itself parallel to the slot, loosen the two bolts or screws in the top of the fence, align the fence precisely with the length of the slot, and retighten the bolts or screws.

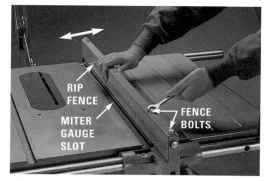

Align the rip fence with a miter gauge slot.

Blade Guard Adjustment

Place a square alongside the blade and splitter. Use a hand screw-type clamp to gently bend the splitter in line with the blade. For major adjustments, add or subtract a washer where the guard fastens to the saw.

Make sure the splitter lines up with the blade.

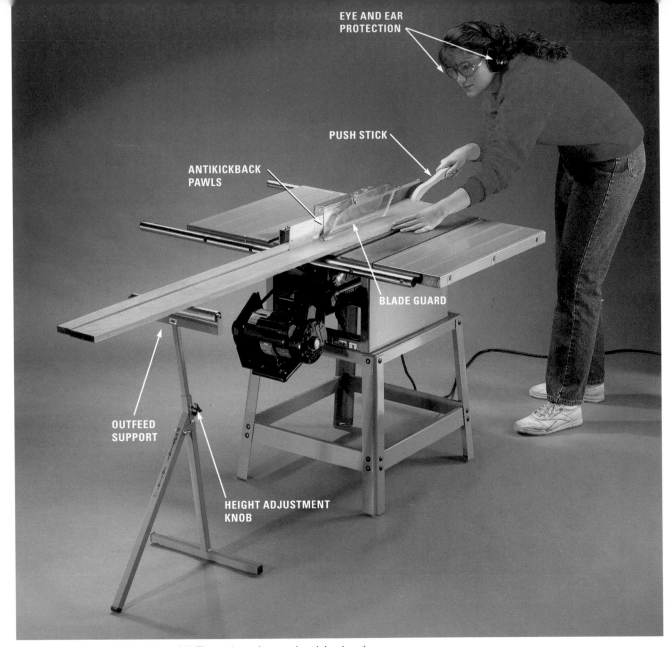

EYE AND EAR PROTECTION

PUSH STICK

ANTIKICKBACK PAWLS

BLADE GUARD

OUTFEED SUPPORT

HEIGHT ADJUSTMENT KNOB

Use safety devices and aids without fail. Those shown here and explained on these two pages include the blade guard with antikickback pawls, a push stick, outfeed support, and eye and hearing protectors.

Saw Safely

The table saw is one of the most dangerous tools in the workshop, if you are not very careful. Being cut by the blade and getting hit by kicked-back boards are the two most obvious dangers. Avoid boards that are wet or green, twisted, bowed, or contain splits and loose knots; these are likely to kick back unpredictably. In addition, take the following safety steps:

▶ Set the blade so it protrudes only about 1/4 inch above the wood being cut. Some professionals claim that setting a carbide-tip blade so the entire tooth clears the work produces a cleaner cut, but that should be the limit. Setting the blade higher exposes more of it for potential accidents, creates more strain on the blade and motor, and leaves a rougher cut.

▶ Use your blade guard. Most guards contain three safety features: a plastic housing to keep fingers away from the

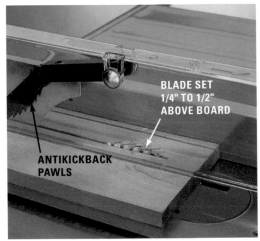

BLADE SET 1/4" TO 1/2" ABOVE BOARD

ANTIKICKBACK PAWLS

Set the blade to reach just above the top of the board, and make sure the antikickback pawls work freely before starting to cut.

blade and prevent splinters or loose knots from flying back at you; a splitter that keeps the cut open after it passes the blade to prevent pinching; and antikickback pawls with little teeth that allow the board to pass in the cutting direction, but bite into it in case it tries to kick back. If you must remove the blade guard for dadoing or some other operation, replace it as soon as possible.

▶ Use a push stick or push shoe *(below)* any time your fingers must pass within 4 inches of the blade. You can buy or make push sticks and featherboards (see page 50) to help you hold boards safely against the saw table and fence as they are being cut. They are important to help avoid kickback, which occurs when the part of the board between the fence and blade gets pinched (or drifts away from the fence as you're cutting) and the blade, spinning toward you, catches it and hurls it back at you. The antikickback pawls don't always prevent this, especially if the wood is very hard or you're cutting skinny strips.

▶ Support long boards with outfeed rollers *(below),* and resist the impulse to reach over the blade to catch a board as it falls off the table at the end of a cut. Rollers and stands cost little, but you can make a substitute from scrap (see box at right). Side and front rollers make handling large pieces of plywood easier.

▶ Above all, use common sense: Always wear sight and hearing protection, and use a dust mask when cutting pressure-treated wood. Never reach over a spinning blade. Don't wear loose clothing. Unplug the saw when making adjustments or changing blades.

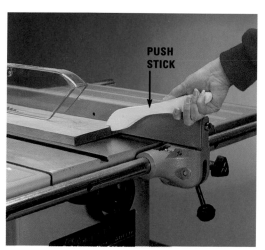

Use a **push stick** or shoe, and featherboards if needed, to keep your fingers away from the blade as you move wood through a cut; see page 50.

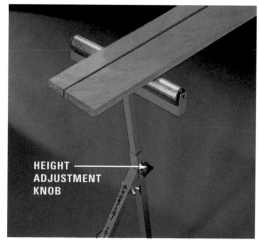

Support long boards and large panels on an outfeed roller or similar device (see box at right). They are very likely to cause kickback if not supported.

Outfeed Supports

Here are two easy-to-build supports for long boards or panels that extend over the edges of the saw table.

Mount a plywood top on an old ironing board. Turn it lengthwise to support long boards, or crosswise for large panels. The height is adjustable, and it folds up for storage when not in use.

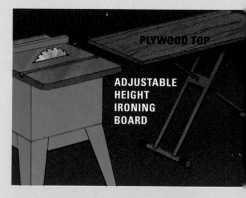

This versatile support uses 360° swivel-ball casters, available inexpensively at home centers. Screw six or more casters to a 3/4-in. board in a zigzag pattern so they don't touch or rub together when they pivot. Screw and glue this caster platform to a plywood frame and clamp it to a sawhorse at the required height. Because the casters swivel, the support is equally useful behind the saw table or at either side.

Making and Using Push Sticks and Featherboards

Use scrap 1x stock or plywood to make these pushers that keep your fingers away from the blade. Engage the work-piece with the notch of the push stick or shoe.

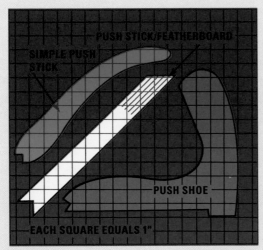

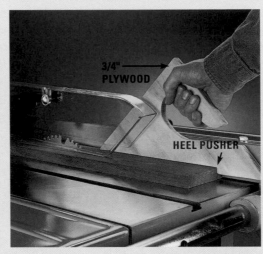

Cut push sticks or shoes from scrap wood. Sand the handle edges smooth and paint them bright colors so they are easy to find.

Use plywood for push shoes. This shoe is made from a 10-in. corner cut from a panel. Sand the handle for a comfortable grip.

Guide wood with push shoes. Use one with a heel notch to push the wood through the blade, and one with a nose notch to keep it against the rip fence.

The fingers of a feather-board exert spring pressure to keep a work-piece against the saw fence or table, so you can use both hands to control the cut.

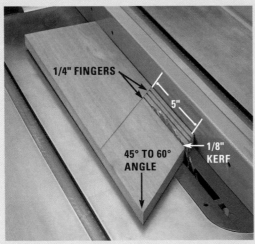

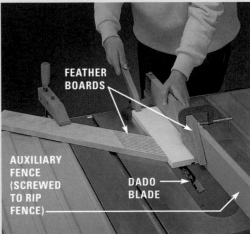

Cut the end of a 3/4-in.-thick board at an angle and then cut a series of 1/4-in.-wide fingers. The kerfs between will give them a springy action.

Move the rip fence 3/8 in. after stopping each cut with the blade in the kerf. Then back the board out and make the next cut.

Clamp one featherboard to the saw table to press work to the fence; clamp another on an auxiliary fence to hold the work down. Use a push stick, too.

Table Saw Blades

Table saw blades bolt on a spindle below the saw table. In addition to the basic types shown below, there are special-purpose blades, such as a dado blade (page 56). Here is what to consider in choosing a blade.

Blade and tooth composition. Steel blades are inexpensive but need to be replaced or resharpened frequently. A sharp steel blade can cut soft woods cleanly, but it will dull quickly when cutting particleboard or tough woods like oak and birch.

Carbide-tip blades last 50 to 60 times longer than steel blades. They can cut particleboard, hardwoods, plastic laminates, and even some metals. Carbide teeth are of various quality: you get what you pay for.

CARBIDE TOOTH

Blade thickness. Carbide blades are available in standard and thin-kerf styles. Thin-kerf blades remove less wood per cut and create less drag on a motor—making them a good choice for benchtop saws. However, thin-kerf blades tend to become distorted when hot and have a shorter life than standard blades.

Number and pattern of teeth. Saw blades have from 20 to 100 teeth, arranged in a number of ways and with a variety of tip angles and bevels. For cutting boards to length or mitering across the grain, use a blade with 60 or more teeth. For ripping boards to width, where speed is more important than smoothness, use a blade with fewer teeth.

Your best starting choice is a good-quality 40- or 50-tooth, carbide-tip combination blade; it has groupings of four or five closely spaced teeth (for crisp cross-cuts) separated by a larger gap (for easy ripping). If you own a benchtop saw, buy a thin-kerf blade.

Changing Blades

When you need to change to a blade best suited for the job at hand, first UNPLUG THE SAW. Then remove the table insert around the blade. Crank the blade to maximum height and immobilize it. Use a clamp with padded jaws *(below)*, or jam the teeth into a piece of scrap wood. Then use the blade wrench to remove the retaining nut.

INSERT REMOVED

PADDED JAWS

To change the blade, unplug the saw and remove the table insert. Clamp the blade as shown or jam a piece of wood in the teeth. Then remove the retaining nut with the blade wrench.

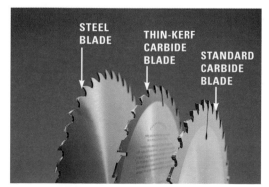

STEEL BLADE

THIN-KERF CARBIDE BLADE

STANDARD CARBIDE BLADE

Table saw blades are all made of steel, but those with carbide tips on the teeth *(top)* have superior cutting qualities and very long working lives.

Saw Blade Rack

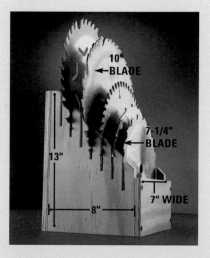

10" BLADE

7-1/4" BLADE

13"

8"

7" WIDE

You could hang your expensive carbide-tip saw blades on a nail, but here's a better idea. Build a topless and bottomless box from scrap plywood as follows:

▶ Cut side pieces about 8x13 in. with one end slanted 45°, as shown.

▶ Cut matching parallel slots 2 in. deep, spaced 1 in. apart in the slanted edges of the sides.

▶ Assemble the box with the sides set between front and back pieces cut 7-1/4 in. wide.

The resulting rack will hold table saw, circular saw, radial arm saw, and dado blades from 7-1/4 to 10 in. in diameter. The slanted sides make it easy to remove each blade, and the wood won't dull the blade teeth.

Making Accurate Cross Cuts

Although the miter gauge of your table adjusts for both 90° and angled cuts, its small size limits its usefulness. Here are three devices to provide greater versatility in making cross cuts.

Rub paraffin on runners so they will slide smoothly in the miter gauge slots in the saw table.

Cut-off Guide

Attach a 1x3 to the face of the miter gauge as a guide board *(below)*. Set the gauge in the left table slot and run the right end of the guide through the saw. Shift the gauge to the right-hand slot and cut off the left end of the guide. Now you have a taller, longer guide for cross-cutting with ends that show you exactly where the blade will make the cut.

Guide Base

For a wider, long guide, cut a base of 3/4-inch plywood that overhangs the table edge on one side *(below right)*. Fasten it to a hardwood strip that fits and runs

smoothly in the miter gauge slot on that side. Fasten a second hardwood strip on the bottom of the base to run along the table edge. Add a fence across the rear edge that extends above the top of the base. Run the assembly through the saw to cut it to length. Make a similar base to run on the opposite side of the saw table.

Cut-off Box

Cut two hardwood runners to slide smoothly in the miter gauge slots of the table *(right)*. They should extend 1/8 inch above the table. Drop the saw blade below the table, run a thin bead of glue along the runners, then press and clamp a piece of 3/4-inch plywood to them. This is the box bed. When the glue is dry, screw a shaped 2x4 fence to the front edge. Add another shaped fence along the rear edge with a screw only at the left end.

Put the box on the saw, and with the saw running, slowly crank the blade up through the center of the bed. Turn off the saw and use a framing square to set the

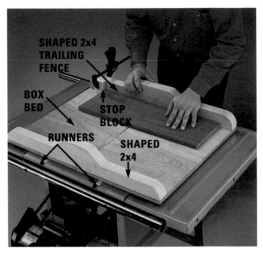

Cut-off box.

rear fence at 90° to the blade. Add a screw at the right end and make test cuts in scrap wood. Adjust the rear fence until you get a right-angle cut every time, then screw it to the bed all along its length.

To make repeated cuts to exactly the same length each time, clamp a stop block to the rear fence at the left or right, as needed.

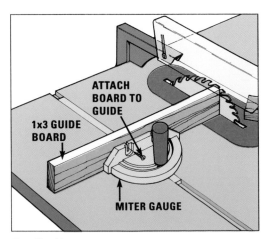

Cut-off guide.

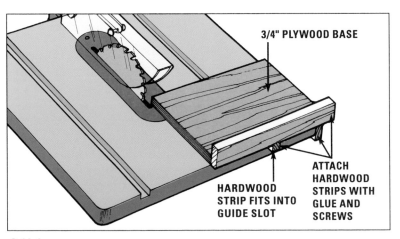

Guide base.

Using Jigs for Straight Rip Cuts

You can make long straight cuts in pieces with untrue edges or irregular shapes using one or another of these jigs.

To straighten the edge of a curved or irregular board, tack it to overhang a base board with a true edge *(below)*. Run the true edge of the base against the rip fence.

Use the same idea to split a spindle or other odd-shaped piece. Tack it to a base piece and run the edge of the base against the rip fence *(bottom)*. You'll cut into the base piece each time with this method.

To cut a long, straight taper, use the jig shown below. Mark the cut line on the workpiece. Put the workpiece on a base board and match the marked line with one edge of the base. Screw a narrow fence strip against the edge of the workpiece. Add a stop block at the rear end of the fence, to keep the workpiece from sliding. Push the base through the saw against the rip fence and the blade will cut on the marked taper line.

When you need to cut a true line in a board wider than your jig base, you can't use the rip fence as a guide. The jig below avoids that problem. It is reusable and is fine for narrower boards, too.

Cut a wood runner to fit the miter slot on your saw table. Attach it to the underside of a piece of 3/4-inch plywood. Set the runner in about 1 inch from the edge so the plywood base extends beyond the saw blade. Turn the saw on, set the runner in the miter slot, and cut the edge of the plywood. This gives you an accurate reference line for cutting with the jig.

Complete the jig by attaching a cleat across the end with three screws protruding (exaggerated in the photo at bottom right for clarity). Glue coarse sandpaper on top of the jig *(below right)*. These two features will give a good grip on a board.

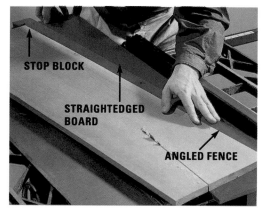

Make a taper jig to cut long, slanted straight lines. Use screws to fasten the jig fence so you can reposition it for other taper angles.

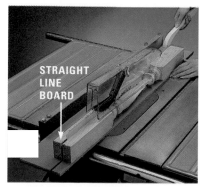

Use a board with true edges as a jig base. Fasten the workpiece overhanging the jig to cut along one edge *(top)*. Cut through the jig to split a piece *(bottom)*.

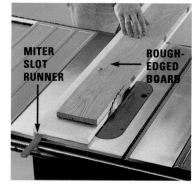

Fasten the bottom runner to run in either the right or left table slot, as you prefer.

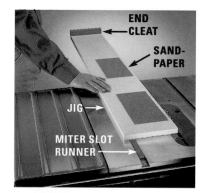

Use sandpaper and an end cleat to hold work without slipping in the jig.

Making a 45° Miter Jig

For an occasional miter cut, simply set the saw miter gauge at 45° and hold or clamp your board against it as you guide it past the blade. But when you need to make a lot of matching cuts—for example, for a set of picture frames, or molding for several windows and doors—the miter jig shown below is a much better solution. It is more accurate, easier to guide, and is always set to make matching 45° cuts from the left or the right.

The pictures show how to build the jig. Fasten the platform to the runners as they sit in the miter gauge slots, for accurate spacing. Cut the blade slot just over halfway into the platform. Mark the 45° lines accurately, and use the carpenter's square again when you attach the cleats, to make sure they form a precise right angle. Rub paste wax on the runners and the bottom side of the platform to reduce friction with the slots and the saw table.

Ripping Narrow Strips

Cutting thin strips safely on a table saw is tricky. The blade guard limits the width to about 1 inch. Cutting without the guard is dangerous, and very narrow strips are likely to be splintered or kicked back at you by the whirling blade. The jig shown at the right makes cutting one or fifty strips fast, easy, and safe.

Cut a 1/4-inch notch along one edge of a piece of 8-inch-wide plywood, leaving a projection to catch the rear end of the board to be cut. Attach a handle to the plywood to help you guide it. To cut a strip, adjust the rip fence so the distance between the edge of the jig and the blade is the width of the strip you want to cut. Nestle the board in front of the notch and cut a strip; place the board back in the notch and rip again. Repeat as many times as you need. The jig serves as a push stick and automatic spacer, and lets you keep the blade guard in place.

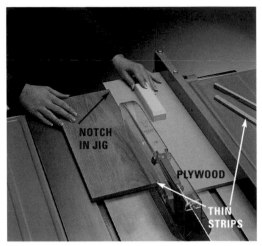

Use 8-in. wide plywood for a strip-cutting jig and position the flat handle on the jig so your fingers will be well away from the blade. A notch 1/4-in. wide catches the board end and pushes it through the blade.

MAKING A 45° MITER JIG

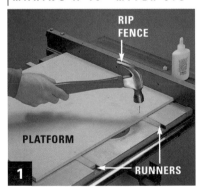

1

Nail and glue a base of 3/8-in. particleboard to two hardwood runners fitted into the miter gauge slots. Use the rip fence to position the platform square to the blade.

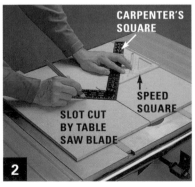

2

Mark two lines at 45° angles to a slot cut just over halfway into the center of the platform. Use a Speed square or 45° triangle to position a carpenter's square.

3

Screw 1x2 cleats along the 45° lines, using drywall screws. Check their alignment with the carpenter's square. Wax the runners and the bottom of the platform.

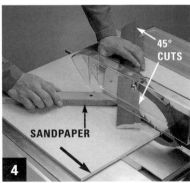

4

Glue sandpaper to the cleats' edges. Cut 45° miters from either side by holding the workpiece firmly against the cleat and sliding the jig across the table and blade.

Using Stop Blocks for Repeated Cuts

A stop block is a measurement gauge that lets you make the same size cross cut again and again. You butt the workpiece against the stop block to position it at the right distance each time, then move it through the blade to cut identical pieces (below) or to make identical cuts in a single piece (bottom).

A "retriever magnet," sold at recreational boating supply stores, or any other large rectangular magnet makes a handy, clampless stop block for repeat cut-offs on the table saw (below). Position it near the front edge of the table so the board loses contact with the magnet just before it reaches the blade as you push it with the miter gauge; otherwise the board could bind between the blade and magnet and kick back. Practice a cut on scrap wood and micro-adjust the magnet with sideways hammer taps. To remove the magnet, grip it with both hands and tip it over sideways or, if you're Hercules, lift it straight up.

You can make a custom stop block for your miter gauge to avoid having a clamp get in the way as you move a workpiece through the blade. The stop block (below) is a 3-inch-wide "box" with an open bottom that slides along an extension board you screw to the guide of the miter gauge.

Before assembling the box, recess a 1/4-inch T-nut in one side and drill a hole through for a 1/4-inch thumbscrew to enter from the outside. Then assemble the box top and sides as shown. This one-piece stop block will cut your setup time to almost nothing.

WORKING TIP

To minimize splintering, cross-cut and rip workpieces with the good side facing up, so the saw teeth cut down into the wood.
If both sides are good, score the cut line on the bottom side deeply with a utility knife before cutting.

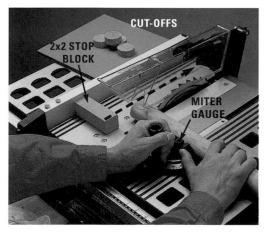

Screw or clamp a fixed stop block in place. To get identical pieces, position the workpiece against it each time you make a cut.

Turn a workpiece each time and butt it against a fixed stop block to cut matching bevels or notches all around.

Align a magnet or other adjustable stop block at 90° to the end of a workpiece so repeated cuts will give pieces of unvarying length.

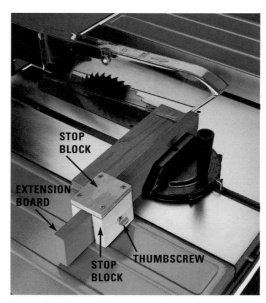

Use 3/4-in. thick wood for the sides of this adjustable stop block, to engage the end of a workpiece securely. The top can be 1/4-in. plywood or hardboard.

Cutting Dados and Finger Joints

A dado is a notch cut into the thickness of one piece to receive the end of another—a shelf, for instance, or railing. You can cut dados with a regular table saw blade by shifting the workpiece slightly each time until the repeated kerfs equal the width of the notch you want. However, it is far easier to use a dado blade—an assembly of two blades and additional cutters placed between them to reach the desired width, so you can cut the dado in one pass. For extra-wide dados you can make additional passes over the dado blade.

You can also use a dado blade to cut finger joints—alternately spaced fingers and notches that are exactly the same width. The strength and simple beauty of these joints makes them a good choice for furniture, boxes, and drawers. The key to cutting them is a simple jig.

To build the jig *(below)* set the dado blade to width—1/2 inch here—and cut a notch in a piece of 1x3, using the miter gauge. Make the notch just tall enough for a square index pin 2 inches long. Glue the pin in the notch. Mark off a space equal to the notch width and cut a second notch that far from the pin. Precise spacing is essential. Make this notch a bit taller than the thickness of the stock you will be cutting.

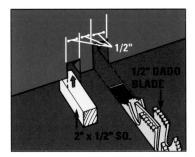

Finger joint jig.

With the saw stopped, put the tall notch over the dado blade and screw the jig to the miter gauge *(Photo 1)*.

To cut the first notch in a board, stand it on end with one edge against the index pin and push the miter gauge and jig to move the board across the dado blade. Lift the board, pull the jig back to the starting position, and place the notch over the index pin of the jig *(Photo 2)*. Cut the next notch, move it over the index pin, cut the third notch, and so on.

Do the same in another piece, then fit the fingers and notches together to see if you need to shift the jig on the miter gauge *(Photo 3)* so top and bottom edges match. On an actual joint, make the first cut so one piece starts with a finger, the other with a notch, so top and bottom edges match.

Glue the joint together. When dry, use a power sander to remove the little ends that protrude at the corners of the box.

CUTTING DADOS AND FINGER JOINTS

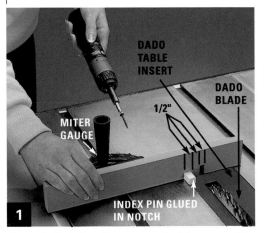

Screw the jig to the miter gauge so that the open notch is aligned exactly with the dado blade. It helps to place the notch over the blade for this step.

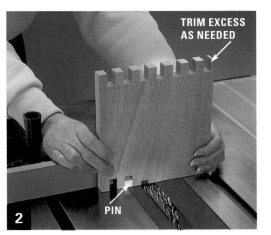

Cut successive notches by moving the just-cut notch over the index pin each time. Keep the workpiece flat against the jig and the edge square on the saw table.

Assemble and check test pieces for a tight fit. You may need to shift the jig slightly on the miter gauge. Glue the joint, then sand off any irregularities.

Cutting Raised Panels

Use your table saw to cut bevels on panels for frame-and-panel doors or wainscoting. You can do it by passing the wood through on its edge, instead of flat, with the blade tilted about 15°. Normally, cutting a wide board on its edge would be very difficult to control and would likely lead to dangerous kickback. A simple vertical fence extension can solve the problem, making this operation comfortable and safe.

Hold the extended fence square to the table saw surface with braces that are notched to fit around the standard rip fence on the saw. Drive a couple of drywall screws through the holes in the metal rip fence, into the back of the taller wood fence. Keep a close eye and a steady hand on your workpiece to make certain it remains vertical as you cut.

Screw a vertically extended fence to the rip fence to guide panels safely for bevels and other edge cuts. Braces on the back keep the fence square.

Cutting Large Sheets

Plywood, plastic laminate, and other large sheets can be difficult to guide through a table saw. Here's how to cut them accurately and cleanly.

Tack a cleat on the bottom side of the panel you are cutting, such as a plywood sheet *(below)*. Keep the cleat against the table edge throughout the cut.

For unmounted plastic laminate, clamp a wood fence to the rip fence, tight against the saw table to keep the laminate from slipping under it *(bottom)*. Use a carbide blade and keep the laminate face up to avoid scratches.

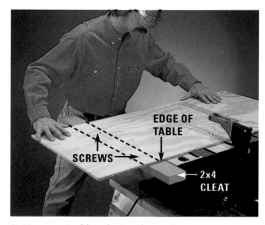

Guide a panel with a cleat underneath.

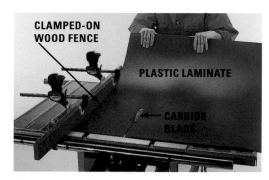

Clamp a board to the rip fence to guide laminate.

Benchtop Table Saws

Smaller and lighter weight than a stationary table saw, a benchtop model has a number of attractive features. It can be conveniently stored when not in use, it is affordable, and you can tote it easily to where you need it or mount it on a roll-around stand *(right)*. Blade size is commonly either 8-1/4 or 10 in. in diameter, and you can make the same kinds of cuts as with a larger saw. The extent of blade tilt for angle cutting may be a bit more limited, and the motor may not be as powerful as in larger saws, but those things should not be a problem unless you are cutting thick, heavy materials or trying to do production work. All in all, a benchtop table saw may be the perfect choice for a do-it-yourselfer.

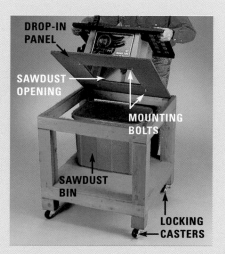

Build a stand with a 2x4 frame to give your benchtop saw roll-around versatility and convenience. Size the stand to hold a piece of 3/4-in. plywood that is 6 in. bigger than the saw base on all sides. Make it tall enough to put the saw table at a comfortable working height, with casters. Put locking casters on two adjacent legs. Cut a hole in the plywood saw base so sawdust can drop through into a removable bin. Leave all four sides of the stand open for easy access to the bin and saw accessories you store there.

Radial Arm Saws

With its swinging, tilting, and rolling motor head and easily adaptable fence, this versatile machine can saw, sand, and shape.

With just a few simple adjustments, you can use a radial arm saw to rip a board to width, trim it to proper length, bevel its edges, miter its corners, cut rabbets and dados in it—and even sand it. Using some ingenuity and perhaps a couple of accessories, there is almost no limit to what you can do with a radial arm saw.

However, you do have to make adjustments for each operation. That long arm and heavy, rotating motor head can flex, and settings can creep, making this saw somewhat less precise than single-purpose tools. But careful maintenance will keep a radial arm saw running well within the limits of most shop needs, so if you have room for only one stationary tool, this might be your best choice.

Getting Set Up

Whether your saw is new or used, it's essential that you spend the time (probably a solid afternoon) to set it up and adjust it properly. Most owner's manuals include this "tuneup" information. A high-quality 40- or 60-tooth carbide-tip blade is a must.

Acquaint yourself with the operations of the saw. Switching from one type of cut to another usually involves loosening, adjusting, then retightening two levers or cranks. With practice, you can switch from one operation to another in less than a minute. And, of course, learn where the safety locks are and how they work.

Crosscutting

A radial arm saw with a 10-inch diameter blade can cut boards up to 3 inches thick and 14 inches wide with excellent results. Pull the saw firmly and evenly toward you *(above)* for the crispest cut. The spinning blade wants to pull itself toward you, so maintain a "stiff" arm as you pull.

Cut boards with the good side up. To prevent splintering the back side, place a scrap piece of plywood beneath the workpiece. For safety, support both ends of long boards with sawhorses or roller stands, and never place your arm in the path of the saw blade.

Ripping

Radial saws do a fair job of cutting boards and sheets of wood to width. Always feed the board against the rotation of the blade *(below)*. Use extreme care, wear goggles, and employ all safety devices, such as antikickback levers. Ripping can be a two-person job, especially for large panels.

Keep in mind that the fence can be set farther back on the table to increase rip capacity; the maximum width of cut is 24 inches. It often is best to rough-cut large panels to approximate width with a circular saw before ripping them on the radial saw.

To make rip cuts, turn and lock the motor and blade 90°. Move the motor along the arm to set the rip width. Feed the work against, not with, the blade rotation.

Mitering

A miter is simply a crosscut at an angle other than 90° *(below)*. A radial arm saw can cut miters on wide, thick pieces of wood, even at angles exceeding 45°.

Cut the board about 1/16 inch too long on the first pass, then slice it to exact length with a second pass for a smoother, more accurate cut. Be careful: The blade can extend beyond the main worktable on a long left-hand miter, exposing the teeth.

To make miter cuts, swing and lock the saw arm left or right at angles up to 45° or more. Check the auto-lock 45° settings for accuracy often if you cut a lot of miters.

Bevels and Compound Angles

Few tools are better than the radial arm saw for cutting bevels using a tilted blade *(below)*, or making compound—combination bevel and miter—cuts *(below right)*. At a compound angle the blade must cut through more wood than usual. Pull the blade slowly so it doesn't bog, and hold or clamp the board firmly so it can't move out of position.

For each new angle cut, first make a small groove in the fence and table by lowering the rotating blade into them, then raising it slightly.

Keep in mind that odd angles make odd cutouts in the rip fence; you'll need to replace the fence more often.

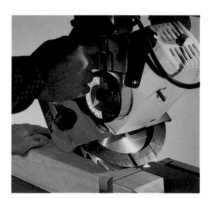 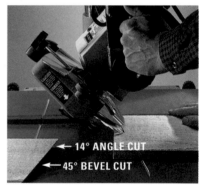

For a bevel cut, tilt and lock the motor to set the angle. Place the work to the left or right as required. Clamp a stop block to the fence to cut matching bevels in identical pieces.

For a compound cut, swing the arm and tilt the motor. Lock both settings and make a trial cut in scrap wood. Pull the blade slowly through the work; it has a lot of wood to cut.

Dadoing and Rabbeting

A dado is a groove cut in the middle of a board. A rabbet is a notch along the edge of a board. Both cuts are widely used in making bookcases and furniture.

The easiest way to make these cuts is with a special dado blade *(below)*, which can be adjusted to various widths. A radial saw lets you watch depth, length, and position of the cut as it is being made.

When cutting a deep groove or notch, make two or three passes, lowering the blade a bit each time. This will avoid tears and splintering of the wood, and reduce strain on the blade and motor.

You can also make these dado and rabbet cuts with a normal blade. Make the outside cuts first, then remove the center waste with a series of cuts.

Use a dado blade to cut both dados and rabbets. For the cleanest results, cut to the required depth in two or three passes, lowering the blade each time.

Sanding and Using Accessories

You can remove the blade from your radial arm saw and mount a variety of accessories on the motor spindle. Many of these can be used in combination with the tilts, swings, and in-out movements the saw permits.

One of the most useful accessories is a drum sander *(below)*. Various diameters and lengths are available, in several grits. You can sand with the motor in the usual horizontal position, tilt it vertically as shown, or use it at an angle. Add scrap wood under the workpiece to raise it to a fresh section as the drum surface fills up with sawdust, or reverse the sanding sleeve when the lower edge becomes worn.

Shaper or molding cutter accessories are available, but setting them up with a safe, properly aligned fence is often tricky. You can do most such jobs faster and easier with a router.

Sand edges as well as surfaces by mounting a sanding drum on the spindle on the other side of the motor from where the blade mounts. Tilt the motor to position the drum for sanding.

Pro Working Tips

Accurate Miters

Use a jig to cut accurate miters in round stock or molding. Install two guides on a plywood base at opposite 45° angles to the saw blade. Place the round stock against the guide for the correct miter angle and press a square holding block against it while cutting. This will keep the piece upright and avoid the chance of its creeping while being cut.

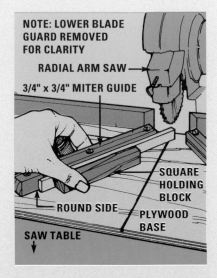

Better Blade Adjustment

For precise alignment, replace the saw blade with a flat piece of 3/4-in. plywood about 10 in. square. Use a try square to get a right-angle setting between the plywood and the saw table. Then lay a carpenter's square flat on the table with one leg butted to the fence and adjust the motor until the board is aligned with the other leg. This will provide a perfect right-angle adjustment with the fence.

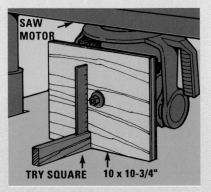

Power Miter Saws

Unequaled precision and speed in making straight and angled cuts are the features of this special-purpose tool. Finish carpenters swear by it.

Note: Throughout, the hand holding the workpiece is farther from the blade than it appears to be in the photographs.

The power miter saw is preeminent at cutting trim: baseboards, window and door casings, cornice moldings, and stair railings. It cuts accurate miters and perfectly square cutoffs. Some models can even cut compound miters—left or right angle cuts with the blade tilted to make a bevel cut at the same time. With the right blade, the cuts are silk-smooth. It's also fast, and you can nibble tiny slivers off the end of your material with great control, to make joints fit perfectly.

You can also use this saw to quickly and accurately cut 2x4s and 2x6s for framing, 4x4s for decks and fences, 2x2s for deck railings, clapboard siding, planks for hardwood floors, picture framing, face frames for cabinets, and even plastic pipe for plumbing. Because the saw is a single compact unit, it's easy to carry to the spot where you are working and set on any convenient surface, even the floor. The biggest limitation of power miter saws is that they can't cut wide boards easily.

Basic Operation

A power miter saw is mounted on a pivot above a table that has a rotating center section and a fixed fence (above). You hold a board or piece of molding in position against the fence, grasp the saw handle with the other hand, then pull the trigger switch and lower the whirling blade into the workpiece.

For an angled cut, you swing the saw left or right and lock it in position at the angle you want to cut. All saws have positive stops at the 90° and 45° settings; some also have stops at 22-1/2°, and a few at 30° as well. The following pages show you how to get the most from a power miter saw.

Miter Saw Techniques

Operating a miter saw is simple and straightforward, but the following professional tricks can make some kinds of work even easier and more accurate.

Mitering Molding

'Corner miters for molding that lies flat against a wall, such as a picture frame, or door or window trim, are simple: Just cut the two pieces at half the total angle: 45° each for a right angle, 30° each for a 60° finished angle, and so on.

Crown molding, which sits at an angle —between wall and ceiling, for example— requires a special technique. Put it in the saw upside down, at the same angle at which it will be installed (below). Think of the table of the miter box as the ceiling of the room, and the fence as the room's wall.

To help hold the molding at the proper angle without slipping, tape sandpaper or a small cleat to the saw table.

Supporting Work

The saw table is not very long, less than 24 inches on most models. That means unsupported long boards and strips of molding will sag and drop, pulling the end at the saw up and making it hard to hold the workpiece in position for a clean cut.

A simple solution is to make a few T-blocks (below). Use 1x6 stock for the base piece to give it stability against toppling over. Cut the upright so its top edge is exactly the same height as the surface of the saw table.

When doing a lot of work, tack-nail or tape the T-blocks in place so you can

quickly move work in and out of the saw without knocking the blocks out of position.

Increasing the Cut

You can't cut work as wide as the diameter of the saw blade, because there is a limit to how far the saw body can be lowered. As a result, the cut can never equal the full size of the blade.

However, you can increase the length of the usual cut by raising the workpiece above the surface of the saw table. For 2x stock, place a piece of scrap 1x wood underneath (below). For thinner stock, use thicker support under the workpiece.

How much you can lengthen the cut depends on the individual saw design, but often just a bit more is all you need, especially when cutting at an angle rather than straight across a board.

Lock the angle setting and move work in from opposite sides for accurate corner joints. Turn crown molding upside down and hold it at its mounting angle when you miter the end.

Support long work with T-blocks so it will lie flat on the saw table. Make the blocks the same height as the table, with wide bases. Tack-nail or tape them in place if necessary.

Raise a workpiece to increase the length of the cut. Use scrap 1x or 2x softwood under the piece to be cut. Be sure to also add equal thickness under a T-block or other support at the far end.

Repeating Cuts

Many projects call for several parts to be cut to precisely the same length. Examples are spindles for a railing, trim for cabinets or stiles and rails for their doors, and toy blocks.

The solution is to fasten the saw in position with clamps or temporary screws through its feet and set up a stop block at the proper distance from the saw blade *(below)*. When you butt one end of each piece against the block the other end is right where you want to cut it. Of course, you must fasten the stop block so it can't move, and you need to support the workpiece at that end so the other end will lie flat on the saw table.

Use a stop block to position pieces for identical cuts. For convenience, fasten the stop block and a support piece on a base that can be clamped at any distance from the saw.

Cutting Compound Angles

Not all miter saws permit cutting a compound angle, but the ability to do so greatly increases the usefulness of the saw. To make such a cut, you tilt the saw body for a bevel cut and swing it right or left so you can also make an angle cut in the same pass *(below)*.

Because the saw body is on the right, the blade tilts to the left. You place the work on the table from the right or the left to get the bevel sloping in the direction you want. The maximum tilt is 45° in almost all models.

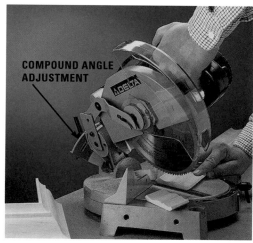

COMPOUND ANGLE ADJUSTMENT

Tilt the saw body and swing it left or right to make a compound angle cut. That makes a 33° vertical by 27° horizontal cut, for example, easy to do when you need it.

Pro Working Tips

▶ "Nibble" to your cutting line by making three or four cuts, working up to the mark. Usually this is more reliable than trying to get it exactly right with the first cut.

▶ Cut to fit. Often the quickest way to get a tight fit is to mark the piece a bit long, cut to the mark, make a trial fit, then cut off the excess in one or two passes. Make angle adjustments as you cut to fit.

▶ For the cleanest cut, hold the saw down until the blade stops after making a cut. Most saws have a brake that stops the blade in a few seconds. Lifting the saw while the blade is still spinning often tears up the grain near the cut.

▶ Get a saw with a dust bag and a large blade guard, and that uses a 10-in. diameter blade. Some 8-1/4 in. models are available, but they can't cut 1x6 or 2x6 stock in a single pass. Large 12- and 15-in. models are too heavy and expensive for nonprofessional use.

▶ Use a fine-tooth carbide-tip blade for smooth cuts. A 10-in., 50- to 80-tooth carbide cutoff blade will be perfect for fine trim work. An 80-tooth blade *(below)* produces cut edges that are almost silky to the touch.

Carbide blade teeth.

▶ Use a carbide-tip blade—but not the same one as for fine trim work—to cut shower door tracks, suspended ceiling grids, and other aluminum building materials. Do not use an abrasive cutoff wheel for ferrous metals or masonry in a power miter saw designed for cutting wood.

▶ As with all power saws, wear eye and ear protection when cutting.

Band Saws

Nothing can match a band saw for cutting curves quickly and smoothly. It's just what you need to create toys, furniture trim, and odd-shaped pieces.

BLADE TENSION LEVER

UPPER BLADE GUIDE AND GUARD

BLADE TRACKING KNOB

RIP FENCE

A band saw has a blade that is a continuous loop of toothed metal. The loop runs over large wheels or rollers above and below a table where you feed work across the blade for ripping, cross-cutting, and angled and curved cuts. The major adjustments are shown in the photo above right. The upper blade guide and guard can be raised or lowered to saw wood of different thicknesses. It provides the best blade support and most accurate results when set within 1/8 inch of the wood surface.

The rip fence can be removed and a miter gauge inserted in a slot in the table to guide square or angled crosscuts. The table can also be tilted for angled vertical cuts (bevels).

There are large stationary band saws *(above)* and smaller benchtop models that can be moved to wherever you are working. The larger the band saw, the larger its throat—the distance from the blade to the body—and so the larger the workpiece the saw can handle.

Large saws, some of which accept blades up to 3/4 inch wide, can accurately rip large materials to width. A well-adjusted, high-quality band saw can slice 1/16-inch veneers from a piece of stock with consistency. Narrow blades *(right)* are required when cutting tight curves.

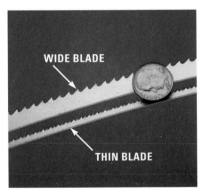

WIDE BLADE

THIN BLADE

Choose the right blade. Use a wide blade with fewer teeth to cut through thick wood, a thin blade with many teeth to cut tight curves. A blade change takes about five minutes. The dime indicates the relative width of the blades.

Making Crosscuts

You can make short crosscuts guiding the work freehand, but for a clean, straight cut line use the miter gauge. This is especially important for "dead end" cuts such as a square tenon *(below)* and for notches, when two pieces of wood need to fit together snugly.

For cuts at a vertical angle, tilt the saw table *(bottom)*. Use the angle indicator for accuracy and be sure to lock the table in position before starting the cut.

Use the miter gauge for straight crosscuts.

Lock a tilted table securely before cutting.

Cutting Curves

The secret to cutting curves on a band saw is to first make relief cuts. You can space them fairly widely for outside curves *(below)*, but tight inside curves require very closely spaced relief cuts *(bottom)*. Adjust blade guides as close to the blade as possible for support, and the blade guard as low as possible to the wood.

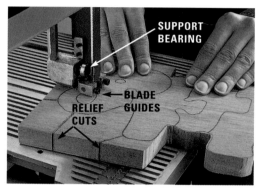

Make relief cuts for outside curves first.

Use very close relief cuts for tight inside curves.

Pro Working Tips

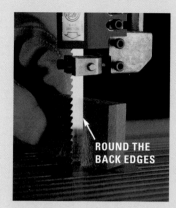

Tightly Curved Cuts

To get more tightly curved cuts with a band saw, gently round the back edges of the blade. With the saw running, touch a medium grit sharpening stone to both corners of the back edges of the blade for just a few seconds. Wear eye protection, and make sure there isn't wood dust in the lower part of your saw, or the sparks may cause a fire.

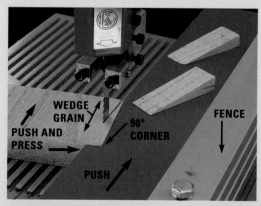

Cutting Wedges and Shims

Here's a fast way to cut a lot of same-size wedges and shims. Make a jig from a 12-in.-long scrap board (red in the picture). Cut a notch with a 90° corner in the edge of the board. The width of the bottom of the notch determines the taper of the wedge. Put one end of the wedge stock in the notch and push the two boards through the blade, holding the stock in the notch as you saw. After one pass, flip the stock over and cut another wedge. Do the same each time. Cut wedges with the grain running along their length.

Scroll Saws

Cutting intricate shapes in wood, plastic, or metal is a cinch with a scroll saw. Whether you're making toys, jewelry, puzzles, letters for signs, or some other project, it's fun too!

In many craft and small construction tasks there are parts that are too small, and curves and corners that are too tight to cut on a band saw (pages 64–65), and too difficult or numerous to attempt by hand, using a coping saw. If you have lots of parts to cut—for a puzzle or a model train set, for example—hand sawing may well take far more time than the project is worth. What you need is a scroll saw, a benchtop power tool that makes precision, small-scale cutting not only easy but a pleasure to do.

A scroll saw is really a motorized coping saw: The vertical blade moves rapidly up and down through a hole in an adjustable table. You place a workpiece up to 2 inches thick on the table and push it against the teeth of the blade. Because the blade is so thin and narrow, you can cut very tight curves, sharp zigzags, and all kinds of other shapes just by turning the work-piece as the saw blade cuts continuously. A hold-down leg keeps even very thin wood, metal, or plastic from vibrating and tear-ing, and a blower tube keeps the cutting line clear of chips and sawdust.

Operating a scroll saw is very easy, and quite safe compared to most other power tools. You need to wear eye protection and a dust mask because of the sawdust produced. But if you keep your fingers from being nicked by the blade, there's little else to worry about. The next three pages tell you how to choose and use a scroll saw. The more you use it, the more rapidly you'll become skilled at doing all sorts of intricate things—and the more fun you'll have.

Scroll Saw Features

A good-quality scroll saw will cost $100 to $300. Look for these features:

Quiet operation, little vibration. Run the saw before you buy. Some are quieter than others. If the blade looks blurred when the saw is running, there's too much vibration.

Blade adjustment. See if it is easy to change blades and secure the blade clamps. Check for easy-to-operate blade-tensioning, either lever-action or knob-controlled.

Good hold-down leg. It should be easy to move out of the way without having to remove the blade.

Multispeed motor. Look for a variable- or two-speed saw. Different speed settings give you better control.

Maximum capacity. Most saws have a 15-inch throat (blade-to-arm) capacity, so they can cut to the center of a 30-inch workpiece.

Tilting table. Not essential, but very helpful for cutting bevels and slanted edges.

Scroll Saw Blades

Scroll saw blades come with two types of ends. Pin-end blades have a cross-pin that slips into a recess in the blade holders above and below the saw table. Plain or straight (flat) end blades are held by clamps. Most saws have attachments to use both types, and most take 5-inch-long blades. The three major designs of blades are shown below. Coarse-cutting scroll blades are used for straight cuts through thick or hard materials. They have regular-style saw teeth. Fret blades, preferred by most scroll saw users, are much narrower and are used for fine and intricate cuts. They have a skip-tooth pattern: tooth, space, tooth, space, and so on. The space carries more sawdust out of the cut so that the blade cuts cooler because there's less friction. Spiral blades are fret blades twisted so the teeth point out in different directions. They're used mostly for cutting extremely tight curves. Spiral blades cut a wider kerf than the other types and require skill in maneuvering the workpiece, something you can only gain with experience.

Setting Up a Scroll Saw

A benchtop saw can be mounted either on a separate stand or directly on your workbench. Either way, it must be bolted down securely or vibrations will make it unusable. If vibration noise is a problem, put a piece of rug, carpet pad, or similar material between the saw and the bench.

Before making any cuts, use a combination square to make sure the blade is square to the saw table. Place the square on the table behind the back edge of the saw blade as shown below. You may need to remove the blade of the combination square. Correct the alignment by loosening the table's tilt knob and adjusting the table-to-blade angle. Also, set the hold-down leg for the thickness of the material before beginning a cut. Basic sawing techniques are shown on pages 68–69.

Use a combination square to make sure the scroll saw table is at right angles to the blade. Do this before starting to use the saw, and each time after tilting the table to cut at an angle.

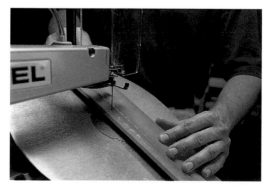

Look for a tilting table. It's versatile and great for cutting moldings, or parts that require slightly beveled edges, such as jigsaw puzzle pieces.

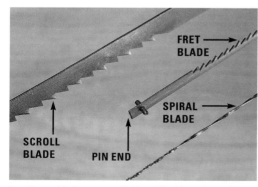

Scroll saw blades are available with either pin ends or plain ends, and different numbers of teeth per inch.

Marking Workpieces

You can draw straight lines and simple curves directly on a workpiece to guide your cuts. For more complex patterns, it is best to draw them on paper. If you need to enlarge a pattern or the drawing you are copying, take it to a photocopying machine that offers variable size changes. When you have the size you need, attach the pattern to the surface of your workpiece with spray adhesive *(below)*. You can cut out the paper shape either before you mount it or afterward with a razor knife.

If you need to cut several duplicate shapes, make a master pattern on heavy paper, then trace it on sheets of tracing paper, one for each duplicate. Spray-mount the tracing paper to the workpiece and cut right through it when you saw out the pattern.

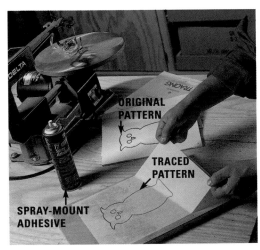

Attach a paper pattern to a workpiece with spray adhesive. Make multiple copies on tracing paper if you need to cut out duplicate parts. You can saw through tracing paper; cut away waste sections of heavier paper with a razor knife before sawing.

Making Straight Cuts

Start all straight cuts at the corner of the shape or pattern *(below)*. Use both hands to guide the workpiece, and feed it slowly into the blade for the smoothest and most accurate cut. Cut slightly to the waste side of the line, so you can sand precisely to the line when cleaning up the edge.

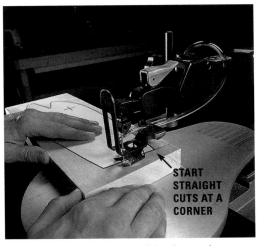

Begin straight cuts at a corner of the shape to be cut out. Reposition the piece to make another cut crossing the first one, unless you are using a spiral blade. Don't try to turn a right angle with a scroll or fret blade.

Making Curved Cuts and Sharp Corners

Use a loop pattern to change directions when cutting a curve or turning a sharp corner, in order to keep sawing continuously with either a standard scroll blade or a fret blade.

Carry the first part of the cut past the end of the curve or corner and out into a loop in the waste portion of the workpiece *(below)*. Continue the loop to bring the blade back to the pattern in the direction in which you want to continue the cut. Make the loop large enough for easy cutting, and don't try to hurry through the loop cut; move at the same speed as when cutting along the pattern lines.

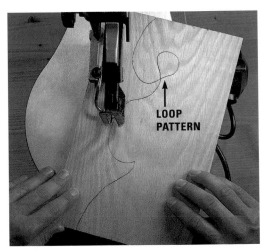

Make a loop cut in a waste portion of the workpiece to change curve directions or to cut sharp corners. Keep the cutting speed constant, and don't force the piece against the blade.

Making Inside Cuts

To cut out the inside of a pattern, such as the hole in the center of an "O," make a pierced cut. Drill a pilot hole through the area to be cut and sand the bottom edge smooth to make sure the workpiece will lie flat on the saw table. Unhook or unclamp the saw blade, stick it up through the hole, and secure it again *(below)*. Then make the cut, following your marked pattern lines. If you want the hole to have beveled edges—for example, to hold a lift-out plug—tilt the saw table before beginning the cut.

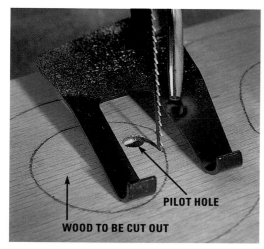

PILOT HOLE

WOOD TO BE CUT OUT

Drill a pilot hole in order to make a pierced cut that removes an inside shape. For intricate shapes, back up to the pilot hole or drill more holes where you need to change direction easily.

Pro Working Tips

Saw Blade Saver

The upper teeth of a scroll saw blade often stay sharp while the lower teeth are dulled by use. To get longer blade life, build an accessory table to raise workpieces up to the unused teeth. Glue 1/2-in.-square blocks about 2 in. long on the underside of 3/4-in. plywood as shown. Drill a 3/8-in. hole for the blade and cut a slot to the front edge so you can place the raised table without removing the blade.

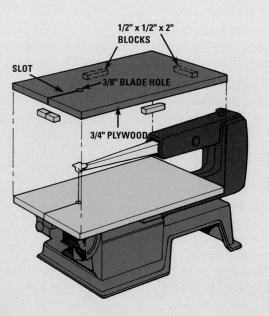

1/2" x 1/2" x 2" BLOCKS

SLOT

3/8" BLADE HOLE

3/4" PLYWOOD

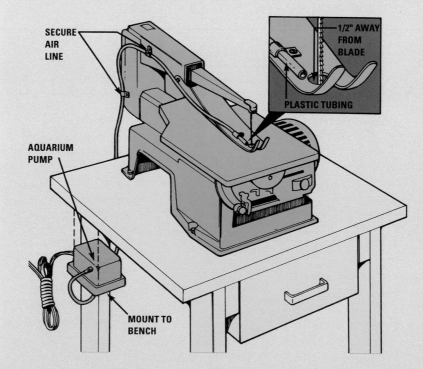

SECURE AIR LINE

1/2" AWAY FROM BLADE

PLASTIC TUBING

AQUARIUM PUMP

MOUNT TO BENCH

Sawdust Blaster

If your scroll saw does not have a dust blower to keep pattern lines visible, make your own. Buy an inexpensive aquarium pump and mount it close to the saw. Run the plastic tube along the saw body to the hold-down leg and secure it 1/2 in. away from the blade, so it blows dust away. You'll find it a lot easier to follow the pattern this way.

Reciprocating Saws

This workhorse tool cuts anywhere, fast. For rough work and heavy-duty jobs, there's nothing better.

HANDLE NOSE GRIP SHOE STARTER HOLE

A reciprocating saw is a grown-up jigsaw, with muscles. It isn't a tool you need for many kinds of projects, but when you tackle any serious renovations it can make tough, rough work go so fast that you'll never want to be without one. For such jobs as sawing through walls, sheathing, or subflooring, removing plumbing or heating pipes, cutting a new doorway, or making an opening in the roof for a skylight, nothing can beat this tool. You can also use it for jobs that are usually done with a chainsaw, such as cutting posts and pruning tree limbs.

When you first need a reciprocating saw, consider renting one; the cost is about $15 a day. That will give you a chance to evaluate its future usefulness, so you can decide whether you want to buy one or to rent again when necessary.

Keep in mind that the reciprocating saw is not a tool for fine carpentry. It's at its best on fairly rough construction, such as cutting away studs and slicing through plaster and lath. It can cut through exterior walls and interior studs in one pass, and with just a little practice you'll be able to saw accurately enough to install door jambs or window frames directly into those openings without further trimming.

A Maneuverable, Versatile Tool

The first big virtue of the reciprocating saw is its maneuverability. It can get into corners and tight spots that a circular saw can't reach. You can work with it overhead or in almost any other position without difficulty, and more safely than with any other power saw. Because you use a two-handed grip to operate the saw, you have good control as it cuts. Most basic models offer two-speed operation; other, more versatile models have a variable speed motor, so you can select what is best for the material you are cutting.

A second virtue of this tool is versatility. Professional contractors and remodelers know that with a reciprocating saw they no longer need a separate hand saw, keyhole saw, or hacksaw. The design of the saw, with an unrestricted blade extending straight out, like the "saw" of a swordfish, is one key to its versatility. Circular saws and jigsaws have blade guards and shoes around their blades that limit their maneuverability and the depth of cut. But a reciprocating saw doesn't have these limits. The blade extends through a shoe at the front and moves rapidly in and out from the body, traveling anywhere from 3/4 to 2 inches, depending on the make and model. On most saws you can adjust the shoe to shorten the effective length of the cutting stroke for greater efficiency or to keep the blade tip from hitting an obstruction.

Another key to the versatility of the reciprocating saw is the wide variety of types and lengths of blades available (see page 73). Whatever you need to cut, there's a blade that's just right for it.

Cutting Techniques

Hold the saw with both hands, one on the handle at the rear, the other on the grip at the front, as shown below. If necessary, drill a starter hole *(opposite page)* for the blade. Press the shoe at the nose of the saw firmly against the workpiece, then pull the trigger.

NOTE: Some pictures show the shoe not touching the work. That is simply for visual clarity. When you work, hold the shoe against the workpiece to minimize vibration and give you maximum control in guiding the saw.

In open work—for example, cutting into wall framing after the drywall paneling has been removed *(below)*—press the bottom of the shoe against the work with the blade angled upward. Start the motor and raise the handle to bring the shoe flat against the work and the blade level across the top, then move the saw downward to make the cut.

The saw's design makes it easy to turn the body so the blade is horizontal *(below)* or at whatever angle is required. Use a blade long enough to reach entirely across or through the work and extend 1 to 2 inches beyond when at the shortest point in the stroke; blade lengths range from 3 to 12 inches for various kinds of work. When cutting "blind" into just one side of a wall, choose a blade short enough so that the tip will not hit the other side. For sawing through a combination of materials, such as wood and plasterboard, use a coarse-toothed blade. Its more widely spaced teeth and a fast cutting speed will clear the kerf better and faster.

SHOE AGAINST WORK

Start a cut on open work with the blade angled upward and lower it into the work. Use a bimetal blade for wood-plus-metal cutting.

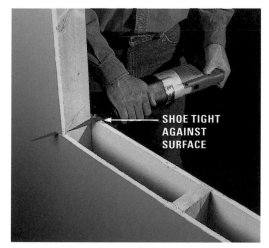

SHOE TIGHT AGAINST SURFACE

Use a long blade to cut through a wall or thick workpiece; it should extend 1 to 2 in. beyond the piece's opposite side. Keep the saw's shoe tight against the work surface.

Sawing Tips

Determine the amount of cutting pressure to apply by trial and error; a little practice will give you the feel of it. Too little pressure will cause vibration and broken blades. Too much pressure will give you a rough, inaccurate cut.

Here are some other tips to keep in mind while sawing:

Rock the blade. To make sawing go faster, pivot the handle up and down to rock the blade as it cuts *(below)*. This helps clear sawdust or chips, which tend to bind the blade, out of the kerf and puts the blade teeth at angles where they can cut into the material most efficiently. When cutting through any old construction, be sure to use a bimetal blade rated for both wood and metal; you'll be cutting nails and perhaps even screws as well as the wood framing.

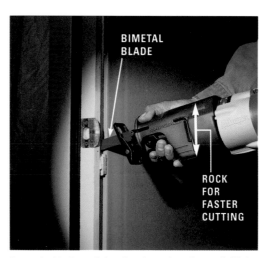

BIMETAL BLADE

ROCK FOR FASTER CUTTING

Insert the blade until the shoe is against the work. Make sure the tip won't hit anything. Speed cutting by rocking the saw.

Make a plunge cut. To save the time of drilling a starter hole, begin by making a plunge cut. Hold the bottom edge of the shoe firmly against the surface with the tip of the blade just above it *(below)*. Start the saw and rotate the tip of the blade down into the wood by slowing pulling up on the handle. Keep a firm grip on the saw so the blade doesn't cause the body to jump as it enters the work. To cut curved shapes, use a narrow blade in the saw, so it won't bind as the direction of cut continuously changes.

NOSE DOWN

PULL UP ON HANDLE

SHOE AGAINST SURFACE

Make a plunge cut instead of drilling a starter hole. Place the shoe on the work and lower the moving blade tip slowly. Grip the saw firmly to avoid bouncing.

Make preliminary straight cuts. To get a precise straight-line cut in thick stock, first make a cut with a circular saw to maximum depth, then finish with a wide blade in the reciprocal saw. The wide blade won't wander in the kerf the way a narrow one often does.

Reverse the blade. For overhead work or to cut tightly to a surface between boards *(below),* reverse the blade so the teeth point up toward the top of the saw body, instead of down. If you can't press the shoe against the work, keep the hand that holds the nose of the saw pressed firmly against the surface.

REVERSE BLADE

Reverse the blade so the teeth point upward to cut nails behind siding or tight trim. Pry the work loose to insert the blade without damage.

Tips for Safety

The reciprocating saw is a bulky tool. Since you'll often use it overhead or in confined spots, keep safety in mind.

▶ Never operate the saw holding it just by the rear handle. The rapid reciprocal movement will cause the saw to buck and bounce, breaking or bending the blade. If the saw jumps out of the workpiece, its weight will cause the nose to drop, where the blade can scar up adjacent surfaces or swing into your leg or body.

▶ Before cutting into walls, always check for electrical and water lines. If you're not sure what's back there, cut a small hole first and probe with a wire coat hanger. Most saws have a rubber boot covering the nose to give you a good, sure grip, and to minimize the danger of electrical shock.

▶ If the blade binds or bends when cutting, don't grab the blade to straighten it. It's likely to be sizzling hot and will give you a nasty burn.

▶ Watch where your extension cord runs, so you don't accidentally cut through it.

▶ Always unplug the saw before switching or cleaning a blade. Blade changing is a two-handed operation that requires a hex key on most reciprocating saws.

▶ As with all power cutters, wear safety goggles every time you use the saw.

Reciprocating Saw Blades

The reciprocating saw is a workhorse tool, but only if you use the right blade. The type of material you're cutting, its thickness, and the shape of the cut—that is, straight or curved—all influence blade selection.

There is an enormous range of types and sizes of blades to choose from—more than 90 by one count— but the following information can help you narrow the choice.

The cheapest blades, stamped from coil steel, are no bargain because they bend easily and dull rapidly. Better-quality toothed blades for cutting wood or metal are made either of high-speed tool steel or of a bimetal combination of tool steel and spring steel. Tool steel blades are inexpensive—$1 to $3—and have hard, durable teeth, but they are brittle. Overheating, twisting, or the tip hammering into a hard surface can cause them to break.

Bimetal blades are about 25 percent more expensive, but they will last four to eight times longer than other blades. In part this is because the two metals dissipate heat more rapidly and effectively, which reduces the rate of dulling as well as metal fatigue. In addition, they are flexible, not brittle. If one is bent, you usually can lay it on a hard, flat surface and tap it with a hammer to straighten it. Whenever you need to cut through both wood and metal, such as nails, be sure to use a bimetal blade.

Blades are 3 to 12 inches long, with 3 to 32 teeth per inch. Use the coarsest-toothed blades for cutting soft woods and green wood such as tree limbs. Use blades with 10 or 18 teeth per inch for cutting hard and finished woods. Metal-cutting blades have the finest teeth, like hand-hacksaw blades. To minimize clogging, choose a blade that will have at least three teeth in contact with the metal at a time. Highly efficient tungsten carbide blades—steel blades with carbide-grit edges—are also available for cutting metal or ceramic materials.

Choose blade length and blade width to suit the size of the material and the line of cut—straight or curved—as described in the text.

High-speed steel blade for metal

Carbide grit blade for cast iron, stainless steel, ceramics

Bimetal blade for wood with nails

Pruning blade for trees

Drilling

Electric Drills

Electric drills are the most frequently used power tools because they are easy to operate and can do a variety of jobs. Learn how to choose and operate yours to best advantage.

76

Hammer Drills

Hammer drills are for those hard-to-drill holes that would ruin a regular drill. Use this tool—along with the right bit—to make holes in concrete, stone, mortar, cement block, brick, or tile.

84

Drill Presses

A bench-top drill press can drill accurate holes in pipes and wooden balls; help you drill rows of holes for bookshelf pegs; and even smooth, sand, and shape, with the help of accessories.

88

Electric Drills

You need a drill for almost every project; it's the No. 1 power tool with do-it-yourselfers and homeowners. Here's how to get the most out of yours.

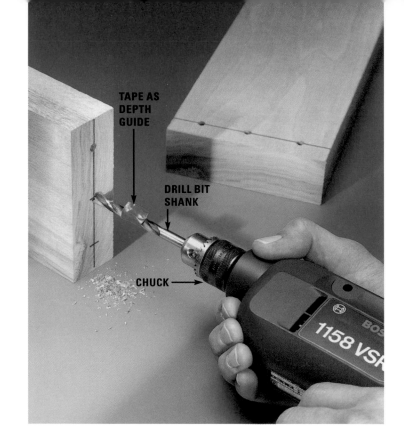

TAPE AS DEPTH GUIDE

DRILL BIT SHANK

CHUCK

1158 VSR BOS

An electric drill is the first power tool most people buy; it certainly is the one they use most—not just for boring holes, but to drive screws, sand, clean metal, polish, and even stir paint. If you don't have one, you should. It is inexpensive and so easy to use that you'll find it indispensable. The next several pages show you basic drill operation and lots of simple working tips that make it easy to do complex jobs.

Selecting a Drill

A drill is the most basic of all power tools. A chuck clamps around the shank of a drill bit or accessory and a motor spins it around. The chuck may be keyed—you turn it with a little T-handle wrench with a gear-toothed end—or keyless, which you can open and close by hand.

A keyless chuck is more convenient, because you don't have to make sure a key stays with the drill all the time. If you have a keyed-chuck drill, you can easily change it to a keyless type (see page 83).

A good first choice is a 3/8-inch, variable speed, reversible (VSR) drill. It accepts bit and accessory shafts up to 3/8 inch diam-

eter. It can spin a bit slowly or quickly (0 to 1,200 revolutions per minute is a common range) for the most efficient drilling in various materials. And it can run in reverse, to back a bit out of a hole where it is binding or to remove a screw. Consider these features, plus the weight, balance, and feel of the drill in your hand as you shop.

A 1/2-inch drill, the next larger size, can accommodate larger bits and more accessories, but generally it revolves slower, weighs more, and is more difficult to control. If you need a large drill from time to time, or a special-purpose drill, you can rent one for very little.

Drilling Holes

There are three keys to drilling a hole that is precisely located, straight, and clean:

1. Start with a clearly marked center point. No matter what material you're dealing with, mark the center point for the drill bit. In soft wood, use a pencil to mark the center with an "X" and put the tip of the drill bit on it *(below)*. In hard wood or when pinpoint accuracy is required, dimple the center of the X with a nail set or even just a nail. In metal or concrete, mark the point where you want to drill using a metal punch.

2. Keep the bit perpendicular to the work. There are various commercial drill guides and doweling devices for aligning the bit accurately, but there are also practical DIY ways. Stand a small try square on the workpiece next to the bit to see if it is vertical. Or ask a helper to assist in the "two hands, four eyes" approach. You each hold the drill handle as you watch the bit—one from behind, the other from the side—and you each gently adjust the drill so the bit is boring straight from your own viewing angle *(below)*.

3. Stop before it's too late. To keep from going all the way through a workpiece or to drill a series of holes all the same depth, wrap tape around the bit *(opposite page)* as a depth guide. For more precise control use a stop. You can buy an adjustable stop—a collar that fastens onto a twist bit—or make your own from scrap wood *(right)*.

If you do want to drill all the way through, you still need to stop before it's too late. The side of the workpiece where the drill bit enters is usually cut cleanly, but the back side is subject to splintering as the bit emerges. This is especially likely with large-diameter twist bits, with paddlelike spade bits, and with hole saws.

Make depth stops from scraps of 1x1. The length of bit extending beyond the stop is how deep the hole will be. This is more accurate than using tape on the bit.

To eliminate tearout, drill the hole until the tip of the bit just barely emerges from the far side, then remove the drill bit and finish the hole from that side *(below)*. You can also clamp a scrap board tightly to the back of the piece to prevent tearout.

Keep the bit headed squarely through the workpiece. Two people can adjust the drill while cross-sighting the bit at 90°.

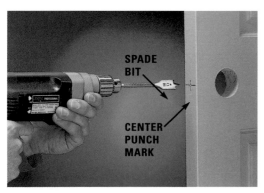

Clearly mark the center point for a drill bit of any type. Punch a small hole with a nail set, awl, or nail to keep the tip from wandering.

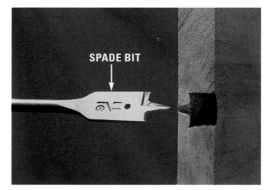

Make splinter-free holes by drilling from one side until the bit tip just goes through, then finish from the other side, as shown.

Drill Bits

Bits for handheld drills are commonly sized by the diameter of the hole they bore, from 1/16 inch to more than 1 inch. Among the types most widely used are twist and combination bits, masonry bits, and brad-point and spade bits.

Twist and Combination Bits

Some very useful bits are shown below. The most common type is a twist bit (A). Only high-speed steel (HSS) twist bits are worthwhile, because they stay sharp longest and resist bending or breaking under the stress and high heat of drilling. Lesser-quality bits are a false bargain because they have such short working lives.

In sizes up to the maximum a drill accepts, the shank and the cutting portion—the shaft or flutes—of twist bits should be the same. For larger sizes, get twist bits with the largest possible shank for your drill—a 1/2-inch bit on a 3/8-inch shank, for example.

Combination bits solve the problem that a flathead wood screw requires holes of different diameters for its head and tapered shank and threads. You can get that in two steps by first using a countersink bit (B) to drill a tapered hole for the head, then using a twist bit to drill the screw pilot hole. Combination bits drill both holes at once. Bit (C) has a countersink and a tapered shaft, with depth adjustments for each. Bit (D) has a depth adjustment only for the drill bit but drills a pilot hole more suited to the profile of a wood screw. Bit (E) is an adjustable combination bit to drill holes for untapered drywall screws, which are widely used to fasten wood as well.

Masonry Bits

For tiles, masonry, and concrete, there are masonry twist bits with carbide tips *(below)*. In hard concrete, drill a starter hole with a small masonry bit, then use a larger bit to reach final size. These bits are not suitable for drilling holes in wood.

Brad-Point and Spade Bits

Standard twist bits have a triangular tip *(below)*. A brad-point bit has a longer, sharp center point to hold it precisely in position at the start, and scalloped cutting edges. You can buy brad-point bits or make them: Grind the tip of a twist bit flat, then use the grinder or a grinding wheel clamped in a drill to cut the scallops. Be careful not to burn the bit; it could lose its original temper. Make the outer cutting tips a fraction shorter than the brad point in the center. They should be even when you view the bit from the side. A brad-point bit cuts fast and clean, so don't force it.

Spade bits *(page 77, bottom right)* have a flat, paddle shape, with a point in the center and, in large sizes, cutting spurs at the outer corners. They are lighter weight and have longer shafts than twist bits, and come in larger maximum sizes.

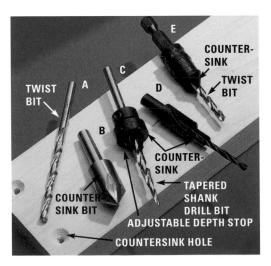

Drill tiles and masonry with a carbide-tip masonry bit. A starter hole keeps the bit from skidding and speeds the process of making larger holes.

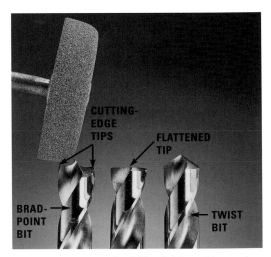

Choose brad-point bits for drilling finish work in wood. You can make them, but it is easier and not very expensive to buy them.

Electric Drill Accessories

A variety of devices can make your drill useful for much more than boring holes. Here a few of the most popular accessories.

Screwdriver Bit

A magnetic bit holder is a steel tube with a magnet inside. It fits into the drill chuck and holds interchangeable flat Phillips head, and square-drive screwdriver tips at the other end. With a variable speed drill, slowly rotate the screw until it bites into the wood, then increase the speed. As you near the end, slow down again so you don't bury the head too deeply. Wood screws need pilot holes; drywall screws cut their own way into the material. A magnetic driver tip will hold a screw for one-hand drill operation while the other hand holds the workpieces tightly together *(below)*.

Hole Saws

Hole saws cut only the perimeter of a hole, making them useful only for going all the way through the material. These saws require a center pilot bit to get them started and keep them on target. Some use simply a twist bit, others use a mandrel or arbor—a bit with a locking nut to secure it to the hole saw. Standard cup-shaped hole saws *(below)* cut to a depth of about 1-1/4 inches; deep cutting versions cut 1-3/4 inches or more. You need different diameters to cut holes of different sizes. An adjustable hole saw *(bottom)* can be set to cut holes from 1 to 4 or more inches in diameter, but is slower working and harder to control.

Sanding Drum

Interchangeable sanding drums come in many lengths and diameters. Use small sizes for tight inside curves and narrow edges *(right)*, large sizes for long curves and surfaces. Some drums take abrasive sleeves, others take self-stick sandpaper; both are equally useful.

Wire Brushes

For removing rust, cleaning garden tools, or even scraping down a barbecue grill, a wire brush will save you lots of time and effort. You can get various sizes of disk and cup-shaped brushes *(below)* with stiff, coarse wires for heavy-duty work and thinner, softer wires for cleaning and polishing aluminum or brass. Be sure to wear eye and hand protection—rust, paint, surface material, and bits of the brush will fly as you work.

SANDING DRUM

Sanding drum.

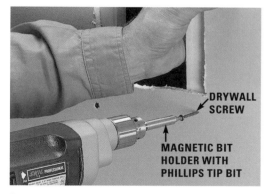

DRYWALL SCREW

MAGNETIC BIT HOLDER WITH PHILLIPS TIP BIT

Chuck a magnetic bit holder into your drill to convert it into a power screwdriver. Straight and Phillips head hex-shank bits fit the holder. A variable-speed drill gives the best control.

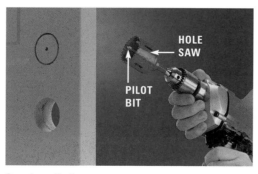

HOLE SAW

PILOT BIT

Cup-shaped hole saw.

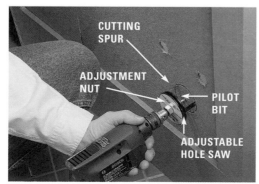

CUTTING SPUR

ADJUSTMENT NUT

PILOT BIT

ADJUSTABLE HOLE SAW

Adjustable hole saw.

Disk-type wire brush.

WIRE CUP BRUSH

Cup-shaped wire brush.

Cordless Drills

Whether you're up a ladder, wriggling around in a crawl space, or trying to do jobs in several spots quickly, you'll find that using a cordless drill is an enormous convenience. A cordless drill can do just about everything a standard corded model can; in addition, it is safe to use in wet or damp conditions without fear of shock. There are three categories of cordless drills: small, light duty; full size, heavy duty; and new high-power models we will call "super duty." Here is some basic information about each category.

Small, Light-duty Drills

Lightweight and compact, these are the handiest and least expensive models. Their built-in 4.8- or 6.0-volt batteries provide 10–15 minutes of operating time, then have to be recharged. The charger plugs into a household AC outlet and into a terminal on the drill body (below). Recharging takes up to three hours.

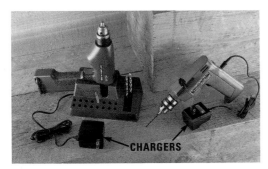

Small, light-duty drills are inexpensive and good for many home improvement tasks, but their built-in batteries provide short operating times, and you can't use the drill during the three hours recharging takes.

Full-size, Heavy-duty Drills

A cordless drill in this category is the best choice for almost all kinds of DIY work. Larger, heavier, and somewhat more expensive (typically $75–100), it has the power to drive screws; drill holes with twist, spade, and Forstner bits with ease; and use accessories such as hole-cutting saws for extended working periods.

A full-size drill has a removable 7.2- or 9.6-volt battery that can be removed and recharged in an hour or less (below). That means you can work continuously, using one battery while an extra one recharges. Many full-size cordless drills have features such as dual or variable speeds, a keyless chuck, and a clutch for controlled screwdriving.

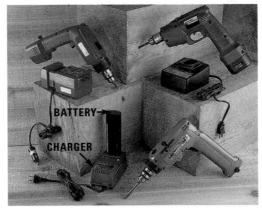

Full-size, heavy-duty drills can handle all kinds of jobs. Their removable batteries provide long operating times and can be recharged in one hour. Many models have special features that increase their usability.

"Super-duty" Drills

These new drills are the largest, heaviest, most powerful—and most expensive—of all (below). Equipped with a 12- to 18-volt battery, a "super-duty" drill can typically drill ninety-five 7/8-inch holes in 2x lumber on a single charge or drive 3/8-inch lag bolts one after another with ease. And when needed, the battery can be recharged in 15 minutes.

Not everyone needs super capability or wants to spend as much as this professional-level drill now costs, but similar models at consumer prices may well be available when you are shopping. If you have major work to do and will not be hampered by its size and weight, this kind of drill may be exactly what you need.

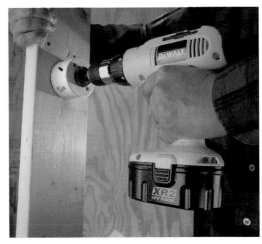

"Super-duty" cordless drills are professional-level tools. Their powerful batteries can handle the heaviest work for three or four hours without difficulty, and can be recharged in as little as 15 minutes.

Features to Look For

Some cordless drills are basic, no-frills models; others have sophisticated features you should consider when you shop.

Design. Drill body shapes are similar, but weights range from 2 to 5 lbs. and more. In addition, the size, shape, and placement of a removable battery affect the comfort and balance of using a drill. Get one that gives an easy, one-hand grip.

Reverse and on-off switches. A reverse switch located near or above the trigger switch is indispensable for backing out screws or removing stuck bits; you'll use it a lot. A drill with a built-in battery should have an on-off switch for safety and to save battery power when not in use.

Chuck. In a keyed-chuck drill, look for a convenient, snap-in holder for the key on the drill body or handle *(below)*. Far more convenient is a keyless chuck, available in many models.

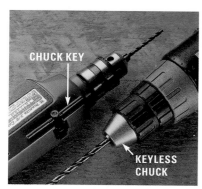

Chucks—keyed and keyless. A drill with a keyed chuck should feature a holder for the key, because there's no cord to fasten it to. A keyless chuck provides the quickest, easiest way to change bits.

Variable speed. This feature is great for driving screws or drilling hard materials like metal or tile. A two-speed switch is helpful, but a variable-speed trigger switch is much better *(below)*. A drill with both features has great versatility.

Clutch. This mechanism on a full-size or super-duty drill limits the amount of force (torque) delivered to a bit. You can use it to control screwdriving into drywall, plywood subflooring, or wherever a uniform depth is desired. A six-setting clutch, usually with five sensitivity levels and one lock mode for full-strength drilling and driving, is a common feature *(below right)*.

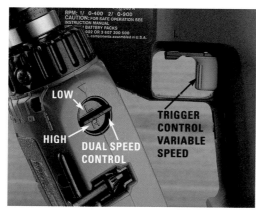

Variable operating speeds greatly increase the usefulness of a cordless drill. Choose at least a dual-speed model. Variable speed operation is even better.

Accessories

Cordless drills can use all common accessories, such as hole saws, sanding drums, and wire brushes. There are some additional items you will find valuable as well.

The first is indispensable: an extra battery for a removable-battery drill. You can't work efficiently without one. Next is one or more magnetic screwdriver bits in various sizes for Phillips head and slotted screws. Another useful accessory is a carrying case to keep everything in place. Finally, a holster to slip the drill into is immensely helpful when you need both hands free or when you are working on a ladder or a roof, where there is no place to put the drill down without it falling or sliding out of reach.

A clutch lets you adjust the force, or torque, of the drill to drive screws to a uniform depth in different kinds of materials. In combination with variable speeds, it provides almost infinite drilling control.

Pro Working Tips

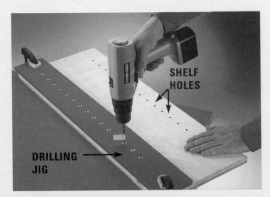

Shelf Pin Drilling Jig

A strip of perforated hardboard (pegboard) makes a quick and easy drilling jig for a series of holes, if the spacing is right. But the drill bit quickly wears the holes too large. For a wearproof jig, drill the threads out of metal nuts—hold them in locking pliers or a vise. In 1/2-in. hardwood or plywood, drill a line of precisely spaced holes the same size or slightly smaller than the width of the nuts, measured across opposite flats. Hammer two nuts into each hole, and your jig is ready to use.

Drill Case

To keep your power drill handy, cut a 12-in. section of 4-in. diameter PVC pipe. Saw a notch in the top about 2 in. wide to receive the drill handle. Mount the holder in a convenient location on your workshop wall.

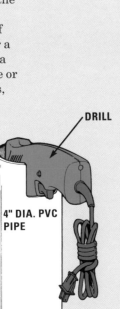

Crank Out the Plug

The cut-out plug often gets stuck in a hole saw and is almost impossible to chisel or hammer out. This is especially true of new hole saws because of the coat of paint inside. To remove the plug, drive a screw into the plug near its outer edge, clamp the saw spindle in a vise, and crank the screw gently until the plug breaks free. Next time, spray some wax inside the saw before cutting.

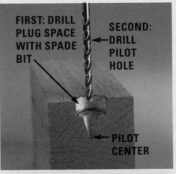

Double-stage Plug Holes

Where screws are to be covered by wood plugs, drill the plug hole first with a spade bit, then follow with a bit for the screw pilot hole. The point of the spade bit leaves a perfectly centered starter hole for the pilot bit, so you can drive the screw straight in without touching the sides of the plug hole. Glue and sand tapered plugs in place to hide the screw heads.

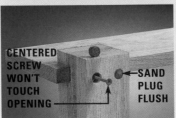

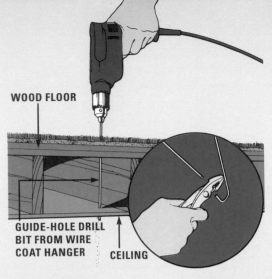

Long Guide-hole Bit

When drilling through a floor and ceiling, or the walls of adjoining rooms, it's hard to get the holes lined up. Make a long drill bit for guide holes by cutting the long straight section from a wire coat hanger with pliers; this will leave a chisel-like tip. Drill a small guide hole through the first surface. Chuck the wire bit in the drill, insert it through the first hole, and drill a guide hole slowly through the far surface. The guide hole on each side will be easy to find and you can enlarge it with an ordinary bit when the location is right.

Fix a Too-small Hole

A spade-bit hole that is too small is hard to make larger because there is no wood left in the center to guide a larger spade bit—so use the edges: Grind chamfers on the corners of the larger bit. They will center the new bit in the hole.

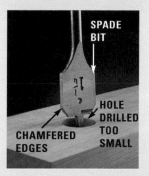

SPADE BIT

CHAMFERED EDGES

HOLE DRILLED TOO SMALL

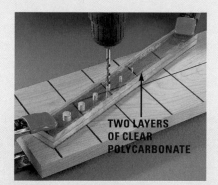

TWO LAYERS OF CLEAR POLYCARBONATE

See-through Drill Guide

For a portable jig to keep bits at 90° to the board when drilling, glue two strips of 3/8-in. clear polycarbonate together, just along the edges, to make a 3/4-in. thick strip. Drill a line of holes—one for each bit you use most often—at a true 90°. The most accurate way to do this is with a drill press (see pages 88–91). Label the hole sizes with a permanent marker. To use the guide, clamp it in place on the workpiece as you sight through it.

KEYLESS CHUCK

TAPER FINAL WRAP

Impromptu Keyless Chuck

Wind several turns of plastic electric tape around your drill's chuck, and you'll be able to quickly hand-tighten and loosen it for drill and screwdriver bits. This can save a lot of frustration when you've lost the key in the middle of a project. Taper the end of the final wrap of tape and firmly press it in place. That way your hand won't loosen the tape as the chuck tightens. And wear a glove to get a firmer grip.

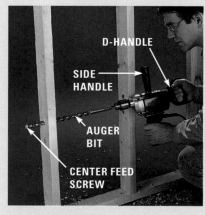

D-HANDLE

SIDE HANDLE

AUGER BIT

CENTER FEED SCREW

Long-reach Bits

Use long auger or self-feeding bits to get a shallow angle of penetration where a drill and bit won't fit. Rent a 1/2-in. drill with D- and side handles to give you plenty of control. If a long, hard-biting bit grabs, it can snatch a one-hand drill out of your hands with great force.

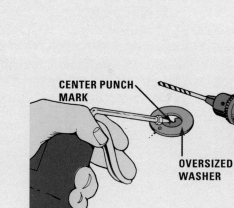

CENTER PUNCH MARK

OVERSIZED WASHER

Keep It Cool

When drilling a flat metal surface, keep the drill tip constantly lubricated, so the heat of friction is reduced. Put a large washer over your center-punched drilling mark and fill the center with oil. The washer will hold the oil around the bit and you can drill all the way through without stopping.

NOTE: SMALL HOLES

3 IN ONE HOUSEHOLD OIL

Oil for Holes in Metal

Use plenty of household or motor oil and a high-speed steel bit to drill metal. For a hole 1/2-in. or larger in thick metal, it's much easier to work up in stages: first 1/4 in., then 3/8 in., and so on.

Hammer Drills

For fast, clean holes in concrete, masonry, and tiles, this is definitely what you need. But it's not a single-purpose tool—you can drill wood and other materials with it, too.

At some point in your do-it-yourself life, you will have to drill precise, neat holes in very hard materials. The project may be putting up a towel or grab bar in a tiled bathroom, hanging a trellis on a brick wall, or running a pipe through a foundation for an outside hose connection. An ordinary drill with a masonry bit will work fine for an occasional hole in a mortar joint or cement block, but heavy drilling of this sort can quickly burn out the motor.

If you're planning to poke a lot of holes in concrete, stone, mortar, cement block, brick, or tile, the tool that can handle the job with ease is a hammer drill.

A hammer drill has two ratcheted disks in its internal drive line that generate a pulsating hammer action. These disks turn against each other, providing up to 50,000 hammer beats per minute in a drill turning at top speed. This hammering action, combined with the rotary motion of the drill bit, breaks up the material and expels the dust and small particles up along the spiral shaft of the masonry bit.

Hammer drills range in size from the models that take 3/8-inch bits to large industrial types. A 3/8-inch or 1/2-inch drill will handle just about any masonry drilling you'll run into around the house.

For example, drilling into a ceramic tile floor that has a concrete base may seem pretty daunting, but with a hammer drill and masonry bit you can glide through with ease. You can also install iron railings on concrete steps, cut patio stones, anchor electrical conduit, fasten plumbing fixtures, attach a ledger to a foundation for a new deck, and install shelving and wall framing on a variety of hard surfaces like concrete, stone, or tile.

You can rent a hammer drill when you need one. But if you're in the market for a new drill, a hammer drill also works as a conventional drill with the turn of a dial. For a comparison of drills, see page 87.

Operating a Hammer Drill

To use a hammer drill properly, hold it firmly and apply only enough pressure on the bit to guide it. Let the drill do the hard work; too much pressure can overload the motor. Most hammer drills have an auxiliary handle and an adjustable depth stop to help you.

Auxiliary Handle

The auxiliary handle usually screws into the side of the drill body; it lets you get a good, two-handed grip. When you drill in concrete or stone and you hold the drill even slightly off center, the bit often binds inside the hole and jars the drill in the direction of rotation. A firm two-handed grip minimizes this. When drilling into a floor or other horizontal surface, keep the bit vertical *(below)*. When drilling into walls, keep the bit perpendicular to the surface both left–right and up–down.

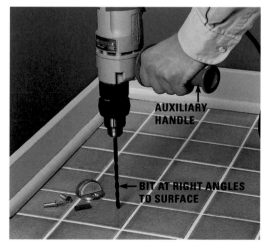

Keep the drill bit perpendicular to the work surface. On tile, mark the starting point with a punch that breaks the glaze, to keep the bit from skating at the start.

Depth Stop

Almost all hammer drills have a depth stop attachment, which is an adjustable rod *(below)*. You preset the position of the rod to get the exact hole depth you want by measuring the difference between the tip of the bit and the tip of the rod.

An exact hole depth is important when drilling into masonry to install screw or bolt anchors—one of the various types shown on page 86. Most anchors require a precise depth to give them stability and to prevent them from extending too far into the hole.

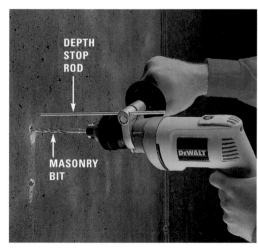

Set a depth stop so the distance from the end of the stop rod to the tip of the masonry equals the hole depth you want. Always hold the drill firmly with both hands.

Holes for Other Purposes

Most often, you make a hole to stick something into—a fastener or mounting pin, for example—or to put something all the way through, such as a pipe or cable. But drilling holes can also be a step in another procedure. The most common example involving a hammer drill is in breaking stone cleanly *(below)*. To do this with the drill, mark out the line along which you want to make the break and drill a hole every inch along it. Then, wearing safety goggles, strike along the line, between the holes, with a masonry chisel.

Do not use the hammer function of the drill on wood, plastic, or metal, since this can cause premature wear on the ratchet discs. Set the drill in standard, non-hammer mode to drill these materials.

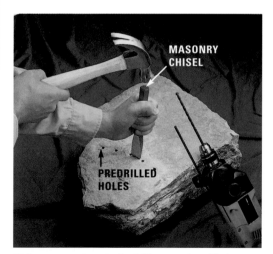

Make stone work easier by drilling a series of holes about 1 in. apart along the intended break line, then use a masonry chisel. Wear eye protection throughout such work.

Hammer Drill Bits

Most hammer drill bits look like ordinary masonry bits, with two wing-shaped, pointed carbide tips at the cutting edge *(opposite page)*. However, the package should specify that they are for percussion or impact drilling, or for use in a hammer drill. They are readily available at most hardware stores and home centers. In the sizes you're most likely to use—1/4 inch to 5/8 inch—the bits cost about $2 to $5 each.

WORKING TIP

To drill more easily in very hard concrete or stone, start the hole with a small bit, then switch to the larger diameter needed to finish the job.

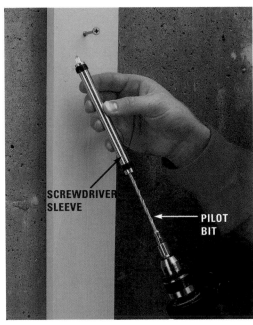

SCREWDRIVER SLEEVE

PILOT BIT

Fasten directly into concrete with a Tapcon bit and driver, and special hardened, self-threading Tapcon screws. The screwdriver sleeve slips right over the pilot bit.

Often the cutting tips of the bit are wider than the shaft end that fits into the drill. In fact, you can get percussion masonry bits with a 3/4-inch cutting tip and a 3/8-inch shaft end. However, even a hammer drill has its limits; you would overwork a 3/8-inch drill if you used a bit with a tip larger than 9/16-inch diameter.

There is one specialty drill bit that is worth particular attention. The Tapcon bit *(left)* is specially designed to quickly and securely attach a furring strip, bracket, or other object to a masonry wall. In one operation, it drills a pilot hole through the furring strip and into the masonry. You then drive in special hardened Tapcon masonry screws that have threads designed to cut into and lock themselves directly to the masonry without any need for an anchor. A sleeve with a screwdriver bit at the end is also available. The sleeve snaps in place over the drill bit, as shown in the photo, so you don't need to change bits or have another drill on hand.

You can buy a combination set of Tapcon bit and screwdriver or, for much less, just the pilot drilling bit. Then after drilling the holes, use an ordinary driver bit in your drill to install the screws. Tapcon screws are inexpensive and are available at most home centers and building supply outlets, and some hardware stores.

Masonry Fasteners

To use conventional screws and bolts in masonry, you need to drill a hole and insert a plastic or lead anchor for the threads of the fastener to bite into. There are several kinds of anchors *(below);* some come with matched fasteners, others take standard size screws and bolts. Plastic anchors are for small holes and fasteners; lead anchors are required for large bolts and screws.

Whatever its material, the anchor expands inside the hole when the fastener is driven in and binds with extreme force against the sides. So for the anchor to grip properly, the hole must be the correct diameter. Check the package or instructions with the product to see what size masonry bit you should use.

Use anchors to hold standard screws and bolts in masonry and stone. The hole must be the proper diameter and depth for the anchor to hold safely and securely.

Drills Compared

Drilling concrete is a lot of work and can be quite trouble-some if you do not use a hammer drill. The comparison shown here makes that very clear.

To see how effective standard and hammer drills and drilling techniques were, a test was made drilling 3/8-in. diameter holes 1-1/2 in. deep in concrete. One hole was drilled with a standard drill and a single 3/8-in. masonry bit. A second was drilled in stages with the standard drill and three masonry bits: 1/8-in., 1/4-in., and 3/8-in.

The third hole was made with a hammer drill and a 3/8-in. percussion (impact) bit—four times faster than the second hole, and ten times faster than the first!

The individual bits cost from $2.50 to $4.00, so only the price of the drill is economically significant. A hammer drill costs about 60 to 80 percent more than an equivalent standard drill, but it is a heavy-duty tool and can also be used as a standard drill.

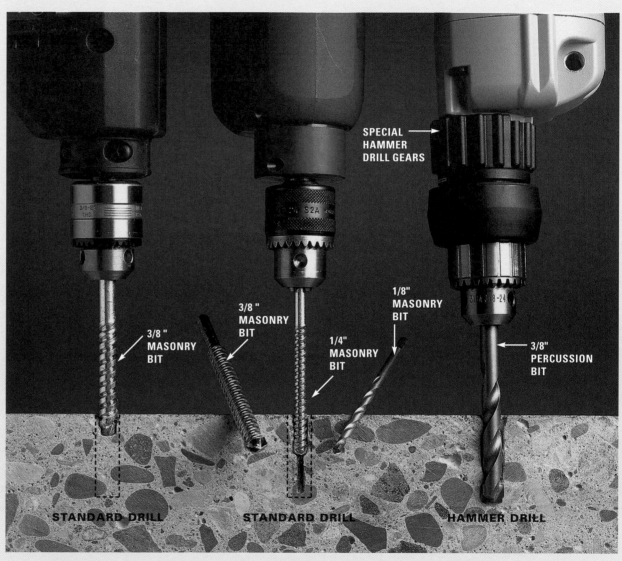

SPECIAL HAMMER DRILL GEARS

3/8 " MASONRY BIT

3/8 " MASONRY BIT

1/4" MASONRY BIT

1/8" MASONRY BIT

3/8" PERCUSSION BIT

STANDARD DRILL

STANDARD DRILL

HAMMER DRILL

3/8-in. masonry bit
Drilling time: 5 minutes

1/8-, 1/4-, and 3/8-in. masonry bits
Drilling time: 2 minutes

3/8-in. percussion bit
Drilling time: 30 seconds

Drill Presses

Drill identical holes—two, ten, or a hundred—with absolute, precise control of angle and depth, in any material. A drill press will tackle that—and more—with ease.

Some projects demand a great deal from a do-it-yourselfer. Consider these tasks: bore holes accurately through metal; drill row after row of holes for cabinet shelf pegs; drill a hole in a piece at an exact 37-1/2° angle; drill straight through the middle of a wooden ball. There is no way you can do those sorts of things well with a hand-held drill. But they are a breeze when you can take advantage of the precision of a benchtop drill press.

Drill Press Features

A drill press is an electric drill mounted on an upright column (*above*). The drill chuck holds a bit in a vertical position, pointing down toward a worktable that can be moved up and down the column, and swung and tilted left or right. To drill a hole, the spinning drill bit is lowered by a feed handle at the side of the drill. In addition to the maximum bit shank size (3/8 or 1/2 inch), the critical dimensions of a drill press are its throat and its throw. Throat is the distance from the chuck to the support column. Drill press capacity is

commonly given as twice the throat size. A "10-inch drill press," for example, can bore a hole in the center of a 10-inch-wide board; the actual column-to-chuck throat dimension is 5 inches. Throw is the maximum downward travel of the drill bit; you can't drill through a piece thicker than the throw without turning it over to complete the job. Drill press operating speed can be changed to suit different types of material, and various accessories, such as a sanding drum, can be mounted in the chuck.

Operating a Drill Press

Using a drill press is very straightforward:

▶ Choose the size and type of bit needed for the hole and the material you want to drill and mount it in the drill chuck. Check to be sure that the drill is at its upper position.

▶ Raise the table so it will hold the workpiece an inch or so under the tip of the bit, closer if it is thick work and you need as much bit length as possible.

▶ If you plan to drill all the way through the workpiece, make sure the hole in the center of the table is under the bit. If you tilt the table, it may be easier to position one of the slots in the table under the bit.

▶ To drill only partway into the work, set the depth stop on the drill press and make a test in a piece of scrap wood before boring into the finish piece.

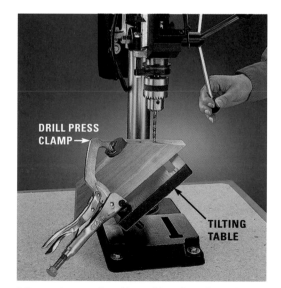

Adjust and secure the table position, then clamp the work to it. Be sure the bit is aligned with a hole in the table, or put scrap wood under the work, if you will drill all the way through.

▶ Clamp the workpiece in position on the table, with the marked drilling point under the tip of the bit. Clamping will keep the work from shifting even slightly as the drill bit enters and leaves, and of course is essential when the table is tilted *(below left)*. Even more important: Clamping is a safety measure, whatever the table position. The whirring drill bit can grab a block of wood or piece of metal and send it spinning into your arm or across the room.

▶ To guide a piece for a series of holes, clamp a fence to the table *(opposite page)*.

▶ Put on eye protection before starting to drill. With the work held firmly in place, turn on the switch. Take hold of the feed handle and move it downward, lowering the bit into the work.

▶ When the hole is the proper depth, raise the drill until the bit clears the work, then turn it off. Then, and only then, start to unclamp and move the workpiece.

Changing Speed

Various materials and bits require different operating speeds for the most efficient drilling. Changing speed on most benchtop drill presses is a matter of shifting the belt that runs between a set of pulleys on the motor and a set of pulleys on the drill *(right)*. Follow the directions in your drill manual. In general, the procedure is: Unplug the machine, open the access panel, and loosen the belt tension knob. Then pull in on the motor while shifting the belt. Retighten the belt tension knob before plugging the motor back in and starting the drill.

Handy Tip

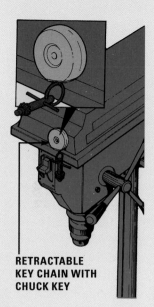

The chuck key for a drill press is small, but essential—you can't mount a bit securely without it. As every drill press owner knows, the key can easily be misplaced or become hidden under tools and scrap material on the bench. To end constant searching, clip the chuck key to a retractable key chain and permanently mount the key chain case to the cover of the drill press. The key will always be within reach, yet safely out of the work area.

RETRACTABLE KEY CHAIN WITH CHUCK KEY

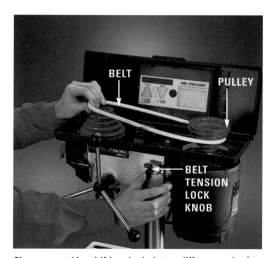

Change speed by shifting the belt to a different pair of pulleys. Unplug the motor before loosening the belt tension knob. Check your owner's manual for directions and speed recommendations for various materials.

Drill Press Techniques

Drilling a hole in a flat piece of work is simple, but in finish work, such as building furniture or cabinetry, there are two advantages to doing even such a basic task with a drill press: accuracy and stability. A bit in a hand-held drill will often follow the path of least resistance and be thrown off by a streak of hard grain or the edge of a knot; a bit in a drill press will bore precisely where you want it to. There are other tasks best done with a drill press. Here are some of them.

Drilling Dowels, Tubes, and Pipes

Cylindrical work is hard to hold in position for drilling. Enough clamp pressure to hold the piece firmly can distort its

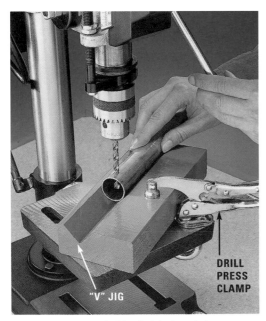

Make a V-notch jig to hold cylindrical workpieces. Center the valley of the V under the bit and clamp the jig in position before putting the workpiece in place.

shape, too little pressure will let it shift. The solution is a simple jig *(below left)*. Rip a 90° V-notch in a piece of 2x4. Hold the workpiece in the V and drill away. Cut the V to one side of the centerline of the jig so there is ample space to clamp it to the drill press table.

Boring Flat-bottomed Holes

Flat-bottomed holes are often required to receive rungs, spindles, and dowels in wood joinery. Similar holes drilled at an angle provide positive, recessed seating for screws in table and cabinet frames. The tapered points on ordinary bits create valleylike bottoms in holes; Forstner bits *(below)* cut holes with clean, straight sides and flat bottoms, except for a small spot left by a spur in the center of the bit. It's tricky to use these bits hand-held, but a drill press makes it easy to control the location, angle, and depth of holes drilled with a Forstner bit.

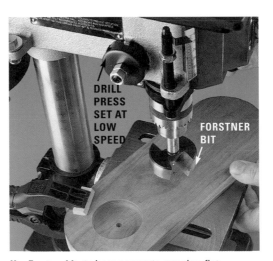

Use Forstner bits to bore accurate, precise, flat-bottomed holes. The bits are available in many sizes. Clamp the work securely; these bits exert great torque.

Drilling a Ball

For a ball-drilling jig, first make a hole half to two-thirds the diameter of the ball in a piece of scrap wood *(below)*, using a spade bit or a hole saw. Leave this jig clamped in position and change to the drill bit you want to use in the ball. Set the ball in the hole, hold it with a hand screw clamp as you drill *(bottom)*. Not moving the jig ensures that the hole will be dead center in the ball.

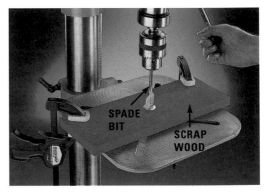

Drill a large hole in a piece of scrap as a jig to hold a ball for drilling. Don't move the jig after boring the hole.

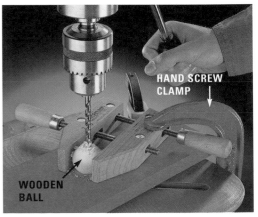

Change bits and hold the ball steady with a hand screw clamp to prevent it from revolving in the jig hole.

Drill Press Sanding

Equipped with an abrasive drum, a drill press makes an excellent sander. As with other stationary sanders, you must move the work against the direction in which the drum turns. Otherwise the drum can snatch the workpiece out of your hands and send it flying across the room.

Since the drum can't touch the drill press table, build an auxiliary table with a hole in it large enough for the drum to stick down into it *(below)*. That way the full edge of a workpiece can be sanded. Be sure to clamp the auxiliary table in position, and run the drill press at a slow speed to avoid edge burning.

Big and Tall Drum Sanding

When you need an extra-long sanding drum for your drill press, buy a 4-1/2 inch long drum and abrasive sleeves designed for an oscillating spindle sander *(below)*. You'll find these items at home centers.

Put a 6-inch x 1/2-inch carriage bolt through the drum and compress it with a washer and nut so it spreads out to hold the sleeve tightly. Put the threaded end in the drill chuck and sand away. For a work surface, drill a hole just big enough for the end of the drum in a piece of 3/4-inch plywood; clamp it to the drill press table.

Pivot Press Drum Sander

Build this simple device *(below)* to edge-sand long, straight pieces of wood. Drill a plywood platform with a hole for the sanding drum and a hole off to one side for a 1/2-inch dowel to serve as a pivot pin. Cut a fence board with a 1/2-inch hole near one end and slip it over the pivot pin. Place the workpiece against the edge of the fence and swing the fence until the other edge of the workpiece touches the face of the drum.

Remove the workpiece, move the fence 1/32 inch closer to the drum, and clamp the free end in position. Start the drill and gently push the workpiece through against the spin of the drum.

Adapt a tall spindle sander drum for use in a drill press by mounting it with a long bolt. Stand boards up to 4-in. wide on edge to sand their faces on the drum.

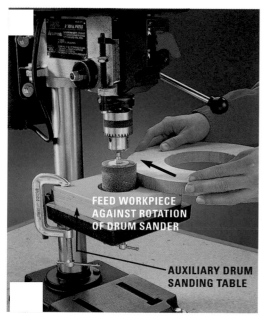

Smooth, sand, and shape using a drum sander and a homemade auxiliary table. Switch to a slow speed and move the workpiece against the drum's rotation.

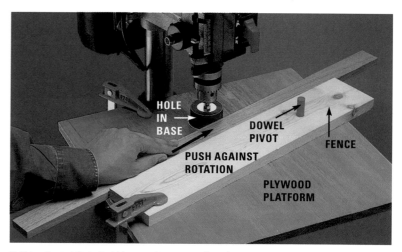

Build a pivoted jig to hold long strips pressed against the drum as you push them through for edge sanding. Always move the work against the drum rotation.

Shaping & Sanding

Routers

A router adds finishing touches to home woodworking projects—the decorated edge, the recess for a cabinet back. Use this tool to transform a plain-Jane project into an elegant work.

94

Lathes

The spinning lathe is the tool that makes a chair leg or a baseball bat out of an ordinary block of wood. Once you have the hang of working on a lathe, learn to shape a bowl from green wood.

100

Random Orbital Sanders

Use this tool for scratchfree finish sanding, general smoothing, and even stripping paint. It can be gentle and accurate, or vigorous and aggressive—whatever your project needs.

108

Belt Sanders

Nothing beats a belt sander for fast sanding and working on flat surfaces. You can use it for large and small pieces, and even to sharpen hand tools.

112

Thickness Planers

Make rough boards satin smooth on both faces, reduce boards to exact thickness, eliminate warp. A thickness planer can do it all on stock from 1/4 in. to 6 in. thick.

116

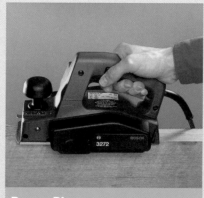

Power Planers

Smooth surfaces and trim boards to fit on the spot, even while they're fastened in place. A power planer is portable, and a lot faster to use on some kinds of jobs than a sander.

118

Jointers

Precision-finished edges are the key to fine craftsmanship in cabinetry and furniture making. You can produce them easily with a jointer; no other tool can do this important task.

121

Routers

Shaped edges, raised panels, fluted columns, and turned spindles—these are features that distinguish truly fine work. You can make them, and more, with a router.

Not many people have the space for a fully equipped workshop, but a router can be used anyplace you have room to clamp down a workpiece. Furthermore, a router is portable, so you can work on door jambs, deck railings, and other pieces in place. With that convenience and versatility, you get a tool that will do most jobs that a professional shop would give to a large, expensive stationary machine.

In addition to shaping edges and grooves, you can use a router to cut and trim plastic laminate, cut mortises for hinges, carve flutes in flat or round workpieces—even turn spindles! Here's how to choose and use this truly exceptional power tool.

Choosing a Router

A router is simply a single-speed, high-rpm motor with a metal collet, or clamping collar, that holds a revolving cutting bit. It also has an adjustable base that lets you control the depth of the cut.

A router with a 1 to 1-1/2 hp motor is the best DIY choice. It has enough power to do most any woodworking project, yet is easy to handle. There are two types of routers: fixed-base and plunge. In a fixed-base model the motor is clamped to the base and the bit protrudes below it at all times. In a plunge router the motor is attached to a spring-loaded work surface that holds the bit above the base until you push it down into the work. Both types let you set the cutting depth of the bit before

starting. A fixed-base unit is a good choice for DIY work for its ease of use and economy. With the proper technique you can make the same cuts as you can with a plunge router.

Many routers have collets for both 1/4-inch and 1/2-inch diameter bit shanks. There is an astonishing variety of bits, but you will seldom need more than four or five different shapes (see pages 96–97), and most of them will have 1/4-inch shanks.

When you choose a router, look for a model that will accommodate the accessories you'll be using. Also look for good balance and an easily accessible on–off switch.

Fundamental Technique

To use a router, first make sure it is unplugged. Then:

▶ Insert a bit all the way into the collet, pull it out 1/8 inch, and tighten the collet securely; this lets the collet get the best possible grip.

▶ Set the depth for the first cut. There are locking controls and a scale on the router to let you do this. To remove a lot of material, start with a shallow cut and increase the depth slightly on succeeding passes.

▶ With the workpiece held securely in place and the router plugged in, place the router base on the workpiece—but with the bit not touching the wood—and start the router. When it is at full speed, bring the bit in contact with the work and immediately move the router from left to right as you face the cut. Carry the cut past the far end of the piece before turning the router off.

▶ Always move the router from left to right as you face the piece being cut. If you are going around the outside edges of a board or a frame, that moves the router in a counterclockwise direction. (Around the inside edges of a frame, the movement will be clockwise. To see why this is, stand facing each of the inside edges and trace the left–right movement the router must make along the edges.)

Basic Edge Cuts

The basic edge cuts are shown below; additional setups and cutting tricks are shown on pages 97–99.

To minimize tearout, cut across end grain before cutting edges parallel to the grain *(below)*. When working on a narrow surface, clamp an auxiliary board alongside to support the base *(bottom)*.

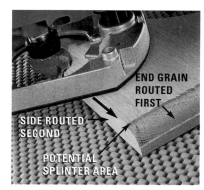

Rout end grain first, then the sides of a board, to avoid rough corners and splinters. Move the router from left to right as you face the cut.

Stabilize the router base when working on a narrow board by clamping a support board to the workpiece. Make sure the clamp's jaws are not in the path of the router bit.

Trimming an Edge

To trim wood with a router, first measure the distance from the edge of the straight-cut bit to the edge of the router base *(below)*. Next, clamp or screw a straightedge that distance from your cutting line. Then run the router base along the straightedge to make the cut *(bottom)*.

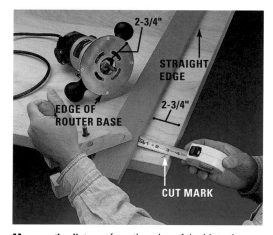

Measure the distance from the edge of the bit to the edge of the router base. Clamp a straightedge at exactly that distance from the work.

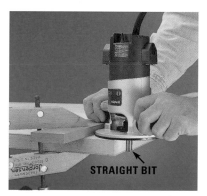

Guide the router base along the straightedge to trim the workpiece edge.

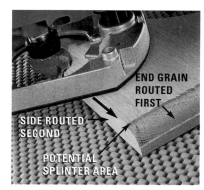 **END GRAIN ROUTED FIRST** / **SIDE ROUTED SECOND** / **POTENTIAL SPLINTER AREA**

Router Bits

Router bits are made either of all high-speed steel (HSS), or of HSS with carbide cutting edges. HSS bits are cheaper, but they dull quickly when cutting plywood, particleboard, and hardboard, or plastics, and are likely to burn the edge of solid wood. Carbide bits seldom burn the workpiece and may never even need to be sharpened. There are two basic types, straight bits and profile bits.

Straight Bits

Straight bits *(photo bottom right, page 95)* cut a vertical straight line. Use them to true the edges of a board, cut dados, and cut plastics, laminate, and other materials. The first two router bits you need are 1/4- and 1/2-inch diameter carbide straight bits. Since they don't have a guide nub or bearing, you must guide the router with a straightedge or use a router table.

Profile Bits

Edge-shaping or profile bits have cutting edges that cut curves, grooves, or angled edges. Carbide profile bits have ball-bearing guides that follow the edge of the workpiece; HSS bits usually have only a guide nub on the shaft. There is a great number of different profile designs; the four most useful shapes are shown below and on page 97.

Round-over and Beading Bits

These bits *(below left),* available in a variety of radiuses, can create uniformly finished edges on everything from bread boards to picnic tables. A round-over bit simply rounds the edge *(below center);* a beading bit rounds the edge, but adds a squared-off lip or ledge on each side of the rounded bead *(below right).*

A round-over bit can be converted into a beading bit simply by switching ball-bearing guides. Remove the hex head screw, then take out the bearing and install a smaller one. Some round-over bits are packaged with a second ball-bearing guide for this purpose.

The thicker the wood, the larger the bit you'll want to use. Four different-radius round-over bits—1/8, 1/4, 3/8, and 1/2 inch—should meet most of your needs. It's amazing the difference in edge appearance you get with only a 1/8-inch difference in the radius of the bit.

When you need to create a deep rounded edge, make two shallow passes instead of one deep one. This technique is easier on your router and your arm, and it reduces the likelihood of tearing the grain. You'll also get a smoother edge.

TOOL TIP

To keep router bits handy but separated so their cutting edges don't nick one another, stick their shafts in the 1/4-in. holes in a piece of perforated hardboard.

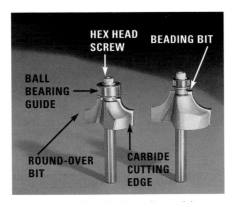

Round-over and beading bits soften and decorate edges. Change the ball-bearing guide to switch from one bit to the other.

HEX HEAD SCREW

BEADING BIT

BALL BEARING GUIDE

ROUND-OVER BIT

CARBIDE CUTTING EDGE

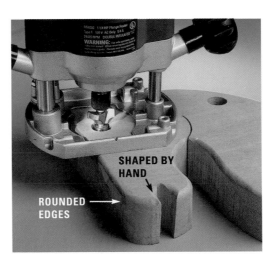

SHAPED BY HAND

ROUNDED EDGES

Choose a round-over radius suitable for the function of the piece: a toy might need more rounding than a bookcase edge, for example. Finish areas the bit can't reach.

2x2 SUPPORT

BEADED BASE MOLDING

Cut decorative molding edges on boards with beading bits. Add a support board for the router base when cutting a narrow edge; hold the workpiece securely upright in a vise.

Rabbeting Bits

Rabbeting bits *(below)* cut a rectangular recess along the edge of a board or interior of a frame. That recess can be used to hold a door panel, a picture, or a drawer bottom. It's ideal for hiding plywood edges or covering the end grain edges of boards.

Most rabbeting bits will cut only 3/8 inch deep, but you can make a second pass with the base of the router raised higher (so the bit protrudes more below the bottom) to create a deeper rabbet. On a frame, the inside corners of the rabbet will be rounded *(bottom);* square them up with a few taps of a sharp chisel. You can create a dado in the edge of a board by raising the base of the router so the groove is cut below the top surface of the board *(middle top)* rather than right along the board's edge. To cut a dado in the face of a board, use a straight bit and guide the router with a straightedge.

Rabbeting bit.

Cut a recess for a mirror, picture, or door panel to cut into by moving a rabbeting bit clockwise around the inside of the opening. Square up inside corners with a chisel.

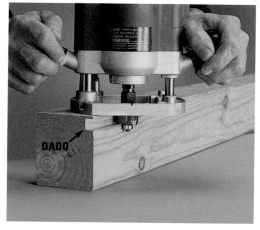

Cut side-edge dados by setting a rabbeting bit to cut below the surface of the work. To do this, raise the router base to adjust the bit position. Lattice or paneling could fit into the groove.

Chamfer Bits

Chamfer bits *(below)* excel at creating 45-degree bevels around picture frames, tabletops, railings, and other projects. They are ideal for turning sharp edges and corners into gentler ones so that the wood or finish is less likely to chip or break off.

Because the end grain edges of a board are more likely than the other edges to chip at the corners, when possible chamfer the ends that have end grain first *(right top)*. That way any chips created at the corners of the board can be cleaned up when the final two edges are routed.

Chamfer bit.

When making a deep chamfer, a shallow pass followed by a full-depth pass will be easier on the router and the workpiece.

For a professional-looking job when butting ends of tongue-and-groove boards together, chamfer the ends of the boards to create a V-groove where they meet *(bottom)*.

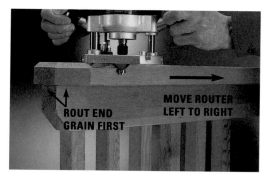

Chamfer deck rails for a clean, custom-built appearance. Cut end grain first, then rout the long edges. Move the router left to right as seen when you face the edge being cut.

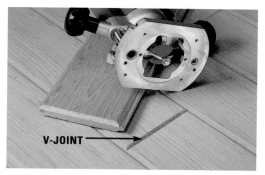

Create V-joints by cutting chamfers on the ends of boards that butt together. This looks best on tongue-and-groove boards that have V-joint edges.

Router Tables

For large pieces and working on pieces in place, a hand-held router is excellent. But a router table is better for routing small, difficult-to-clamp pieces, for edging narrow boards, and for cutting face flutes and dados. You can buy a table *(below left)* or make your own *(below right)*. The router, with base plate removed, fastens to the underside of the table and the bit sticks up through a hole. You can guide work with a fence or a miter gauge. Do not try to move the work freehand past the bit. This is dangerous, because it is very hard to control the piece. In all cases, move the work from right to left—the opposite of what you do with a hand-held router—because the table-mounted router is upside down.

WORKING TIPS

• Use bits with 1/2-in. diameter shanks in a table-mounted router. They cut with less vibration and resist the stress of table-routing better than 1/4-in. bits.

• To rout shapes using a template guide and template on a table router, attach the template to the bottom side of the work-piece, not the top.

• When you rout the full thickness of an edge, set the outfeed fence just enough offset from the infeed fence to properly guide the narrower board after it passes the bit.

• Whenever possible, use push sticks (see page 50) to push work along the fence, past the bit.

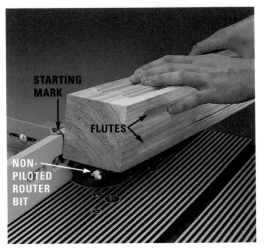

Cut flutes and stopped dados with a nonpiloted bit and a fence. Mark starting and ending lines (concealed by the work here) on the fence to show where to lower and raise the piece over the bit.

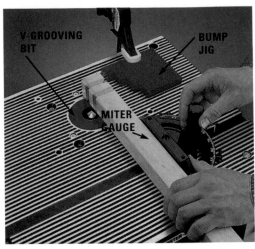

Use a stepped bump jig for accurate repeat spacing. Set the piece against the first step to position it for the first cut. Move it to other steps to space subsequent cuts.

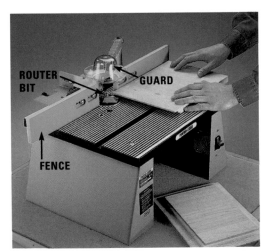

If you buy a router table to which you can attach your own router, look for a bit guard, removable fence supports, and a slot for a miter gauge.

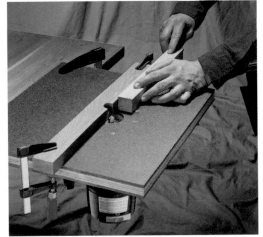

Make your own router table from 3/4-in. plywood. Glue on a hardboard top to make work slide easier. Rout a recess in the bottom for your router and mount it using long screws.

Pro Working Tips

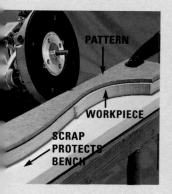

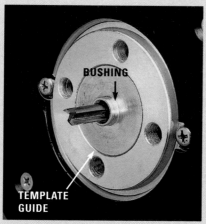

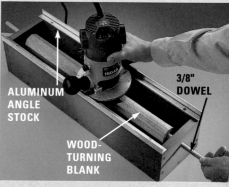

PATTERN

WORKPIECE

SCRAP PROTECTS BENCH

BUSHING

TEMPLATE GUIDE

PUSH COUNTER-CLOCKWISE

PIVOT NAIL

1/4" PLYWOOD COMPASS ARM

SCREW INTO BASE

ALUMINUM ANGLE STOCK

3/8" DOWEL

WOOD-TURNING BLANK

Template Routing

To rout pieces to match a pattern, first make a template of the shape from 1/4-in. hardboard or plywood and clamp it to the workpiece. Use a straight-cutting bit and an accessory template guide in the router. Keep the bushing on the guide in contact with the edge of the template as you move the router. Make the cut in a series of gradually deeper passes.

The routed piece will be about 1/16 in. larger than the template, so experiment first to determine how much smaller to make templates for exact-size results.

Big Circles

Use your router as the tip of a big compass to cut large wooden circles. Remove the router base plate and screw the router to a long arm of 1/4-in. plywood. Using a straight-cutting bit, pin the compass arm at the center of the required circle with a single nail or screw. Do this on the bottom so the hole won't show on the finished side of the workpiece. Cut through in three or more passes, increasing the depth each time. Support the circle for the final pass for a clean edge and so it doesn't drop to the floor.

Perfect Laminate Joints

Clamp the two sheets of plastic laminate you want to seam to a support board with a 1/4-in. space between their edges. Make a shallow pass right down the middle of the seam with a 1/2-in. straight carbide bit in the router and a straightedge fence. Even if the fence wasn't absolutely straight, the two edges of the laminate will mate perfectly when you butt them together.

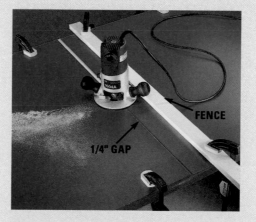

FENCE

1/4" GAP

Router Woodturning

Use your router as a lathe to turn wooden cylinders. Make a box with removable ends and just wide enough to hold your router in guides of aluminum L-channel angle stock.

Drill 3/8-in. centered holes in the box ends and in the ends of your turning blank. Rough-cut the blank on a table saw so it's somewhat round, glue 3/8-in. dowels in the end holes, and place it in the box. Move the router back and forth along the blank, using a 3/4-in. diameter straight bit and slowly turning the blank. Lower the bit slightly as needed until the cylinder is the diameter you want.

Lathes

Balusters, spindles, table legs, bowls—
using a lathe, you can make
these graceful shapes emerge like
magic from pieces of wood nobody
else wants.

TOOL REST
POSITIONED
SLIGHTLY
BELOW CENTER
LINE OF LATHE

OVERHAND
GRIP

A lathe is a slender power tool that takes up little space in a garage or basement; and, unlike most power tools, it runs almost silently, even when you're turning wood.

No matter what you make on a lathe, the process is the same: You hold a sharp tool to a square piece of spinning wood, called a blank, and make it round. Basic rough shaping is shown in the photo above; refining the shape to a finished piece is essentially the same, using other cutting tools—three or four are all you need for almost any project.

Turning technique is easy, but like any tool that involves freehand work, a lathe offers the challenge and reward of developing advanced techniques and skills. The next several pages show you how to get started, and how to do some advanced work, too.

Preparing Wood

Most lathe projects require a thick piece of wood, so you may need to glue together two or three boards to get a blank for the item you want to make. You can also buy ready-to-turn blanks in a variety of woods at many woodworking stores.

Nearly all wood turns to a smooth finish, from softest pine to hardest ebony, but it must be free of knots. Hard knots can cause your tool to jump, creating gouges; they will break out of the piece, leaving unwanted holes; and they can damage the cutting edge of a tool. So be sure to buy "select and better" grade lumber, and keep your tools sharp.

If you glue together your own wood blanks, match the grain direction of the pieces before gluing them. For a uniform appearance, use pieces of the same color;

for a decorative effect, try alternating light and dark woods. Use good-quality wood glue and clamp the pieces together until the glue is dry. You don't want the blank coming apart on your lathe!

Trim the glued blank so it is square, not rectangular, when seen from the end. This is important for proper centering and to avoid irregular vibration as the blank spins. To speed up initial rounding and to lessen tool wear, moderately bevel the four corner edges of the blank with a plane or band saw.

Setting Up for Turning

Securing a blank in the lathe for turning is called "loading." The procedure explained here is the same for all lathes, but be sure to check your machine's manual, too, especially regarding how to choose the best speed for various kinds of turning.

The lathe holds a workpiece between a headstock and a tailstock *(below left and right)*. The headstock, powered by the lathe's motor, spins a spurred drive center, a removable claw that bites into the blank when you tighten it in the lathe. The tailstock slides and clamps on the lathe bed to fit the length of the blank. The center pin in the tailstock is not powered, but merely keeps that end of the workpiece in place.

To load a blank, follow these steps:

▶ Draw an X across the corners of both ends of the squared-up blank to locate its center axis. Also lay out scribe lines on all four sides from a measured drawing or prototype to tell you where to begin and end various cuts. The scribe lines are easy to see as the blank spins.

▶ Place one end of the blank against the drive center on the headstock; make sure the point of the drive center goes into the center of the marked X *(below left)*.

▶ With the center pin of the tailstock retracted partway—adjust it with the center crank—loosen the clamp and slide the tailstock along the lathe bed *(below right)*. Push the point of the center pin into the center of the X on the end of the blank. Push a bit harder to seat the blank on the points at each end, then clamp the tailstock in position.

▶ Turn the center crank on the tailstock to extend the center pin, forcing the pin and the spurs on the drive center at the headstock firmly into the ends of the blank. Grip the blank in your hand and check for a tight fit. Use the center crank to take out any play.

Tools for Turning

The tools you will use most *(right)* are:

Parting tool. The narrow, double-beveled edge cuts vertically into the blank, making a groove. It can cut through a blank in seconds, so use only light inward pressure.

Skew. The skewed (slightly angled) double-beveled straight edge smooths the roughed-out blank. This tool is also handy for shaping the round bumps (beads) on a turning.

Roughing gouge. Its curved, thick edge removes wood rapidly, so pause frequently to check the changing size of the blank.

Small gouge. The narrower, more delicate shape of this gouge is just what you need to shape inside curves (coves).

Sandpaper. Lathe purists frown on this "tool," but it gives wood a glassy smoothness, unlike any cutting tool.

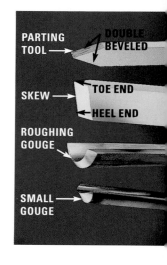

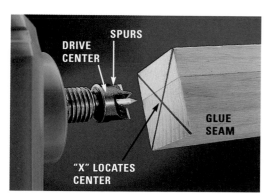

Headstock. Make sure the blank is centered on the drive center of the headstock. Use the X marked on the end of the square blank to align it properly.

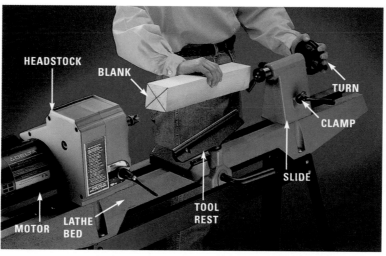

Familiarize yourself with all the lathe controls and adjustments before loading a blank for your first experience in turning. The lathe manual is essential reading.

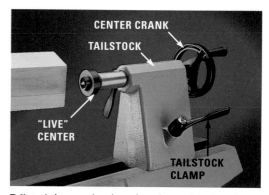

Tailstock. Loosen the clamp in order to slide the tailstock to put the center pin against the blank. Reclamp, then turn the crank to tighten the blank onto the head and tailstock centers.

- **Always wear eye protection and a full-face shield (see pages 12–13).**

- **Wear a long-sleeve shirt. Keep it tucked in and the cuffs buttoned.**

- **Stand to one side when you first turn on the lathe, in case any chips are thrown off.**

- **Turn at the lowest speed until you feel confident about using the tools.**

Learning to Turn

With a blank in the lathe, adjust the tool rest so its edge is at or below the center axis of the blank and is as close as possible to the spinning blank without touching it. Reposition the rest left or right as needed.

Basic use of the gouge is shown below. Stand upright with your feet well apart for a wide base and sway your torso from side to side as you move the tool along the wood. If you are right-handed, hold the cutting-edge end of the tool with your left hand in an overhand grip (photo, page 100) and the tool handle in your right; if you are left-handed (below), reverse these positions. The heel of the gouge's bevel (below left) should rest on the work; the edge is brought to bear against the wood by raising the tool handle. Raise the handle for a deep cut, lower it for a shallow cut.

Making cuts with the parting tool and skew is shown below and right. Calipers are the best way to measure round pieces; set them from a measured drawing or a prototype piece.

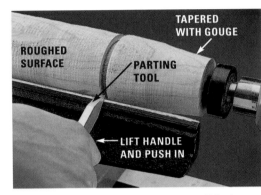

Use the parting tool to cut the rough-shaped blank to specific diameters. Angle the cutting tip upward, then raise the tool handle slowly and push inward. Use a small gouge in a similar way for tapers and inside curves (coves) on short sections.

The skew is a versatile tool. Turn it on its side to cut grooves narrower than those made with a parting tool. Angle the skew from vertical to cut grooves with bead edges. To smooth a shape along the length of a piece, turn the skew on its flat side (below) and move it left and right along the tool rest.

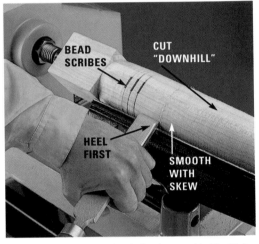

Cut bead edges with the heel of a skew tool held with its narrow edge on the tool rest. Scribe lines for the bead locations before starting to cut. Use the skew turned on its flat side to smooth a roughed-out shape.

Grip the cutting end of the tool overhand, and control it with the other hand. Raise and lower the handle to get the edge at the best cutting angle. Use arm, not wrist, movement to raise or lower the tool; swing it right and left with body movement.

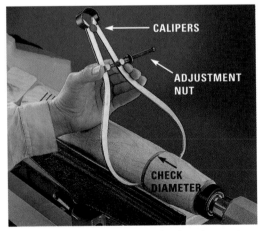

Measure diameters with calipers. Set them from a plan or model piece. You can make measurements as the workpiece turns.

Sharpening Your Tools

A good sharp edge on each tool makes turning a joy, and much safer. Put your bench grinder a step away from the lathe and use it often. Two modifications to your grinder will give you much better results:

▶ Replace the standard gray grinding stone with a white aluminum oxide stone. It cuts cooler, making it easy to grind without damaging the tool from excess heat.

▶ Add a wooden block as a large and steady rest for the tool *(below)*. The angle and design aren't critical, just make it wide and sturdy.

Sharpen the bevel on gouges to about 45°, grinding the tip of the tool either straight across or to a fingernail shape. The fingernail shape is easier to turn with but harder to grind. To grind, start with the heel of the bevel rubbing against the wheel, then raise the handle until sparks come over the top of the edge. Turn and roll the gouge left and right to get the fingernail shape.

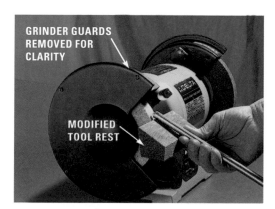

GRINDER GUARDS
REMOVED FOR
CLARITY

MODIFIED
TOOL REST

Grind tools frequently while turning. Use a white stone and screw a modified tool rest to the grinder. Sharpen gouges to a fingernail shape with a turn and roll action.

Turning Bowls

Once you have started to make things on a lathe, you discover that turning wood is totally unlike other kinds of woodworking. There is a kind of magic in the way rough wood takes shape under your hands, fast and spontaneously. Turning wooden bowls is addictive, because you have the freedom to make different shapes and show off the grain and colors of unusual woods—all in a useful object.

The photo at the right shows just a few examples of finished bowls; there are many others you can make, with and without lids. It also shows some bowls in earlier, unfinished states, and the raw material—a chunk of green wood.

Professional turners work with wood straight out of the tree, and you should too. Turning bowls from green wood is not only great fun, but without any doubt it is the best way to learn. The wood is free or cheap; large branches, fallen trees, large pieces of firewood all can be turned into bowls. Green wood is soft and cuts like butter. And when it's free, you can practice all you want, experiment when you're feeling creative, and turn so many bowls you'll be an expert in almost no time.

You'll probably discover that half the fun is the surprise of finding beautifully figured wood inside a log. Weird-shaped, gnarly, bumpy, half-rotten wood that couldn't possibly make decent lumber often will make gorgeous bowls. The following pages will help you start on that journey of discovery.

Turning bowls from green wood requires patience, above all. After roughing out, the bowl must be set aside for three to four months to dry before final turning. But the results can be stunning.

Stages in Bowl Turning

There are three major stages to turning a bowl from green wood. They are illustrated below and explained step by step on the following pages.

The Basic Process

The key to green-wood bowl turning is to first make a "rough" bowl, with fairly thick walls and base, like the unfinished examples on page 103. Then you must let the rough bowl dry.

Drying takes three to four months, during which the green wood will warp, but usually not crack. No chemicals and no kiln drying are needed. By contrast, if you tried to dry a 6-inch-thick plank to the same state before cutting a blank and turning a rough bowl shape, it would take six years. And buying kiln-dried lumber that thick is impossible.

After the rough bowl is dry, you can remount it on the lathe and turn it to final shape. First you turn the inside and outside walls of the bowl. Then you reverse it on the lathe and turn the base. The final small stub in the base is cut off by hand before you apply a finish.

In the diagrams below showing the stages in the turning process, the waste wood that you cut away is shown in yellow.

Gaining Mastery

Turning bowls is as difficult—and as easy—as playing baseball. What you need most is plenty of practice. The best way to get that practice is to try to master the tools while you're making rough bowls. Don't concentrate on getting a finished bowl, just on mastering the tools. By the time your first rough bowls are dry, you'll be pretty good. Don't hesitate to turn your first few chunks of wood into shavings, just for practice. Someone learning to draw makes sketch after sketch that gets crumpled up and thrown away; that's part of the learning process. You are learning to "draw" three-dimensional forms in wood.

STAGES IN BOWL TURNING

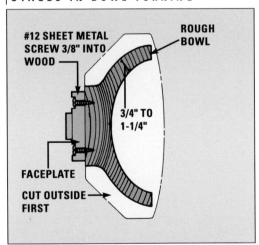

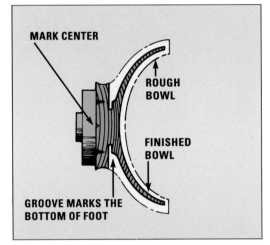

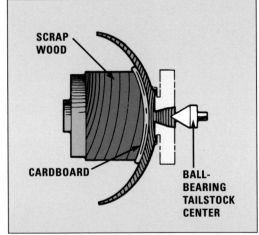

Stage 1. Begin by turning a roughly shaped blank of green wood into a rough bowl. Turn the outside first, then the inside. Details of mounting and turning are explained on later pages.

Stage 2. Let the bowl dry for three to four months. Then remount it and turn it to final shape. Leave the bottom as shown after cutting a groove with a parting tool to mark the foot.

Stage 3. Reverse the bowl and hold it against a turned wood plug with a protective cardboard shim to turn the bottom. Chisel off the last small plug in the center of the bottom by hand.

Tools for Bowl Turning

After you have located a suitable piece of green wood, your first task will be to cut a blank for turning, as explained at right. You will find a chain saw and band saw useful—although not essential—for cutting a log into chunks and giving each chunk a roughly circular shape for turning. Don't buy a chain saw just for turning bowls; rent one for a weekend and you can cut enough wood for months of turning. If you don't have a band saw to roughly shape the blanks, use the chain saw or a hatchet to do that too.

You will need three lathe tools *(below):* a deep-fluted bowl gouge, a round-nose scraper, and a parting tool. These tools can be ordinary carbon steel, but you'll get best results with a gouge of high-speed steel, because it will stay sharp much longer. As for all lathe work, eye protection and a full-face safety shield are mandatory working equipment.

Preparing Blanks

Trees downed in storms, firewood, and orchard prunings are potential sources of bowl wood. For dramatic grain patterns, choose sections where the grain is contorted: bent limbs, crotch wood, flaring roots, and burls. Mineral staining, sapwood (the wood nearest the bark), and the beginnings of rot can all produce interesting colors and patterns.

The diagram at right shows several ways to cut bowl wood from a log. Avoid the heart (center) of the log and the wood for an inch or so around it. This part is almost sure to split in drying. Also, if the grain is very much off-center, the rough bowl will dry with a great deal of distortion.

Mark out a shape that will let you make walls generously thick and cut out the chunk *(below).* Shape that further with a band saw or hatchet. Keep blanks covered and damp until you want to turn the rough bowls, so they won't crack. Just before turning, screw on a centered faceplate that will mount on the lathe headstock *(below right).*

Cutting Bowls from a Log

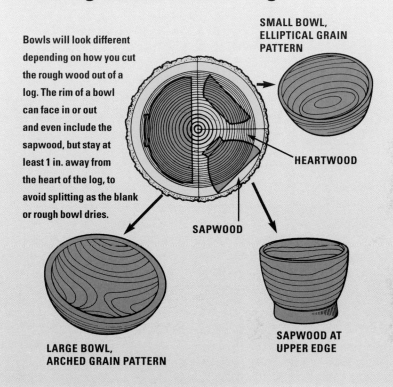

Bowls will look different depending on how you cut the rough wood out of a log. The rim of a bowl can face in or out and even include the sapwood, but stay at least 1 in. away from the heart of the log, to avoid splitting as the blank or rough bowl dries.

SMALL BOWL, ELLIPTICAL GRAIN PATTERN

HEARTWOOD

SAPWOOD

LARGE BOWL, ARCHED GRAIN PATTERN

SAPWOOD AT UPPER EDGE

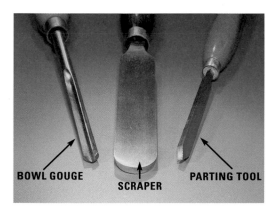

BOWL GOUGE

SCRAPER

PARTING TOOL

Turn green-wood bowls with just three tools: a 3/8-in. high-speed steel bowl gouge, a round-nose lathe scraper tool, and a parting tool. Keep them sharp as you work.

HEART

Cut short sections from a fresh log. Mark the bowl shape on the log to make sure you provide enough wood for thick walls when you turn the rough bowl.

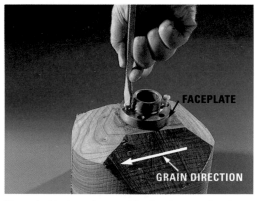

FACEPLATE

GRAIN DIRECTION

Shape the blank as shown with a band saw or hatchet. Attach a faceplate with four screws, two in line with the grain for exact reattachment even after the wood has dried and shrunk.

Bowl Turning Step by Step

Here is how to turn a bowl in twelve steps.

Turning the Rough Bowl

1. Use the gouge to turn the rough blank until the sides and top (face) are round and smooth. Hold the tool securely, because it will be jumpy until the wood is round.

2. Shape the outside of the bowl first, rolling the gouge on its side a bit and moving toward the faceplate. Leave extra wood where the faceplate screws penetrate the blank; you'll remove this waste later.

3. Drill a hole to the bottom of the rough bowl. You can use a bit in a drill, or a gouge inserted while the blank is spinning. Make the bottom about 3/4 inch thick.

4. Hollow out the inside of the rough bowl, keeping the walls 3/4 to 1 inch thick. Mark the thickness with a parting tool first, then cut with the gouge. The drilled center hole will show you how deep to cut.

Turning the Final Shape

5. Remount the bowl after it has dried for three or four months. Use the grain-line screw holes to align the faceplate correctly. Shape the outside first, then the inside, rolling the gouge on its side so the edge makes contact at an angle and shears the wood in a fine shaving.

6. Use a scraper for the final finish cuts. Hold the tool horizontally, with the edge tipped upward for a shearing effect. Take very light cuts, so you don't go too far.

7. As you turn the inside of the finished shape, measure the wall thickness with calipers to get it uniform. Use the scraper to finish the inside of the bottom of the bowl.

8. Make a very light final cut inside and outside with the scraper. Then use the parting tool to make a cut that marks the bottom of the final shape of the bowl.

Finishing the Turning

9. Sand the bowl inside and out as it spins on the lathe. Use a foam-backed sanding disk in an electric drill to reduce sanding time dramatically. Or use a strip of sandpaper held by each end and curved partway around the outside of the bowl, and a folded pad of sandpaper inside.

10. Unmount the sanded bowl and mark the center of the waste on the bottom by eye. Remove the faceplate.

11. Remount the bowl in reverse with a turned wood plug and protective cardboard shim inside (see Stage 3 diagram, page 104), and a live tailstock center outside against the bottom. Cut away all but the very center of the outside bottom waste.

12. Unmount the bowl and chisel off the final bit of bottom waste. Chisel with the grain to avoid tearout. Sand the bottom and apply an appropriate finish.

BOWL TURNING STEP BY STEP: TURNING THE ROUGH BOWL

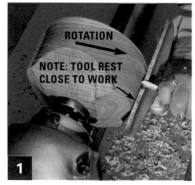

Turn the side and top of the rough-cut blank until they are round and smooth. Take light cuts setting the gouge, with the lathe at its slowest speed. Wear a face mask.

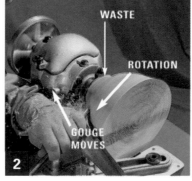

Shape the outside of the bowl first. Work from the wide end of the blank toward the faceplate with the gouge rolled on its side a bit, for cleaner cutting.

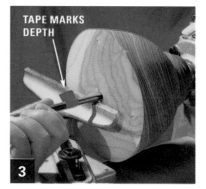

Drill a hole to the inner bowl depth. Use a drill with the blank stationary, or a gouge with it spinning. Mark the depth on the tool with tape. Turn the tool rest as shown.

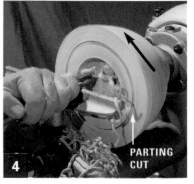

Hollow out the inside of the bowl with the gouge. Mark the inner circumference with a parting tool first, to leave thick walls in the rough bowl for drying.

BOWL TURNING STEP BY STEP: TURNING THE FINAL SHAPE

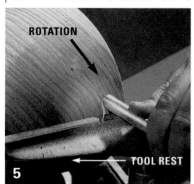

5 ROTATION / TOOL REST

Shape the outside first during the final turning. For the smoothest cuts, roll the gouge on its side. A thin smooth shaving shows the edge is at the proper angle.

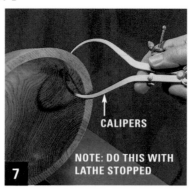

6 ROTATION

Use a scraper for the last cuts. Keep the tool horizontal and firmly on the tool rest. Make light cuts with the edge tipped. The burr left from grinding does the cutting.

7 CALIPERS / NOTE: DO THIS WITH LATHE STOPPED

Measure wall thickness with calipers. It must be uniform at all points on any circumference line to avoid splitting from uneven expansion and contraction.

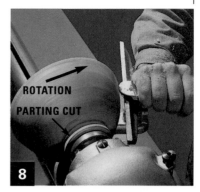

8 ROTATION / PARTING CUT

Use the scraper for very light final smooth cuts inside and out. Position the tool rest so you can move the scraper along the profile of the bowl without stopping.

BOWL TURNING STEP BY STEP: FINISHING THE TURNING

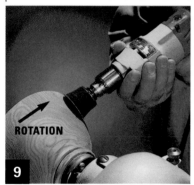

9 ROTATION

Sand the spinning bowl inside and out. The quickest way to do this is with a foam-backed sanding disk in an electric drill, but you can use hand-held sandpaper for equally good results.

10

Mark the center of the waste on the bottom of the bowl before removing the faceplate, after the bowl has been completely sanded. Place the tailstock center on this mark in Step 11.

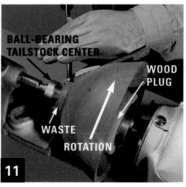

11 BALL-BEARING TAILSTOCK CENTER / WOOD PLUG / WASTE / ROTATION

Remount the bowl between a tailstock center and a turned plug and remove the waste around the bottom. Cover the plug with a piece of cardboard inside the bowl to prevent damage.

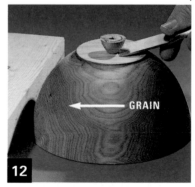

12 GRAIN

Chisel off the little nubbin left after you turn away the waste. Chisel with the grain to avoid tearout. Sand, then apply a finish to the bowl inside and out.

Random Orbital Sanders

From rough work to finish work, these clever tools combine the aggressiveness of belt sanders with the accuracy of hand sanding.

For taking a good deal of the drudgery out of do-it-yourself projects, there's nothing like using a power sander instead of sanding by hand.

There are three basic kinds of hand-held power sanders: belt, finishing, and orbital. Belt sanders (pages 112–115) move the abrasive material in a straight line; finishing sanders move it in a rapid back-and-forth motion, and orbital sanders move it in a circular path. Orbital sanding is not as fast as belt sanding, but can both rough- and finish-sand a greater variety of materials with less chance of leaving gouges or cross-grain scratches. Orbital sanders are generally smaller, easier to handle, and usable in spots a belt sander couldn't reach.

Random Orbital Sanding

A conventional vibrating or orbital sander—whether a disk sander, an accessory disk for an electric drill, or a rectangular or square-pad sander—moves the sandpaper in exactly the same pattern again and again. Even if you keep the sander moving, you can quickly sand that pattern into the workpiece.

A random orbital sander combines the spinning motion of a rotating disk with a secondary orbital motion created by an offset counterbalance. This causes the sanding disk to spin while moving irregularly left, right, forward, and backward *(opposite page, bottom left)*. This random motion ensures an unrepeated path for

the sandpaper. The result is a swirl-free finish even where adjoining grain runs in different directions. And because the random motion also prevents the sandpaper from clogging, you can sand much faster than with a conventional sander.

Handling the Sander

Using a random orbital sander for the first time is like dancing with a new partner. The random motion has a tendency to lead, so take control and you'll get along just fine. Before tackling a real project practice on some scrap material.

Place the sander flat on your workpiece before you turn on the switch. Otherwise you may catch the sanding disc on the edge of your work and tear it—or worse yet, gouge the surface of a veneer or a soft wood such as pine.

To keep a small workpiece from sliding while you sand it, place a piece of foam carpet pad or a router pad under it, or use a clamp. Wear safety glasses, hearing protection, and a respirator or dust mask whenever you use your sander.

Keep the cord away from the action or you could end up nipping or breaking it. If the pad that holds the sandpaper becomes damaged, replace it or the finely tuned balance of the counterweight will be disturbed.

Unless you are using a small palm sander (page 110), which is meant for one-hand operation, grip the sander with both hands—one on the handle at the rear of the body, the other on the auxiliary handle at the side (*opposite page*) or at the front of the sander (*below*).

Guide—don't force—the sander forward along the predominant grain direction of the workpiece. The random motion of the disk will move the sander; your job is to make sure that it covers the entire surface of the piece in overlapping passes.

Sanding Tips

You can use a random orbital sander for a great variety of projects. Here are some applications where it will excel:

Cabinet doors and face frames, where boards meet at right angles to one another (*below*). The sander will smooth the joint without leaving swirl marks across the opposing grains of the wood.

Tabletops, cutting boards, and other flat surfaces. Move the sander in an arcing motion to sand the piece quickly and smoothly. Be careful on plywood and veneer tops; you can sand right through thin wood skin.

Refinishing and preparation for painting. The sander will cut quickly through old paint or the residue left by chemical strippers. A random orbital sander will also remove paint quickly from metal surfaces that need preparation for priming and repainting (*opposite page*).

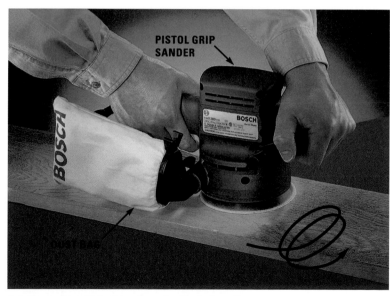

Grip the sander with both hands and guide it along the length of the workpiece. The random orbital action (spiral arrow) avoids scratching and gouging.

Sand with the grain along the principal parts of a workpiece, but don't worry about grain at other angles. Even with coarser grits, random orbital sanding won't leave prominent swirl marks.

Types of Sanders

Random orbital sanders fall into three broad categories:

Palm grip sanders *(below)* are best suited for light-duty work such as finish-sanding furniture and cabinetry. They offer excellent control, and are so small and lightweight that they can be used easily with one hand for hard-to-reach spots.

Right angle sanders *(bottom right)* are the most aggressive. Their powerful motors make them ideal for heavy-duty uses like sanding large surfaces, tabletops, wood and fiberglass boats, and auto-body panels. They are available in 5- or 6-inch diameter pad styles, and in single or variable speeds.

Pistol grip sanders *(opposite page, bottom left)* are often equipped with a D-shaped handle, along with a front handle that may be adjustable for the most convenient position. These tools are less powerful and aggressive than right angle models but are much easier to control. They are the most versatile of the orbitals and can handle every job from smoothing rough-sawn boards to fine-sanding furniture.

Types of Sandpaper

Sandpaper disks are available in all grits. They are secured to the sander either by a hook-and-loop system *(below)* or by pressure-sensitive adhesive *(bottom)*. These prepared disks are more expensive than conventional papers, but they provide the convenience and speed of changing that are worth the extra cost.

HOOK-AND-LOOP STYLE PAD AND DISC
DUST PORTS

Hook-and-loop pads and disks allow you to change and use paper easily. The sander pad has tiny hooks that grasp onto fuzzy-backed disks.

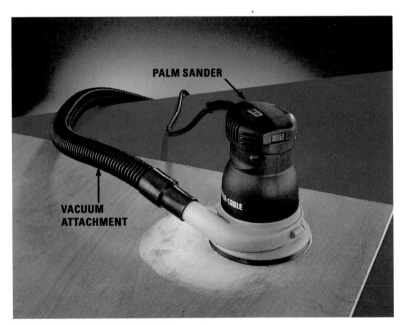

PALM SANDER

VACUUM ATTACHMENT

A palm sander is ideal for finish work and small enough to reach into difficult spots. Use two hands on top if possible, but one-hand operation is sure and easy when necessary.

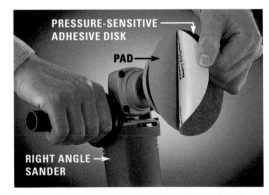

PRESSURE-SENSITIVE ADHESIVE DISK
PAD
RIGHT ANGLE SANDER

Apply and remove pressure-sensitive adhesive (PSA) disks working from one edge of the pad. They adhere far better than disks applied with rubber cement.

Accessories

The accessories available for random orbital sanders include various dust collectors *(right)* and, for some models, a kit to convert from 5-inch to 6-inch disk size.

Among the most popular accessories are polishing bonnets and buffing disks *(below)*. A bonnet ties on over the sander pad; a buffing disk adheres to the pad by whichever system the sander uses for sandpaper, hook-and-loop, or pressure-sensitive adhesive.

If you have a 4-1/2 or 5-inch angle grinder, you don't need to buy a sander. Many grinders have an accessory attachment so you can turn them into random orbital sanders.

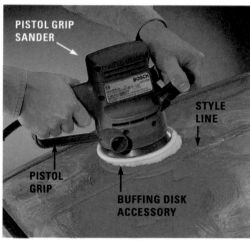

Buff your car or any other waxed surface with a buffing disk or polishing bonnet. Use polishing accessories at low rpm only, and be careful around painted decorations, style lines, and edges. Too much heat could soften and wear away the paint.

Dust Collection

Whatever else sanding may accomplish, it produces plenty of dust. Many sanders have built-in or accessory dust collection devices, and this is definitely a feature to look for when buying a sander.

Sawdust is usually collected through as many as eight holes in the pad and sandpaper disk. Some simple sanders have a removable bin built into the body. Others have a spout on one side to which you can attach a canister *(right top)*, a vacuum cleaner hose *(opposite page, far left)*, or a dust bag (page 109). Not all models permit all three options, but if there is a spout, you can usually attach a bag or a shop vacuum hose with tape if necessary.

If your sander does not have built-in dust collection, you can make a sanding vacuum box for use with any kind of sander *(right bottom)*. Make a box frame of 1x3 pine or scrap wood about 12x18 inches in size. Add a solid bottom of 1/4-inch plywood and caulk all joints from the inside for improved performance. For a top, use either 1/4-inch plywood and drill a grid of 5/16-inch holes as shown, or use 1/4-inch perforated hardboard and drill out every other hole to 5/16 inch. In the center of one side, make a port for your shop-vacuum nozzle. A PVC expansion adapter, available at plumbing supply stores and elsewhere, works well, or cut a hole that accepts the hose nozzle with a tight fit. Hook up the vacuum and you're set for cleaner, healthier sanding.

Collect sanding dust with a canister, bag, or vacuum hose connected to the dust spout on many sanders. Other models may have a removable bin at the rear of the body.

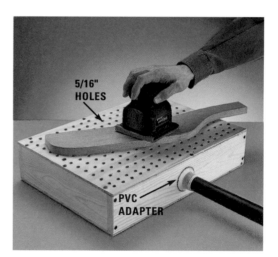

Build a sanding vacuum box if any of your sanders does not have a provision for dust collection. The hose connects to a shop vacuum. Even with a box like this, wear a dust mask when sanding.

TOOL TIP

Don't connect a household vacuum cleaner to a sander; very fine particles of sawdust will probably clog the bag. Use a shop vacuum for direct connection and work-area cleanup.

Belt Sanders

For fast sanding and working on flat surfaces, a belt sander is outstanding. It's also versatile; you can use it to smooth small pieces and even to sharpen hand tools!

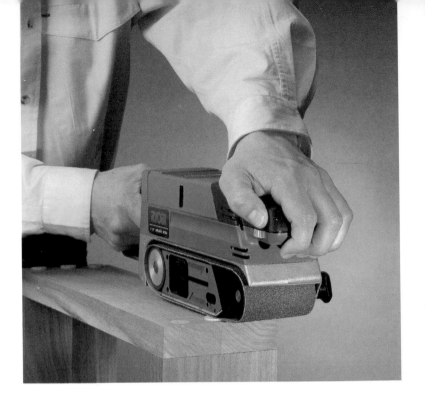

A belt sander is just what its name implies: it smooths by moving a continuous loop of abrasive material at a speed of 450 to 1,100 or more feet per minute over the surface of the work. This speed and the ease of changing belts to use different sanding grits, from very coarse to very fine, makes the belt sander a versatile workhorse tool. It is used in the cabinetmaker's shop, on the job with finish carpenters and installers, and on construction sites. And it is excellent for all sorts of do-it-yourself work. Whether you want to do coarse cleanup, rough smoothing, paint removal, or finish sanding of details, you can do it with a belt sander. It all depends on the belt you select and how you control the tool.

Sanders and Belts

Belt sanders are classified by their sanding belt width and circumference; 3x21 inches, 3x24 inches, and 4x24 inches are common sizes, but there are smaller sizes such as 3x18 inches and even 2-1/2x16 inches as well. A 4-inch belt sander removes stock quicker and levels surfaces more evenly than a smaller model, but its weight (typically 14 lbs. vs. 8 lbs. for smaller sanders) makes it tiring to use.

The size and power of a large sander are just what you need for working on big pieces and over large areas, but those same factors make it difficult to control sanding on small or delicate surfaces. Small belt sanders are good for touch-up work, but they're too small for flattening large surfaces.

A 3x21- or 3x24-inch sander will handle most home improvement or woodworking projects. You can clamp a flat-topped model upside down for use as a stationary sander or for sharpening tools (page 114). A sander with "flush sanding" capability, like the one above, has one edge that can sand directly up to another surface. For instance, when you're sanding a floor, the flush edge can sand directly against the wall or base molding.

Like sheets and disks of sandpaper, sanding belts are available in various grits, or degrees of coarseness, ranging from 36 to 200. Lower numbers designate coarse, quick-cutting belts; higher numbers indicate fine-grit belts.

Basic Techniques

Never underestimate the power of your sander. A coarse belt can remove 1/4 inch of material in seconds, which is fine if that's what you want to do, but not if you've just sanded through the thin veneer of a door or piece of oak plywood.

When you first buy a belt sander, practice on scrap material to get the feel of using it. And whenever you work, remember that the surface you're sanding is below the machine, so stop frequently to check your progress. Here are some techniques for using your sander effectively:

▶ To avoid gouges, turn on the sander and let it get up to its full speed before bringing it to the workpiece.

▶ When smoothing rough or uneven surfaces, sand in large, sweeping strokes at a 45-degree angle to the grain (below).

As the surface gets smoother, use finer belts and start working in long strokes parallel to the grain.

▶ If the belt starts to wander off the rollers or rub against the body, get it back on track with the tracking adjustment knob. Turn the sander on and slowly rotate the knob one way or the other until the belt is centered. Be sure to check this whenever you change belts.

▶ Don't press down on the sander; let the weight of the tool and the grit of the belt do the work. Keep the sander moving or you'll create a depression.

▶ Start and end each sanding pass with the belt flat to the work surface or you risk rounding over the ends or edges of the board. When preparing pieces for finish work, sand the lumber before cutting it to final length (below). That way, any gouges or rounding in the ends of the board will be in the waste that you cut off.

▶ Always wear a dust mask; eye protection is a wise precaution too when sanding wood. Both eye and hearing protection are essential when sharpening tools or working on metal.

▶ Make a series of light pencil marks across the surface of large pieces. As you sand, keep an eye on these marks; if they remain, you've missed that area.

▶ To sand vertical surfaces and edges, brace your arms against your body (below). This will avoid bounces and gouging, which could occur as your unbraced arm muscles tire. It also makes it easy to hold a fixed angle with your sander, which is helpful when chamfering the ends of a board or putting a bevel along the edge of a door so it closes easier.

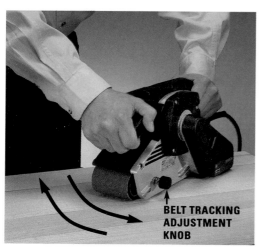

Flatten and smooth surfaces and glued-up boards by starting at an angle with a coarse belt, sweeping the sander in arcs. Finish by sanding parallel with the grain with a fine-grit belt.

Start and end each pass flat to the work surface. Finish-sand boards before cutting them to final length to be sure of getting square edges at the ends.

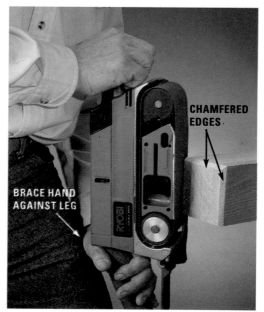

Steady a vertical belt sander and maintain a consistent angle by bracing your wrist against your leg or hip and the other elbow against your upper body.

When using the sander upside down as a stationary tool, use the lock button to hold the switch in the On position. Stand out of the path of the belt, so if it snatches and throws a small piece you will be out of harm's way. Be careful not to contact the moving belt with your fingertips.

Getting More from Your Belt Sander

Here are three special techniques that will let you take advantage of the versatility of a belt sander.

Sanding Laminate and Veneer Edges

When sanding the edges of plastic laminate countertops, veneer-finished panel, or plywood, hold the sander as shown below. The belt should rotate toward the edge and body of the piece, so that it is always pushing the laminate or veneer layer down, against the core or substrate. If it pulls up, you could rip the thin plastic or veneer away from the solid surface beneath, chipping the edges.

Sanding Small Pieces

You can't hand-hold the sander to work on small workpieces and narrow edges. A clamp holding the piece will get in the way, and the bulk and weight of the sander make it almost impossible to sand just a little bit, without going too far. So instead, turn your belt sander into a stationary tool. Turn it over and secure it upside down with a clamp (below), or in a bench vise. Then you can hand-hold the workpiece against the flat or curved portion of the belt to sand just the shape and amount you want.

Sharpening Tools

You can use an upside-down sander to sharpen paint scrapers (below), chisels, and other tools. Use a fine belt and remove the dust bag from the sander so sparks won't ignite the material inside. Hold the tool so the sharp edge points to the rear of the sander, in the direction that the belt rotates. If it points the other way, it can tear open the cross-seam on the belt, ruining it, quite possibly chipping the tool edge, and definitely putting you in danger of injury as the belt ends flap wildly loose.

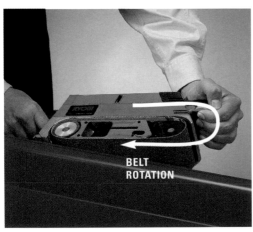

BELT ROTATION

Avoid splintering laminates and thin veneers by holding the sander so the belt rotates and pushes these fragile surfaces against their wood cores.

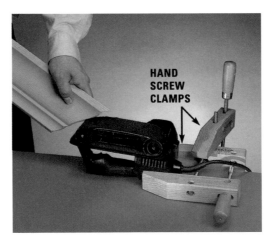

HAND SCREW CLAMPS

Clamp the sander upside down or hold it in a vise so you can smooth small pieces while keeping a careful eye on progress. Lock the switch in the On position.

PAINT SCRAPER

Sharpen and clean edged tools such as scrapers and chisels on a fine belt mounted in the sander. Remove the dust bag to avoid fire from sparks.

Dust Collection

Most belt sanders have a removable bag to collect sawdust. In fact, this is a feature to look for when you buy a sander. But the bag can't collect everything; there is always some loose dust between the belt and the surface being sanded. Especially during finish-sanding, lift the sander frequently and blow off the surface to prevent buildup that could cause gouges. Whether you use a dust bag or not, the trick shown below makes sanding much cleaner. Screw a radiator hose clamp to a scrap piece of 1x3 so it can hold the nozzle of your shop vacuum. Clamp the cleat to your workbench to position the nozzle where the sander throws off the dust.

HOSE CLAMP

Get on-the-spot dust collection by making a simple holder for the nozzle of your shop vacuum. Use a scrap-wood cleat and an automobile radiator hose clamp.

Belt Cleaning

Sawdust and paint will cake up in the grit on a belt. To extend the useful life of the belt, hold a belt cleaner against the belt as it rotates. This inexpensive bar of rubber will clean the grit in short order. You can also use the crepe rubber sole of an old shoe (tennis shoe rubber soles won't work), or even an art gum eraser.

BELT CLEANER

Prolong the life of sanding belts by removing sawdust and gummy deposits with a rubber belt cleaner.

Pro Working Tips

Belt sanders and orbital sanders are excellent for flat surfaces and straight or gently curved edges, but they can't get into close corners or sharp curves. One way to sand those edges is with a sanding drum in a drill or a drill press (page 91), but even that has its limits. For the smallest inside curves, use the method shown below.

To sand small irregular edges and very tight curves, make your own miniature sanding drums. Wrap adhesive-backed sandpaper around short lengths of dowel and chuck the dowels in your drill. Different dowel diameters—1/4 inch, 5/16 inch, 3/8 inch—let you get those tight inside spots smooth and clean. They're good for smoothing the inside of small holes, too.

←SANDPAPER

Thickness Planers

Here's how to turn rough-surfaced wood of uneven thickness into finished lumber with a speed and ease no other tool or hand method can equal.

OUTFEED ROLLER

A thickness planer is one of those tools you can live without, until you have one. Then you may find yourself using it on so many home improvement and wood-working projects that you'll wonder how you ever really did without it.

For woodworkers, owning a planer means being able to: create 1/2-inch-thick boards out of 3/4-inch stock, turn rough-sawn lumber or boards with chatter marks into smoothly planed materials, make a single board a uniform thickness from end to end, or make five boards uniform before gluing them together—and, with some planers, create moldings.

For home-improvement oriented do-it-yourselfers, a planer can create satin-smooth deck railings from ordinary boards, quickly strip the finish from painted boards (although this is hard on the blades), cut crisp edges on boards and moldings, and much more.

Planer Basics

A thickness planer removes a thin, uniform layer of wood—typically 1/16 inch or less—from one side of a board each time the board passes through the tool. Operation is simple because a planer is self-feeding, with power-driven rollers that move boards past a revolving cutter head holding two or three long, sharp blades. The motor and cutter head can be raised and lowered to accommodate different thicknesses of lumber. And the cutter head can be cranked down in small increments when several passes are needed to smooth or thin a board.

Planers are referred to by the length of their blades, which determines how wide a board they can handle. Most benchtop models—the kind most practical and affordable for DIY projects—have 12-inch or slightly longer blades and feed boards through at a rate of about 26 feet per minute. The cutter head on these planers can be raised to take lumber up to 6 inches thick, and can be set to shave off anywhere from 1/32 to 1/8 inch of wood on each pass. Benchtop planers have a short infeed table, called a threshold, and a similar outfeed table, both with idler rollers for smooth board movement.

Planing Boards

A planer can be noisy and it generates piles of shavings, so always wear hearing and eye protection *(opposite page)*. Make sure the planer is bolted down, then go to work using the following techniques:

▶ Remove nails and staples from boards; nicks in the cutter blades will leave small unplaned ridges along the length of a board. If the blades do get nicked, loosen and shift one blade slightly so each blade will plane off the ridge left by the other.

▶ Before starting, use the height adjustment crank to lower the cutter head until it just touches the surface of the board *(below)*. Remove the board and lower the head a bit more for the first cut. Follow that with a series of gradually deeper passes. For soft woods like cedar and pine, remove about 1/16 inch per pass; for hardwoods like oak or walnut, remove even less. To get the smoothest surface, make the last pass a paper-thin one.

▶ Use a helper or an outfeed roller *(opposite page)* to support long boards, to eliminate end gouges, called "snipe." You need more than twice as much working space as the length of a board— over 20 feet for a 10-foot board, for example—so set up outdoors to plane long pieces. That's also a good idea because of the noise and the amount of shavings that power-planing creates.

▶ Feed short boards through the planer one after another, to avoid end snipe *(below)*. Don't feed in boards shorter than the length of the planer base. Instead, plane a long board to the right thickness and cut short pieces to length, or use the tip shown at the right.

▶ Don't try to plane warp out of a board; that will only make the board thinner. Use a jointer (pages 121–123) or hand plane to flatten one side of a warped board, then run it through the planer flat side down *(below right)*.

Handling Short Boards

To safely plane small pieces of lumber, use spots of hot-melt glue to fasten a longer piece of scrap lumber to each edge of the piece to be planed. Use these edge pieces to feed the work through the planer. They will keep your fingers well away from the cutter blades. When you're through, tap the glued-on pieces on the ends to break them free.

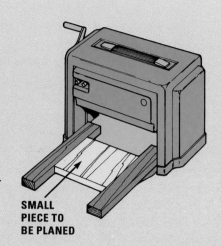

SMALL PIECE TO BE PLANED

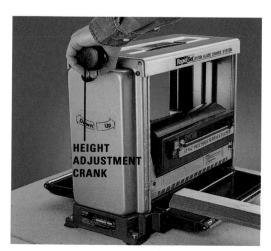

Adjust the cutter head with the height adjustment crank. Set it to remove about 1/16 in. of wood each pass. For maximum smoothness make a paper-thin final cut.

HEIGHT ADJUSTMENT CRANK

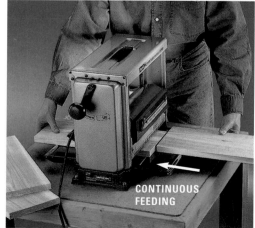

CONTINUOUS FEEDING

Minimize end snipe—gouges on the ends of boards— by feeding short boards one after another. Don't push; let the planer rollers pull each board through.

WEATHERED WOOD CHIPS

WEATHERED WOOD

Work on a warped board as explained in the text before thickness-planing it. Warped or not, you can plane weathered or painted wood to regain usable lumber.

Power Planers

On-the-spot smoothing and trimming to fit are a breeze with a power planer, and a lot faster than with a sander.

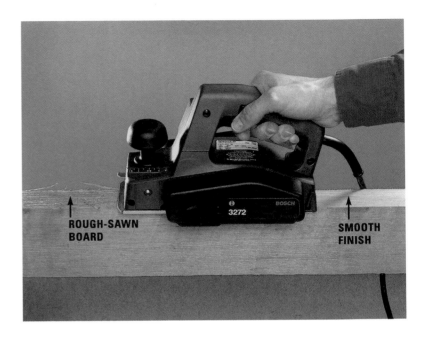

ROUGH-SAWN BOARD

SMOOTH FINISH

A hand-held power planer is a real time-saver for all sorts of jobs that would take far longer with a sander or hand planer. A planer is best at tapering and smoothing boards, fitting doors and trim such as baseboards and window and door casings, and cleaning up the surface of old lumber. It's got a healthy appetite for nibbling wood. You can cut the bulk of the wood with a circular saw and then plane right up to your pencil line with the power planer. It's great for removing high spots on uneven joists before installing decking. When you install cabinets or built-in furniture, you can use the planer to taper face frames or to trim their edges or filler pieces to fit precisely along uneven walls or floors.

Choosing a Planer

Power planers suitable for DIY projects are reasonably priced, but you might want to rent one first, to see what it can do for you. That will probably convince you to get one of your own.

Portable power planers come in various blade widths from 2-13/32 to 6-1/8 inches. The narrower planers are for planing edges of doors, while the big, 6-1/8 inch planers are great for planing large pieces and heavy timbers.

For most tasks, the common 3-1/4 inch width works great and is quite affordable. Some models are equipped with a bevel attachment for planing angled edges, like those on doors. In working around the house, controlling chips is usually a concern, so get a model that has a dust bag attachment. You can always remove the bag at the times when you don't need it. You can buy power planers at home centers, hardware stores, and mail-order tool suppliers.

Most planers come with a set of two or three high-speed steel blades, installed on a rotating cutter head. Some blades can be resharpened (page 120); others are disposable. When they finally go dull (it takes a while), consider buying carbide replacement blades—they will stay sharp for years. You'll be able to detect dull blades easily, because the planer will leave burn marks on the wood surface and the chips coming out of the discharge will look more like sawdust.

Power Planing

The controls and basic operation of a power planer are explained in the diagram at the far right. The power planer deserves a lot of respect. Keep your hands out of the path of the planer; any tool that eats wood this quickly won't be easy on your fingers. A planer is loud, so wear hearing protection. And with chips flying, eye protection is a must! Here are some valuable planing tips and techniques:

▶ Turn on the tool before you make contact with the surface of the workpiece.

▶ Even though the planer can remove more than 1/16 inch with each pass, it's best to take multiple passes of less than 1/16 inch. Move the tool across the workpiece in smooth, even strokes.

▶ When you cut tapers *(below)*, start by making a few cuts near the fat part of the taper, then gradually lengthen the strokes until the taper is even. Think of it as scrubbing away wood.

▶ Always be sure the wood you're planing is free of staples and nails.

▶ For the surest control, use two hands to guide the planer whenever possible.

▶ When planing the long edges of a board, look at how the grain runs to the edge. Plane in the same direction as the grain, not against it. See page 120 for the technique of planing across end grain without chipping or corner tear-out.

▶ To fit an edge to an irregular wall—a common problem when installing a countertop *(below)*—first scribe the cut line on the workpiece. Then start in the middle of the bow and gradually work toward the ends of the line. You can turn the cutting depth adjustment knob as you cut to control the amount of material you're removing.

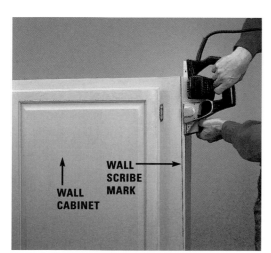

Taper the edge of a cabinet, filler piece, or long board with short strokes on the widest part of the taper, followed by longer strokes to even the edge.

WALL SCRIBE MARK

WALL CABINET

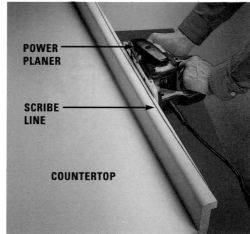

POWER PLANER

SCRIBE LINE

COUNTERTOP

Fit an edge to an irregular wall by working from the middle of the bow to the ends of the scribed line. Turn the depth knob as you cut to control the amount removed along the line.

How a Power Planer Works

Cutting blades that extend across the width of the planer are exposed in a space between an adjustable front sole and a fixed rear sole. The blades rotate at speeds of up to 20,000 rpm to quickly remove wood and leave a smooth, even surface (photo, opposite page).

The rear sole supports the planer on the freshly planed surface much like a jointer. The higher the adjustable front sole is set—by turning the depth control knob—the deeper the cut. Shavings are thrown up and ejected through a port on one side of the planer. Many models have an accessory bag that can be attached to the port to catch the shavings.

For a smooth, chip-free start, place the front sole on the surface of the work and keep pressure on the front as you move the planer forward. Once the planer is completely on the workpiece, shift the pressure to the rear sole and keep the planer moving forward. Best results are obtained, especially with hardwoods such as oak and maple, by making multiple cuts instead of trying to remove too much.

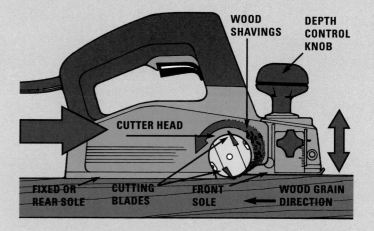

WOOD SHAVINGS

DEPTH CONTROL KNOB

CUTTER HEAD

FIXED OR REAR SOLE

CUTTING BLADES

FRONT SOLE

WOOD GRAIN DIRECTION

Dealing with Planing Problems

Two problems in planing are how to make angled cuts such as chamfers and bevels, and how to plane end grain without chipping or corner damage.

Chamfers and Bevels

A chamfer is an angled cut along an edge that creates a narrow, flat 45° surface in place of the sharp 90° corner. The front sole of most planers has a groove to guide the tool for chamfering the edge of a board. This is a feature to look for when you buy a planer. Most chamfer cuts can be done in a single pass.

A bevel is an angled cut across the whole width of an edge. An adjustable bevel guide attachment makes it easy to cut a consistent bevel along the entire edge of a long board or a door *(below)*. In some cases you can bevel or straight-cut

the edge of a door without taking it off its hinges. Work from top to bottom. The floor will prevent the planer from going all the way to the bottom, so finish the last few inches with a bullnose hand plane, or remove the last bit with a file or a very sharp chisel and finish with sandpaper.

End Grain

To plane the end of a board, or across the top and bottom ends of the rails of cabinet or room doors, work as shown below. Start from the corner at one side and plane to the center. Then plane from the opposite corner toward the center. Never go all the way across or start at the center and go out to the edges. That will cause the end grain to tear away at the end of the cut.

Sharpening Blades

To sharpen or replace power planer blades, you must remove them from the cutter head. Consult the instructions for your planer to see how to do this. Sharpen the blades on an oilstone or whetstone, in the same way as hand plane blades. To maintain the balance of the cutter head, keep the same angle for each blade and remove the same amount of steel.

Most planers come with a handy plastic gauge for setting the blades to the proper height. When adjusted properly, the blades should be set flush with the fixed sole (diagram, page 119). Some manufacturers recommend that their blades be replaced only by a trained technician.

Bevel the edge of a door or board with an accessory bevel guide attachment. Set the guide to the desired angle, and keep it flat against the side of the workpiece.

DEALING WITH PLANING PROBLEMS: END GRAIN

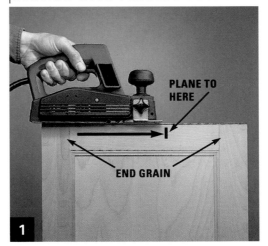

PLANE TO HERE

END GRAIN

1

Plane end grain from the outside edges toward the center of a door or board to avoid corner tearout. Start at one corner and go to the middle.

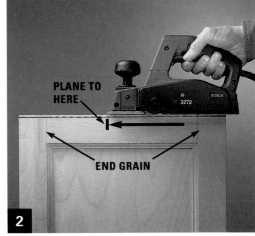

PLANE TO HERE

END GRAIN

2

Finish end-grain planing by working back to the middle from the other corner. Do the same on plywood and other veneer panels.

Jointers

Fine craftsmanship in furniture making demands edges and surfaces finished with precision—the kind of precision only a jointer can attain.

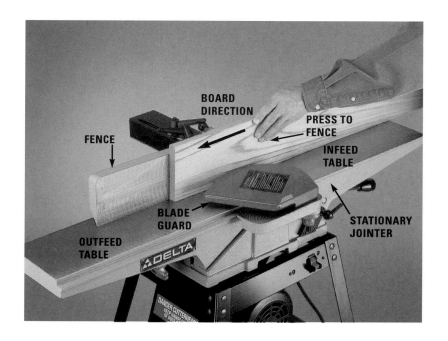

FENCE

BOARD DIRECTION

PRESS TO FENCE

INFEED TABLE

BLADE GUARD

STATIONARY JOINTER

OUTFEED TABLE

Why spend hours planing and sanding rough lumber in a quest for boards with truly flat surfaces and square edges? A few minutes' work with a jointer will give you the boards you need, and you can use your time to finish the furniture, toys, and cabinets you want to build.

You don't have to be a fanatical woodworker to need a jointer. The factory-cut, predimensioned lumber, particleboard, and plywood you use for projects and home remodeling is going to fit where you put it only if you make it fit. Along with the table saw, the jointer is the essential wood-tailoring tool. It can transform you from weekend project maker into a pro with a flip of the switch.

A jointer gets its name because it makes boards flat and planes their edges straight and square to the face; woodworkers call this process "jointing." A thickness planer (page 116) smooths rough lumber and cuts it to exact thickness. The jointer is more versatile. It's designed for accurate edge-planing of boards you're gluing together into larger boards, such as for cabinets or tabletops, but you'll also use it to: straighten an edge of a curved board so it follows the table saw fence as you cut it to width; remove saw marks on the edges of a board; flatten warped board faces; smooth the edges of plywood, particleboard, and Plexiglas; microplane cabinet door edges to get an exact fit; bevel door and board edges; clean up glue joints on stock laminated for lathe turning; and trim fractions of stock from door or window molding when remodeling.

How It Works

A jointer's cutter head spins between a two-part infeed-outfeed table (above). The exposed portion of the cutter head is covered by a swiveling blade guard. The edges of the blades in the cutter head are set level with the stationary outfeed table surface; the adjustable infeed table is set a fraction of an inch lower. As a board passes across the blades, its just-planed edge rides on the outfeed table. The infeed table can be moved up and down to determine the depth of cut. A fence keeps the board positioned at a preset angle to the jointer table and cutter head as it moves through the jointer. If the infeed table is set 1/32 inch below the outfeed table, the jointer will remove precisely 1/32 inch all along a board edge. The new edge will be at the same angle to the face of the board as the fence is to the jointer bed.

121

Jointer Techniques

In basic edge jointing (photo, page 121), grip the board in both hands and push it toward the cutter head, keeping firm pressure downward on the infeed table and sideways against the fence. Feed the work at an even rate; don't stop the cut partway through. As you finish the cut, maintain pressure on the end of the board to keep it firmly on the outfeed table. That's simple enough, but there is more to know and do to use your jointer to its fullest. Here are the most important points:

▶ A precision tool is only as precise as its operator. The jointer may seem harmless because it runs quietly, but be careful. Never remove the swiveling blade guard.

▶ Set the cutting depth at 1/16 inch or less on the infeed table before turning on the jointer (below). If you're planing hardwood, experiment with even shallower cuts to get a smoother board edge and to reduce blade wear and tear.

▶ When possible, cut with the grain—that is, with the grain running down toward the rear end of the board. When you must cut against the grain, the jointer will trim edges smoothly if you don't rush the cut.

▶ Reposition the fence frequently when jointing boards to distribute wear across the length of the blades.

▶ To straighten a curved edge, joint several inches from one end, then as you hear the blades losing contact with the cupped edge, turn the board around and joint the other end. After a few rotations, the curve will be removed.

▶ To flatten a warped board (below), set the infeed for a 1/32-inch cut and make several passes. Keep pressure steady over the cutter head with one hand or a push shoe while pushing the board down on the outfeed table with the other hand.

▶ Check jointer alignment at the beginning of each work session and make any necessary adjustments (opposite page).

▶ When jointing boards 3 to 4 feet long, keep your hands in the same position throughout the cut. Longer boards require repositioning your hands to keep pressure consistently downward and against the fence.

▶ Don't joint boards shorter than 12 inches long. Instead, joint longer boards and cut the lengths you need afterward.

▶ To bevel an edge, set the fence to the desired angle and make multiple passes (below). On the first pass the board will be riding on one corner and that will be cut off at the present angle. Each succeeding pass extends the cut farther across the edge, until the full width is beveled.

CUT WITH GRAIN →
1/16" DEPTH OF CUT
PUSH INTO CUTTER HEAD ←
OUTFEED TABLE
INFEED TABLE
CUTTER HEAD
BLADE

Set the infeed table lower than the outfeed table; 1/16 in. is good for most work. The newly planed edge will be supported by the higher outfeed table.

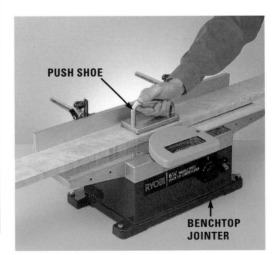

PUSH SHOE

BENCHTOP JOINTER

Flatten a warped board by using a 1/32 in. cut in repeated passes. Press the board down with one hand over the cutter head and with the other hand (not shown, for clarity) on the outfeed side of the board.

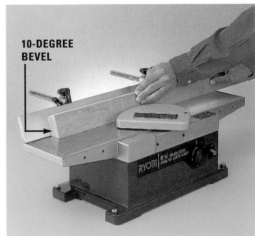

10-DEGREE BEVEL

Bevel the edge of a board by tilting the fence back at an angle. Make multiple passes without changing the depth of the cut until the entire edge is beveled.

Checking and Adjusting Your Jointer

To keep your jointer performing with precision, perform the cleaning and maintenance procedures listed in the instruction manual on a regular basis. In addition, make the checks and adjustments explained here.

Operating Checks

A row of setscrews holds each blade in the cutter head. Check the screws for tightness with an Allen wrench each time before starting to use the jointer.

Also check the joints your tool is making. Joint two boards and place them edge to edge. If you see any gaps in the joint, consult the diagram below to determine the cause and the necessary adjustment to make.

Adjustments

If the jointed edges reveal a misaligned fence, use a high-quality square to realign it *(right top)*. Do not assume that the "automatic" angle stops on the jointer are accurate. Consult the instruction manual to learn how to change the fence setting on your jointer, and adjust it until you see no light between the vertical edge of the square and the face of the fence. Move the square along the table and check at several different points; you may have to make more than one adjustment. Then go back and recheck at each point.

If your test joint reveals misaligned infeed and outfeed tables, don't fret; that happens normally with use. Lay a straightedge on the outfeed table and check the depth from its bottom edge to the infeed table at several points *(right bottom)*. If it is not the same at all points, adjust the outfeed table until the measurements show the tables are parallel. Many jointers have "gibs" (adjustment screws) at the base of the outfeed table for leveling purposes; check the manual.

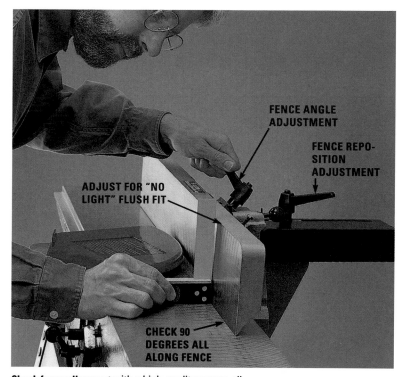

Check fence alignment with a high-quality square all along its length. Adjust the fence for a "no light" fit against the edge of the upright arm of the square.

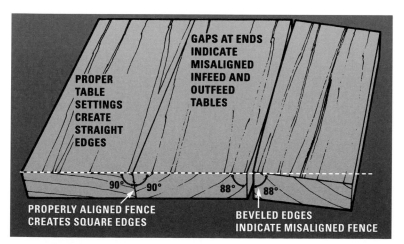

Good and bad jointer joints.

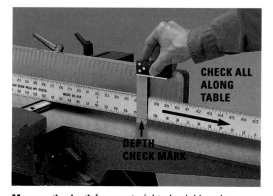

Measure the depth from a straightedge laid on the outfeed table to the infeed table at several points. Adjust the outfeed table until all measurements are equal, indicating the table surfaces are parallel.

Fastening

Plate Joiners

Make invisible corner, edge-to-edge, and miter joints. A plate joiner, glue, clamps, and wooden "biscuits" are all you need for strong, secure results every time.

126

Power Nailers

Avoid hammer fatigue—let air power do the work. From construction framing to installing delicate trim, a power nailer will save you enormous amounts of time and effort.

129

Power Screwdrivers

Use a power screwdriver to avoid wrist-twisting muscle fatigue and aches. There are models for putting up drywall, coarse and fine construction, and delicate craft tasks.
132

Glues and Gluing

Don't get stuck using the wrong sticky stuff for crafts, furniture, or construction. Here is how to choose and use the proper glue for any DIY project.
134

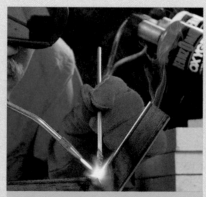

Brazing

Stronger than soldering and both easier and safer than welding, brazing is the ideal do-it-yourself way to join steel, cast iron, brass, copper, bronze, aluminum, and stainless steel.
138

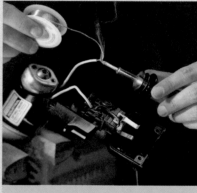

Soldering

For electrical, audio, or video connections with stranded wire or for joining copper plumbing pipes and fittings, soldering is the technique to use. It's fast and easy.
140

Plate Joiners

Corner joints, edge-to-edge joints, miter joints—you can fasten them all quickly, securely, and invisibly with this intriguing tool.

A plate joiner is a specialized machine for joining boards to make cabinets, frames, boxes, shelves, and other woodwork. It is sometimes called a biscuit machine because the joints it makes are fastened with wood plates, commonly called "biscuits."

The tool's working element is a 4-inch diameter carbide-tip cutter, spring-loaded into the base of the tool *(right)*. The front of the joiner can be advanced or retracted to set the depth of cut. An adjustable fence assists in aligning the tool. To make a joint, you butt the front plate against one piece of wood and pull the trigger switch: The cutter plunge-cuts a crescent-shaped slot. You cut a matching slot in the other piece and squirt glue into both slots. Then you insert a wood plate in one slot, slip the slot in the second piece over the exposed half of the plate, and clamp the joint together until the glue sets.

The plates, or biscuits, are shaped pieces of compressed hardwood. This compression is what makes plate joints so strong: The moisture in the glue makes the plates expand slowly in their slots to give a very tight fit and an excellent glue joint. There are three standard sizes of plates (see Tool Tip, opposite page) for making various size joints.

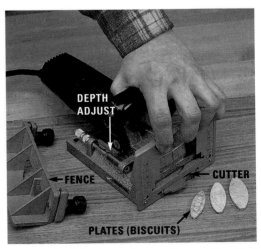

A typical plate joiner has a plunge-action carbide cutter and an adjustable and removable fence. Plates come in three sizes.

Plate Joint Features

The plate joiner is at its best making the corner and butted T joints of plywood and particleboard cabinets. It is particularly useful when the outsides of the cabinet must show, so screws or nails can't be used.

It is excellent for square and mitered frame joints in solid wood *(below)*, though it is limited to pieces over 2-3/4 inches wide to allow for the slot width.

A plate joiner is fast, and the joints are strong: The swelling of the plates inside the slots guarantees a very strong glue line. Because the plates are wide, there is much more glue and wood involved in the joints than in dowel joints. It is also very easy to get perfect joints every time. Until they swell from the moisture of the glue, the plates are loose in their slots, which are always cut oversize, so you can adjust the pieces of wood being joined as much as 1/4 inch to get perfect alignment.

Plate Joint Basics

Slots for plate joints should be centered in the thickness of the wood. When the joiner base and workpiece are on the same flat surface, the slot will be centered in 3/4-inch-thick stock. The fence can be set for other thicknesses. The slots also must be equally spaced along the edge *(opposite page, top)*. You can mark the center of each slot using a ruler or the spacing marks on the joiner body *(right top)*.

For an accurate joint, clamp the two pieces with their edges aligned so you can use one set of marks for both of them *(right top)*.

Use a ruler or the spacing marks on the joiner to get equal distances between slot centers. Cut all the slots in one piece, then go back and cut slots in the other piece *(right middle)*.

Put glue in the slots before inserting the biscuits. You can use a thin scrap of wood, but a thin, flat nozzle on a glue applicator *(right bottom)* is much easier. More details for making specific kinds of joints are given on the next page.

Mark the center of each slot across the workpiece.

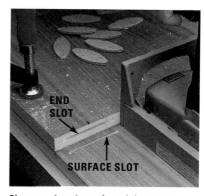

Clamp mating pieces for a joint together. Slot one piece first, then the other.

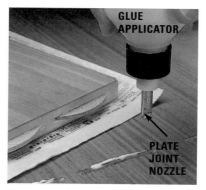

Put glue in all slots before inserting the wood plates.

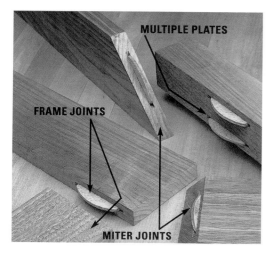

Make frame joints in thin stock with one plate, use multiple plates in thicker stock. Both square and miter joints are possible. Methods for other joints are shown on page 128.

Making Plate Joints

In various projects you will need edge-to-edge joints, T joints, and end joints. Here's how to make them.

Edge-to-Edge Joints

Biscuits help make strong joints, and they help keep the boards flat during clamping. Lay boards with their edges together and make spacing marks across the joint *(below)*. If you have several boards, as for a tabletop, lay them out and mark all the joints at one time. Separate them and cut slots with the plate joiner centered on each mark. Insert glue and biscuits and assemble the boards. Lightly clamp them and tap on the ends to align the marks along each joint, then tighten the clamps.

You may want to leave the boards long and trim the final assembly to length after the joints dry.

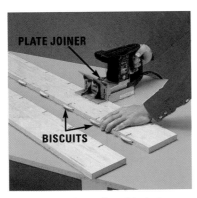

Mark slot spacing—about 6 in. between centers—for edge-to-edge joints with the boards together, then separate them for cutting .

T Joints

Use a T joint to fasten the edge of one board to the face of another, as for bookcase shelves. Clamp the pieces together, mark the shelf, and cut slots in the end *(below)*. You don't need the joiner fence; the body rests on the side workpiece.

Next, turn the joiner vertical and butt the base against the end of the shelf to cut matching slots in the side *(bottom)*.

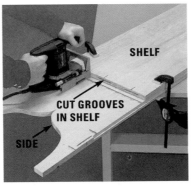

Cut T joint slots while both pieces are clamped together with their outer edges aligned. Remove the joiner fence and cut the end slots first.

Turn the joiner on end and butt the base against the slotted end piece to cut matching slots in the surface of the other piece of a T joint.

Assemble the joint with glue, biscuits, and clamps. Tap the edges into alignment before a final clamp tightening *(below)*.

Tap on a piece of scrap wood to move a joint into alignment before the glue swells the plate—about 5 minutes. You can adjust the joint by as much as 1/4 in.

End Joints

Cut door rails, frame rails and stiles, and narrow stock—square or mitered ends—as required. Then build a simple jig of scrap *(below)* to hold the pieces. The extra width will support the joiner, and you won't have to clamp each piece separately.

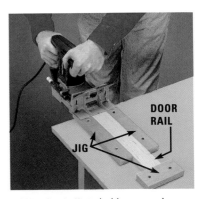

Build a simple jig to hold narrow pieces for end slotting. The jig holds workpieces without clamping and provides good support for the joiner fence.

Power Nailers

Don't pound nails with a hammer, pound them with air! Whether you're using it for construction framing or delicate trim, an air-powered nailer is faster, more accurate, and infinitely less tiring than a hammer.

One of the hardest things in driving nails is to avoid damage. One slip of a hammer and you have dented molding, broken glass or plaster, bruised fingers, or rapidly climbing blood pressure—and perhaps all of the above.

If you haven't experienced such disasters, it's probably because you work slowly and carefully, drilling pilot holes, tapping nails just to above the surface, and finishing off with a nail set. That's the classic way to do it, if you have plenty of time and lots of patience. But many do-it-yourself projects need to be done in an afternoon or during a weekend at most, and classic ways can turn an otherwise quick project into a time-gobbling monster.

The power tool that can make tedious nailing go quickly and make tricky nailing easy is a pneumatic "hammer" called a power nailer or air nailer. It uses compressed air to drive nails into wood effortlessly. You can hold a piece of wood—trim molding, for example—in position with one hand, and drive a nail through it by pulling the nailer's trigger with the other hand. The trim will stay in position when you drive the nail and won't drift away as with successive blows from a hammer. The nailer will even set the nail head below the surface, saving you that extra step.

Power nailers come in a wide variety of sizes; some large models are used to drive large framing nails. This chapter focuses on nailers for installing wood trim, but the basic techniques explained here apply to all sizes.

There are two categories of trim nailers: brad and finish.

Brad nailers *(above)* generally drive nails that are 1/2 to 1-1/4 inches long. They are lightweight (3-lb.) and ideal for small pieces such as decorative cabinet trim, base shoe molding, door casing, small picture frames, decorative shelf trim, and hobby projects.

Finish nailers (page 130) have a larger cylinder to drive bigger, thicker nails that are 3/4 to 2-1/2 inches long. A nailer like this really saves on the arms and elbows, even though it weighs 5 to 6 lbs. It can drive nails through wallboard or plaster into wall studs, and easily handles nailing baseboard, door casing, chair rail, stair treads, crown molding, window casing, and exterior deck or porch trim.

Getting Set for Air Nailing

When you decide to get a nailer/air nailer/nail gun, there are plenty to choose from; a current tool catalog lists more than 80 models suitable for DIY use, and many more for heavy-duty professional use. Be careful: "nail gun" can also mean a construction tool that uses blank .22-caliber cartridges. You also need the following power equipment:

▶ A 3/4-hp or larger tank-type air compressor capable of producing up to 120 pounds per square inch of air pressure.

▶ An air filter and regulator, usually included with the compressor.

▶ Air hoses and connectors.

For more about compressors, see pages 162–164.

Nails for Your Nailer

You'll find almost as many kinds of trim nails for air nailers as for hand nailing. A variety of nail "clips" or strips are used in air nailers. The nails are bonded with a coating to keep them together in a strip, which is loaded into the magazine, where a pressure spring feeds them into position under the driving pin.

Some nails have a galvanized coating to keep rust away, making them great for exterior use, such as with siding, trim, or railings. Don't use interior nails outside or they'll rust and a dark stain will form around the nail hole. Air nailer manufacturers sell their own nails, but some brands are interchangeable.

Nails for power nailing cost about five to ten times as much as standard nails from your hardware store, but the speed and ease of the air nailer will quickly convince you of their value.

Learning to Air Nail

A nail gun isn't as intimidating as it looks. The operating parts and controls are shown below. Find some scrap wood and test the nailer to get comfortable and find your "aim." Proceed as follows (additional techniques are shown on page 131).

▶ With the air hose disconnected, load nails into the magazine.

▶ Connect the air hose and turn the compressor on.

▶ Put on hearing and eye protection. An air nailer operates with a "bang" and its percussive blow can throw off metal or wood chips.

▶ Grasp the handle firmly and position the nailer in the direction you want the nail to go. It travels in a straight line directly out of the cylinder and nose piece.

▶ Push the nailer until you feel the nose piece depress, then squeeze the trigger. You probably won't even realize the nail has been driven, because of the nailer's quick action. Drive more nails one by one. It will take time to develop a feel for the nailing action.

▶ Watch out for repeat action. As long as the trigger is pulled up, the nailer will fire each time the nose piece is depressed against the workpiece. Skilled workers can "bounce" the gun from point to point very rapidly—but it's dangerous. Accidents can happen when tools work faster than your eyes, so work at a reasonable pace and remember that you're already saving time.

Learn the parts of your nailer and their functions before driving your first nail. Read the manual carefully, because not all nailers are alike.

Air Nailing Techniques

Try a test nail or two in scrap wood the same as your finish trim. If nail penetration is too deep, turn the regulator on the air compressor to get a lower reading on the pressure gauge (below).

If the nailhead sticks above the surface, adjust the compressor for a higher pressure. Most air nailers operate at pressures of 70 to 120 pounds per square inch (psi). Check the manual for your nailer and never exceed the maximum specified operating pressure.

Aim the nail gun cylinder directly in line with the "receiving" workpiece and clamp it in place so the impact of the nail won't send it flying (below center). You may have a tough time penetrating hard wood such as oak or maple. When this happens, turn up the air pressure or choose the next shortest nail that will do the job. If all else fails, revert to basic craftsmanship: drill a pilot hole, dust off your hammer, and pound in an ordinary nail; finish with a nail set.

Always find the wall stud locations before nailing. You may not be able to "feel" a missed nail (below right) the way you can when using a hammer, so be sure to mark stud locations before nailing.

Be especially careful about plumbing, gas pipe, and electrical wire runs. Don't drive nails that are unnecessarily long, because they may find a wire or pipe hiding back in the wall. Use a nail length that will drive two-thirds of the nail into solid wood behind wallboard or plaster. If you don't want the nail to show through the back side of a workpiece, do some careful measuring first.

Safety and Maintenance

To make sure your nailer operates properly and safely, do the following:

▶ Keep the nailer oiled. Add a few drops of No. 10 nondetergent oil—No. 30 nondetergent oil in warm temperatures—in the air inlet before each use.

▶ Never load the nailer with the compressor air hose attached.

▶ Never leave the nailer unattended. Children are fascinated by nailers, which can be deadly.

▶ If your nailer isn't firing, disconnect the air hose before you attempt any repairs.

▶ All nailers are not alike. Read your owner's manual thoroughly for specific instructions.

▶ And finally, be sure to keep all body parts and bystanders away from the nail path to avoid serious injury.

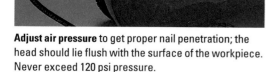

Adjust air pressure to get proper nail penetration; the head should lie flush with the surface of the workpiece. Never exceed 120 psi pressure.

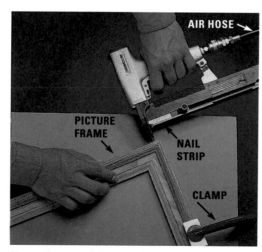

Clamp a loose receiving workpiece to resist the impact of the nail. Aim straight into the work; an angled nail can split the wood, leaving a dangerous exposed point.

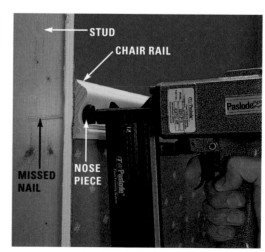

Mark stud locations before driving nails into walls. You won't be able to "feel" that a nail has missed and offers no useful holding power.

Power Screwdrivers

Driving screws with electrical power instead of wrist power has called for new kinds of screws. Together, the tool and fasteners make holding things together a snap.

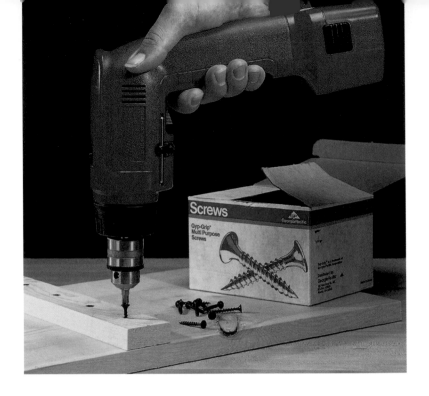

Once the electric drill became common, what might be called the "Great Screwdriving Revolution" was inevitable. Although hand screwdriving is still with us, it is no way to get a job done quickly or to avoid muscle fatigue when you have ten, twenty, or hundreds of screws to drive—for example, in putting up drywall. As a result of the revolution, today there are three power ways to cope with screwdriving:

Electric Drills. Conventional drills with cords have the power to drive long screws all day, as when building a deck. Cordless drills are more convenient and less powerful, but still strong enough for most power screwdriving.

Electric Drivers. Similar to drills, these are designed especially for screwdriving. They are typically cordless *(above)*, with a clutch to adjust how deeply the screw head travels and a low-speed setting for more comfortable and powerful screwdriving.

Cordless Screwdrivers. Pocket-size tools that look like a flashlight *(right)*, cordless screwdrivers are especially convenient where there isn't room for a full-size driver. However, they are slow and are best for small screws.

Drive short, hardened screws like those for mounting hardware with a cordless screwdriver. It's good for working in tight spots, too.

Power Driver Accessories

There are several accessories *(below)* to increase the ease and versatility of power screwdriving:

Magnetic bit holder (A). A steel tube that holds the hardened steel hex-shaft Phillips head and straight bits used in power driving. To avoid damage, use only a bit that fills the single or crossed slots in the screw head.

Flexible shaft (B). One end fits in the chuck, the other holds a bit; the shaft bends to reach otherwise inaccessible spots.

Combination countersinks (C, E). A drill bit-reamer to drill a pilot hole for a screw shank and a larger hole for the head.

Screw-eye driver (D). A Y-shaped "bit" that holds the loop of a screw eye or hook.

Keyless chuck (F). Makes changing accessories fast and easy. You can add one to your old drill; see page 83.

Screws for Power Driving

The speed and torque of a power driver require screws with hardened heads and shafts. Drywall and similar screws *(below)* have a single-diameter shank and a Phillips or square-drive head. A drywall screw—good for fastening wood also—has a large "bugle" head. Trim head screws can be driven below the surface and concealed with putty.

Small size screws for power driving *(right top)* must also be hardened. Use flathead screws to mount hardware. For outside construction, use galvanized decking screws *(right center)*. They are rustproof and especially good to fasten redwood and cedar.

Whatever screws you use, a driver/drill with a clutch has several settings, so you can adjust it to drive screws to a consistent depth *(right bottom)*, usually flush with or slightly below the surface of the workpiece.

Match the bit to the screw size. Small flathead hardware screws usually require a No. 1 Phillips bit; larger sizes take a No. 2 bit.

Choose galvanized decking screws for outdoor construction, to avoid rust streaks. Drive decking screws with a powerful drill and hardened driver bit.

WORKING TIP

Drywall and similar screws do not usually require a pilot hole in softwoods, and only one size of hole in hardwoods. Drive a screw into a scrap piece of your project wood to see if you need to drill a pilot hole.

Use accessories to make power driving easier: (A) magnetic bit holder; (B) flexible shaft; (C, E) combination countersinks; (D) screw-eye driver; (F) keyless chuck.

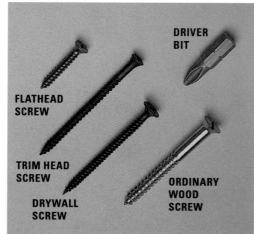

Select hardened screws for power driving; there are many types, most with Phillips heads. Use only hardened driver bits, and use the slowest driver speed with slotted-head screws.

Adjust the clutch of a driver/drill to consistently set screws to a desired depth. The higher the setting number, the deeper the screw goes. Use low-speed operation for extra power and control.

Glues and Gluing

A glue joint can be invisible, and stronger than the wood it joins. There's no mystery to making a joint like that; all you need to do is choose the right glue for your project and apply it properly. Here's how.

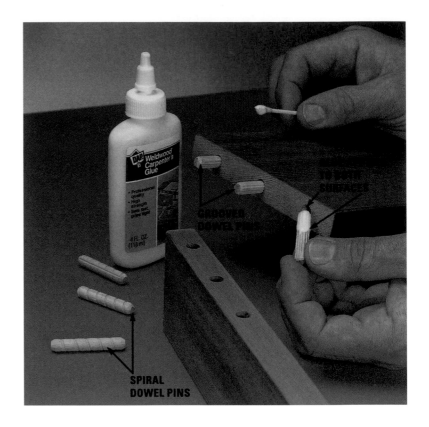

SPIRAL DOWEL PINS

Glue has been the woodworker's best friend for centuries. Furniture and craft pieces assembled with glue are generally superior to those using metal fasteners; repeated movement will cause a screw or nail to wear a hole bigger and loosen the joint. If a glue joint does loosen, you can disassemble and clean it, and glue it back together without damaging the surface and without having to fill ugly screw or nail holes.

Glue lets you join boards edge to edge without fasteners. It also holds mortise-and-tenon, dowel, and plate or biscuit joints (pages 126–128) in a way no metal fastener can. You can use glue to hold square and mitered butt, lap, and T joints. And you can use it to join irregular or broken pieces that a metal fastener would only damage further.

Unlike any other fastener, glue becomes part of the wood it joins. The only difference is that it's stronger.

Gluing Action
Most wood glues are made up of solid glue molecules suspended in a liquid. The liquid carries the glue molecules into the pores of the wood where they lock themselves in. As the liquid evaporates—that is, as the glue sets and dries—the molecules in and between the boards link together chemically, joining the pieces of wood: "glued together" effectively means linked together.

Types of Wood Glue

The five glues commonly used in woodworking are yellow, white, hide, epoxy, and resorcinol. Their strengths and weaknesses are described here. Making glue joints is explained on pages 136–137.

Yellow or carpenter's glue *(opposite page).* This aliphatic glue has a short clamping time—only 30 to 60 minutes—and good tack, meaning it clings well to the materials it is joining. It can be applied in temperatures from 40° to 100° F, and when dry stands up well to heat, so it is less likely to clog sanding belts. Yellow glue's strength, convenience, and affordability make it the logical choice for wood projects that will be used indoors.

White or PVA (polyvinyl acetate) glue. White glue is easy to clean up and dries clear. But it gums up sanding belts more readily than yellow glue, requires a longer clamping time, and isn't as resistant to the solvents found in some varnishes and paints. It is suitable for use on paper, leather, and on wood for crafts and other light-duty projects.

Hide glue. Glues from animal hides are available in melt-and-use form, but the ready-to-use variety *(below left)* is the logical choice for most DIY projects. Its biggest advantage is that it sets up slowly, providing as much as two hours of assembly time for projects with lots of parts; it is often used for constructing and repairing furniture and musical instruments. Clamping time increases proportionately—8 to 12 hours. Hide glue is highly sensitive to moisture and humidity, and the unused portion must be discarded after a year.

Epoxy glue. Epoxies are two-part agents formed by mixing two viscous liquids in exact proportions. They can be "filled" with plastic grains, wood dust, cotton fiber, and other materials to take advantage of their ability to fill gaps in imperfectly matched joints.

Resorcinol and polyurethane glues. Two-part resorcinol glues are created by mixing a powder and liquid *(below).* They're expensive, but amazingly waterproof and extremely strong, making them ideal for use on outdoor furniture, signs, even boats. They're also better at filling gaps than other wood glues, although the resulting glue line is dark and quite noticeable. There's wide variation among products, so read the labels.

Ready-to-use polyurethane glues are meant for exterior use. They're expensive and require long clamping time, but they're completely waterproof and very strong.

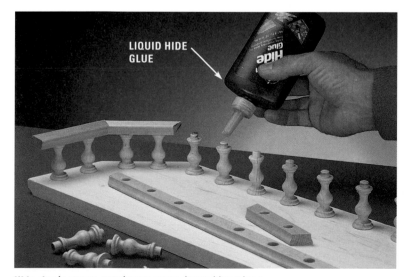

Hide glue is strong, yet slow to set up. It provides a long assembly time for furniture or woodworking projects involving lots of pieces.

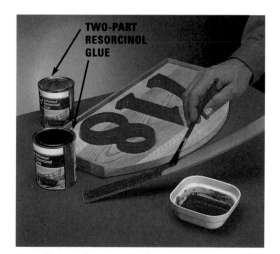

Resorcinol glue is durable and truly waterproof. Ideal for signs, boats, and outdoor furniture, it is created by mixing a powder and a liquid.

Making Glue Joints

The keys to making good-looking, long-lasting glue joints are selecting the right wood and preparing it correctly, applying the glue properly, clamping the workpieces evenly, and being patient as the glue sets and cures.

Be sure to use fresh glue, or to stir older glue if you haven't used if for over a month; the solids can settle.

Select the Right Wood

Use dry lumber, preferably pieces with 6 to 8 percent moisture content. That's hard to determine without a moisture meter, but at a minimum, buy kiln-dried wood, buy it all at the same time, and store it in a dry place. With wet wood, the joint can fail because the glue never really dries and hardens—the moisture in the glue has no place to go. Also, as the wood dries, it shrinks and the wood can split or the glue joint can fail.

Prepare the Wood Correctly

Remove saw marks by planing or lightly sanding. Examine any boards that you take directly from a joiner or planer; surfaces can be so glassy and burnished that glue can't penetrate into the wood pores. In that case, sand lightly with 100- to 150-grit paper to open the pores again. Make sure boards are free of dirt or oils. Test-fit the pieces, keeping in mind that the boards should fit tightly together before clamping. Check edge joints for a good match by holding them up to the light. A tight fit is important because white, yellow, and hide glues are poor gap fillers; spaces even the thickness of a piece of paper will create a weaker joint.

Apply the Glue Properly

Spreading globs of glue creates a thick and therefore weak joint, wastes glue, and makes cleanup a chore. You want a thin, even coating on both surfaces. One way to get it is to apply a thin line of glue down the center of one edge, bring the pieces together, and slide their edges back and forth. Then pull them apart to check that the glue is distributed evenly. Even better, apply glue with a roller *(below)* or a brush to both surfaces to be joined. When you clamp the pieces together, a small bead of glue oozing out on both sides of the joint indicates you have used the right amount of glue; if not, pull the joint apart and apply some more.

If you are making a doweled joint, use parallel- or spiral-grooved dowels (photo, page 134) that fit easily but not loosely into their holes. Apply glue to the dowels, not to the holes. Use a cotton-tip applicator or small brush, or spread a bit of glue on a piece of scrap wood and roll each dowel in it. The grooves in the dowels let the glue fill the joint without oozing out the top of the joint.

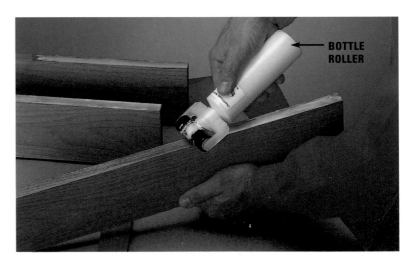

Spread a thick, even line of glue along both surfaces to be joined. A bottle roller or a brush will help you obtain consistent results.

Clamp with Even Pressure

Use adequate and even clamping pressure. Clamps aren't intended to force warped boards into alignment; their function is to hold boards together evenly while the glue sets. Apply clamps 2 inches from each end, then every 6 to 8 inches between when gluing 1-inch-thick stock *(below)*. Space clamps closer for thicker woods. Hard, dense woods, like walnut or oak, require almost twice as much clamping pressure—either more clamps or tighter clamps—as soft woods, like pine.

Keep an eye on the temperature; as it drops, clamping time for proper adhesion and setting increases. Too cold and the glue might not bond at all; too warm and you'll have a shorter time to assemble and clamp the pieces.

You've used the right amount of glue if, after clamping, a small, even bead of glue—or ooze line—appears along both sides of the joint. Remove excess glue immediately by wiping with a damp cloth or by waiting a half hour, then removing it with a scraper *(below)*.

Be Patient

Leave the clamps in place for the length of time recommended on the glue's label. Then set the piece aside, usually overnight, to let the glue cure to full strength before continuing work. If you plane or sand the piece too soon, you'll wind up with a sunken joint; as the glue continues to evaporate, the wood along the joint shrinks and the joint becomes recessed. Before applying a finish, test for glue residue on the wood by rubbing mineral spirits across the joint *(below)*. Sand away the residue with a fine-grit paper or those areas will resist whatever stain or finish you try to use.

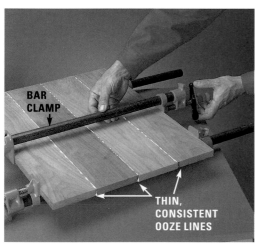

Clamp pieces together, applying even pressure. Thin, consistent "ooze lines" on both sides indicate the right amount of glue.

Remove excess glue with a scraper when it reaches toothpaste consistency, or wipe with a damp cloth immediately after clamping.

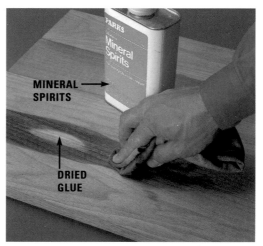

Check for residue by lightly wiping joints with mineral spirits. Sand to remove all traces of glue; it will resist stains and finishes.

Brazing

Far stronger than soldering and far easier and cheaper than welding, brazing is a marvelous metal mender.

Glue, screws, or nails aren't much good for mending a broken lawnmower, fixing a steel porch railing or barbecue grill, and similar tasks. Brazing is what you need. You can teach yourself to do it in a couple of hours for less than $100.

In brazing, the metals to be joined are first heated to about 800° F. Then a filler material, usually brass or bronze rod, is melted so it can flow into the pores of the metal and around the joint, forming a sturdy bond. Brazing lets you join different types and thicknesses of metals easily. Steel, cast iron, brass, copper, bronze, aluminum, and stainless steel can all be brazed using the proper filler rods and fluxes. Brazing uses lower temperatures than welding, so there's less damage and stress to metals. Soldering (pages 140–143) involves lower temperatures than brazing and provides great electrical conductivity, but it forms only a weak structural bond.

What You Need

For brazing, you need a gas-fired torch, flux, rods of filler metal, and eye and hand protection. The least expensive, and most limited, torch setup is a MAPP gas cylinder equipped with a special brazing torch head. With this you'll be able to braze small objects and thin metal.

Higher temperatures and a better-defined flame are produced by a propane-oxygen setup *(above)*. This kind of fuel allows you to join metals up to 1/8 inch thick, and quicker than with MAPP. A propane-oxygen outfit is both convenient and versatile, but the nonrefillable oxygen tanks cost $7 or more each and last only about 10 minutes.

Professionals use oxygen-acetylene gas torches for brazing , welding, and cutting all kinds of metals. These are generally beyond DIY use because of their expense—about $200 for a torch, and $300 for two large gas cylinders—as well as the skill and experience needed to use them correctly and safely.

A can of powdered flux costs about $5, and will last for many, many jobs. Filler rods, available both fluxed and unfluxed, are less than $1 apiece. Both the flux and the filler rod must be appropriate for the material you are brazing. Check the labels or ask the supplier.

Get safety goggles with No. 4 or No. 5 lenses. They are more for protecting your eyes from bright light than from sparks; clear safety glasses are not enough. Sunglasses also are not enough and are definitely not safe! Always wear heavy leather gloves to protect your hands. Welding supply stores can provide both equipment and advice; many large home centers also carry the basic equipment.

Brazing Away

The sequence of operations in brazing is simple: clean, heat and flux, heat and fill. Here's what to do:

1. Clean the joint area of all oils, paints, oxides, or rust *(below)*. Use wire brushes, grinders, and abrasive papers. Brazing dirty surfaces is as futile as gluing boards covered with loose paint.

2. Clamp or position the pieces to be joined. The smaller the gap at the seam, the stronger your joint will be. Don't think about touching the pieces to adjust their positions once they're heated; they'll sear you right through your gloves.

3. Lightly heat the entire joint, then sprinkle powdered flux over the area *(below center)*. The purpose of the flux is to remove any oxides on the metal. Go back and heat a small section of the joint area, moving the torch head in a small circular or zigzag motion *(below right)*. Steel objects will glow a dull red when at the proper temperature.

4. Touch a fluxed filler rod to the joint and continue to direct the flame just ahead of the melting rod tip. (If you have an unfluxed rod, heat it and stick the end directly into the can of flux powder.) The heated base metals, not the torch flame, should melt the rod. If you can't get things hot enough, try raising the metals off your work surface. Or your metals might be too thick.

5. Once started, continue heating the joint evenly and depositing the filler rod. Your first pass should deposit a thin, free-flowing layer of filler material on the joint (the tinning pass). Additional passes, applied in a series of short dabs, will build up the joint and strengthen the connection at the joint.

6. Chip off any excess hardened flux after the piece cools. Be careful; cooling takes a good while.

Safety, Safety, Safety

Brazing can be dangerous—you're dealing with fumes, bright light, and concentrated heat. Yet with the proper precautions you'll be quite safe.

▶ Know what metals you're joining. Avoid cadmium-plated material like electrical conduit and galvanized metals, both of which produce toxic fumes when heated.

▶ Work in an area with adequate ventilation. Outdoors is best. If you braze indoors, do it near an exhaust fan that directs the fumes out and away. Do not rely on disposable masks.

▶ Do not braze near flammable liquids like gasoline or paint thinners. Shops and garages are just where you might need to braze, and also where flammable materials are usually stored.

▶ Wear leather gloves, and goggles with No. 4 or No. 5 lenses.

▶ Work on a nonflammable surface like firebrick and know where your torch flame is at all times.

WORKING TIP

When connecting two pieces with a brazed lap joint, make the overlap area three times the thickness of the metal.

Clean surfaces to be joined by grinding or sanding down to bare bright metal. Brazing cannot form a firm bond over rust, oxidation, dirt, or paint.

Sprinkle powdered flux over the heated area to be brazed. It cleans oxides from the metal surfaces and turns dark and glassy at the proper brazing temperature.

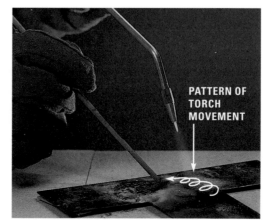

PATTERN OF TORCH MOVEMENT

Keep the torch flame moving just ahead of the fluxed filler rod. If the rod sticks, the temperature is too low; sizzling means the metal is too hot.

Soldering

Soldering is used to make electrical connections or join plumbing parts, which are two very different processes. Here's the lowdown on both.

Solder, a soft, easy-melting metal, is used to join other metals together somewhat in the way glue is used. It has high electrical conductivity, which makes it an excellent material to join stranded wires that carry electrical current, such as extension cords, connections in self-contained electrical and electronic devices, and lines that carry audio and video signals. However, because a soldered connection does not have great physical strength, it is not a safe way to connect solid copper-wire conductors such as those used for home wiring; in fact, its use for that purpose is forbidden by the National Electrical Code.

Solder is an excellent material for joining copper pipes and tubing used for plumbing. Because making plumbing joints with solder is so fast and simple, soldered copper long ago replaced threaded steel as the water pipe of choice. For health safety, building codes universally require using lead-free solder in water-supply piping.

Soldered connections for low-voltage electrical and similar applications are made with an electric soldering iron or soldering gun. Connections in pipe and tubing are easily made with a torch fueled by a hand-sized tank of propane gas. You can't use a gun or iron to solder pipe.

Techniques for both kinds of soldering are explained on the next three pages.

Choosing Solder

Solder is an alloy of tin and a softer metal that melts at a relatively low temperature, less than 800° F. The type of soft solder to use for electrical repairs has a rosin core and is sold in electrical and audio/video departments. Acid-core solder is designed for plumbing work. Never use acid-core solder for electrical connections. It looks similar to rosin-core solder but will corrode small wires.

The rosin or acid core is a flux that helps clean and bond the connections. However, you should also apply paste flux to all areas to be connected. Paste flux is the same for either electrical or plumbing repairs and is commonly carried in the plumbing department.

Preparing the Iron or Gun

The tip of your electric soldering iron or gun must be clean and properly tinned—coated with solder—in order to make a soldered connection.

With the tool unplugged and cool, clean the tip with a medium-coarse (bastard) metal file *(below left)*. Use light strokes to remove any old solder or coating from the tapered surface of the tip and get down to bare copper.

To tin the tip, plug in the iron or hold the trigger switch of the gun depressed to get it hot. Then touch solder to the tip *(below)*. A hot tip will cause the solder to flow immediately. Coat the entire cleaned area of the tip and wipe off any excess solder with a damp sponge. A tinned tip prevents oxides from forming on the heated connectors or wires.

Tinning Stranded Wires

Light-gauge, stranded copper wire, such as 20–24 gauge speaker wire, will work better if the ends have been tinned. It will make a more solid connection in a screw or clamp terminal because all the wires will be held together under the head of the screw or clamp. (Soldering wires to tab connectors is explained on the next page.)

Twist the strands together with your fingers and bend the wire into the hook or other shape you need for the connection. Trying to bend it after tinning will break the solder. Touch the hot tip of the soldering iron to the one side of the wires for a moment or two *(below)* and then touch the solder to the other side of the heated wires—not to the tip of the iron. If the solder doesn't melt, continue heating the wires until it does.

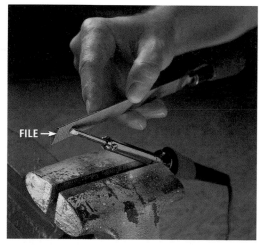

FILE →

Clean the tip of a soldering iron or gun with a file to remove all old solder; get down to bare metal on the tapered surfaces.

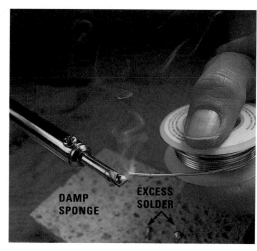

DAMP SPONGE

EXCESS SOLDER

Tin the heated tip by touching solder to it. You want a thin coat on all cleaned surfaces. Use a damp sponge to catch drips.

SOLDERING IRON

TINNED WIRES

TIGHTLY TWISTED STRANDED WIRE

Twist stranded wires together and bend them into shape for the terminal before tinning. Heat the wires, not the solder, until the solder flows and joins them.

Making Soldered Tab Connections

Many devices and components have flat metal tabs for connecting stranded wires.

If the tab has a hole in it, a soldered connection is called for. If the tab is flat, it requires a slip-on connector.

To make a soldered connection to a hole-type tab, first make sure the tab is clean. Use fine abrasive cloth or steel wool to remove any corrosion, film, or dirt. Then twist the wire strands together, insert the wire in the hole, and bend it around the connecting tab.

Place slips of protective material under the tab to catch any excess solder *(Photo 1)*.

Speaker cones, electronic components, plastic cases, and tabletops are easily damaged if hot solder drips onto them.

Apply paste flux to the tab and the wires with a small brush.

Touch the heated tip of the soldering iron against the tab *(Photo 2)*. Keep the flat surface of the tip against the tab to heat it and the wires. Then touch the solder to the wire and tab, not to the tip of the tool. The heated connection should melt the solder; if it doesn't, keep heating the connection until the solder melts and flows freely onto it.

Remove the solder and the tool as soon as a bead of solder has covered the connection. Let the solder cool for a minute before moving the wire. A good job has a smooth, rounded surface *(Photo 3)*. If the solder is jagged or has a rough surface, there was not enough heat and the connection will not be secure or electrically complete. It that case, reheat the joint, wipe away the old solder when it melts, and try again.

MAKING SOLDERED TAB CONNECTIONS

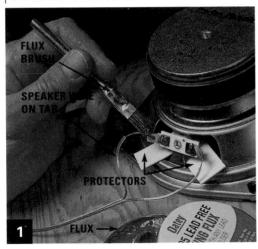

Wrap twisted-together stranded wires through the hole of a cleaned tab and apply paste flux before soldering. Provide a protector to catch drips.

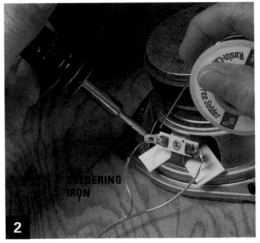

Heat the tab and wire with the flat surface of the tip of the soldering iron or gun, then touch rosin-core solder to the connection. It will flow freely onto properly heated components.

Inspect the connection, but don't move anything for a minute or so. A smooth bead covering the wire and tab end indicates a good soldering job.

Soldering Copper Pipe

Copper pipe and tubing for residential plumbing is connected using threadless fittings with "sweat soldered" joints. Here's how to do it.

Cut the pipe end clean and square with a tubing cutter. (Shut off the water and drain the system if you are cutting into an existing supply pipe.) Ream the inside edges of the newly cut end to remove any burrs. Use the fold-away reaming tool built into the cutter or a separate hand reamer.

If the pipe was a connected water pipe, stuff a bit of bread 4 or 5 inches into it, to prevent any drops from getting to the connection as you work—steam will ruin a soldering job. The bread will dissolve when you turn the water back on.

Now make the sweat-soldered connection in the steps illustrated below.

1. Clean the outside surface where the fitting will be soldered with abrasive emery cloth (Photo 1).

2. Clean the inside of the fitting with a fitting brush. Brushes are available in various sizes and do a better job than emery cloth (Photo 2).

3. Spread paste flux on the cleaned area of the pipe and the inside of the fitting. The flux provides chemical cleaning that is essential in addition to the abrasive cleaning with emery cloth (Photo 3).

4. Place a fitting on the pipe and heat it with the flame of a propane torch. The tip of the flame is the hottest part. Hold lead-free solder at the joint; when the fitting is hot enough, capillary action will draw the solder into the joint. Wipe away excess solder with a wet cloth. There should be a solid shoulder of solder all the way around the joint, with no gaps (Photo 4).

WORKING TIP

When soldering a fitting or adapter with interior threads, raise the threaded end of the pipe so the joint area is downhill and solder will not be drawn into the threads.

SOLDERING COPPER PIPE

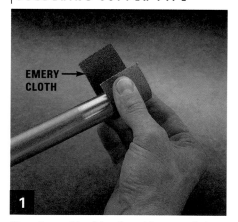

1. Clean the outside of the pipe with emery cloth. Don't touch the cleaned area.

2. Use a fitting brush to clean the inside of the fitting to be soldered on the pipe.

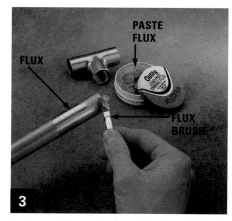

3. Apply paste flux to the cleaned surface of the pipe and the inside of the fitting.

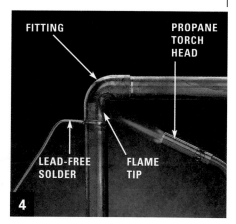

4. Heat the fitting, not the pipe or solder, until solder is drawn up into the joint. Wipe clean with a wet cloth.

Multipurpose Tools

Power Washing

For yearly maintenance or to prepare for painting, power-washing the exterior of your home will save hours, even days, of scrubbing and sanding. Here's what you need and how to do it.

146

Spray Painting

For fast, easy, better painting, spray it on. You can paint small pieces, intricate shapes, and large areas better than with a brush or roller, and do jobs they can't touch.

148

Heat Guns

A heat gun is much more than a paint stripper. It can loosen, dry, soften glue, and thaw ice. Intrigued? Look into what this gun can shoot your way.

156

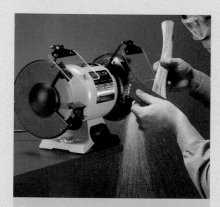

Bench Grinders

A grinder's first job is to keep tools razor sharp for safe, efficient use. It can also clean, buff, and shape metals. Here's how to get the most use from your bench grinder.

159

Air Compressors

All kinds of tools are powered by compressed air. Learn how to choose the right compressor and accessories for jobs from washing and painting to construction and auto repairs.

162

High-Speed Rotary Tool

Small hand work—carving, engraving, sanding, sharpening, drilling, cleaning, and polishing—is easy with this unique tool. It has accessories for literally hundreds of applications.

165

Wet/Dry Vacs

This workhorse can pick up dust, hardware, glass, stones, leaves, liquids, and almost anything else without difficulty. You'll use it constantly in the workshop, basement, and garage.

168

Power Washing

You clean the inside of your home thoroughly at least once a year—why not the outside? A power washer does the job fast, with the least effort. And it gives excellent preparation for repainting.

TELESCOPING WAND

POWER WASHING WAND

POWER WASHER

Power washing uses water under high pressure to clean away dirt, mildew, moss, and peeling and flaking paint on the outside of your house. You can rent a washing unit for a day for a fraction of the cost of buying it. Using a power washer is not difficult, and while you're at it, you can clean a lot of other things, too.

Power washing is an excellent way to prepare your house for repainting. Once the dirt is off, you may discover that you don't have to paint. However, in some cases, repainting will definitely be needed. For example, chalking *(right)* is a problem with most painted siding, especially aluminum siding that is 15 to 20 years old. Power washing gets rid of it so that new paint will adhere.

How long the job will take depends on

the size of your house. A 2,000-square-foot, ranch-style home can be cleaned in a couple of hours. A 3,000-square-foot, two-story home takes considerably longer. The additional surface area, the height of the area to be cleaned, plus the strain of handling the washing wand make the job more tiring and time consuming.

The landscaping of your home is also an important factor. The easier it is to get close to the house, the quicker you'll get done. In any case, plan to devote at least a morning to completely power wash your house; longer if it's large or really dirty.

CHALKED PAINT RESIDUE

Rub your hand over the surface to check for chalking; it is common on painted siding after several years. Power washing can remove it.

What You Need

To clean a house, you need a power washer with sufficient pressure, rated in pounds per square inch (psi), for efficient cleaning. The recommended rating for residential use is 1,200 to 2,500 psi. Units rated less than 1,200 psi won't do the job as effectively; washers rated above 2,500 psi could cause damage if not handled properly.

The nozzle design on the power wand and its size, which determine the width of the spray pattern, are also important. The three recommended sizes for power washing a house are 15°, 25°, and 40°. You'll get good results with either a 15° or 25° nozzle. The smaller spray width will give you the greatest control and least overspray and deliver a thorough cleaning. An accessory telescoping wand *(opposite page and below, far right)* is necessary for reaching upper areas. Don't try to use a ladder. You can't get the nozzle far enough away from the house, and even if you could, the force could knock you and the ladder over.

Whether you need to use a cleaning agent depends on how dirty the house is. A clear-water power washing will usually do the trick. However, if there's chalking, oxidation, moss, or mildew, you'll need to use a general-purpose cleaner, available where you rent the equipment.

You'll want to wear clothes you don't mind getting wet, and rubber-soled shoes or other nonslip footwear. For detergent cleaning, wear goggles, especially when using the usual shorter power wand. Gloves are optional, but you may want a rain hat when using the telescoping wand on high areas.

Preparation

Don't start until you've made everything ready. Cover all plants and shrubs with drop cloths, whether you're using a cleaner or plain water. Move lawn furniture and other portable objects away from the house. Cover all outside light fixtures with plastic bags and all electrical outlets with polyethylene film, and seal both with duct tape. Also make sure that all windows are closed tightly.

Handling the Equipment

You'll be working with a lot of water pressure—1,200–2,500 psi—compared to the average garden hose, which delivers about 60 psi. But with a little practice, you should be able to control the wand. If you plan to use a telescoping spray wand *(below),* be prepared for a battle. Each time you depress the handle to start the water flow, the wand kicks back 3 to 4 feet. With either wand, you'll get tired from fighting the pressure. So when you begin to feel the strain, take a break.

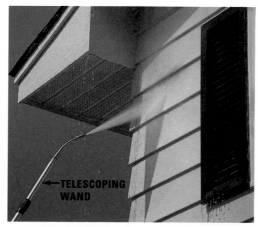

Use a telescoping wand, not a ladder, to reach high places; it's much safer.

Washing Techniques

Wash from the bottom up so that dirt and cleaning agent running down the wall won't cause streaks. Keep the nozzle 10 to 12 inches from the wall and angled downward to the surface, so you don't force water up into the lap of horizontal siding. Move the wand steadily from side to side.

Work in sections. When you have washed to the top of an area, rinse with plain water, working down from top to bottom *(below).* When you're working near the main overhead electrical service line to your house, be extremely careful. Accidentally contacting the wires with the wand can kill you. Keep the wand at least 10 feet from the power line. If necessary, clean around the power line by hand, using a wood-handled scrub brush and extreme caution.

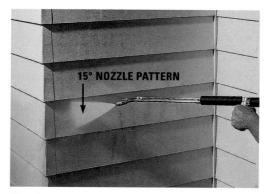

15° NOZZLE PATTERN

Rinse from the top down with plain water to thoroughly wash away residue and avoid leaving streaks on the clean surface.

WORKING TIP

While you have the washer, clean the garage, wheelbarrow and other equipment, and trash cans. Use the washer on decks, walks and driveways, brick steps, and concrete patios. You'll be amazed at how much dirt you can blast away in just a few minutes.

SAFETY TIP

Never put your hands or fingers near the tip of the wand when it's operating, or aim it at a person or animal. The water will penetrate the skin and cause severe injury.

Spray Painting

Whether you're coating small pieces and intricate shapes or large areas, spray painting can make the job go faster, easier, and better than using brushes or rollers.

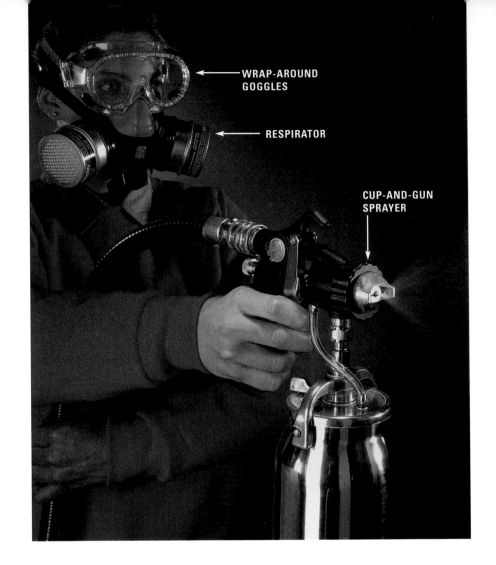

WRAP-AROUND GOGGLES

RESPIRATOR

CUP-AND-GUN SPRAYER

Once, spray painting was expensive, messy, and gave less than first-class results. That's no longer the case. Today's paints, spray cans, and spraying equipment make it easy to get a top-quality paint job fast. Although spraying doesn't make sense for some projects, like painting windows, for others spraying is the only way to apply paint well.

On the following pages you'll learn how to spray paint successfully, whether you're using an aerosol can or a hand-held spray gun. The tips and techniques explained here work for both. You'll also learn what you need to know to rent or buy equipment for a large-scale project, and how to use it efficiently and safely.

Painting with Aerosol Cans

The most common way to spray paint is with an aerosol can. Most of today's spray paints dry fast, or are at least dry to the touch in about 10 minutes. You'll find a wide range of colors, as well as a variety of special-application paints, such as high-temperature spray paint for barbecue grills and wood-burning stoves. No matter what type of aerosol paint you use, here's how to get great results.

Read and Shake

Read the directions on the back of any spray paint can. There is important information about what the paint is suitable for, how to apply it best, and what to use for cleanup. In addition, every aerosol can has the same important instruction: Before spraying, shake the can vigorously for about one minute. Aerosol cans have a metal ball inside that must rattle freely, indicating that the paint is fully mixed, before you spray.

Apply Multiple Coats

Every manufacturer recommends applying light, multiple coats of spray paint. The first coat, called a "tack coat," gets the surface ready. The second coat can usually be applied before the first coat is completely dry. For subsequent coats, though, wait until the previous coat has completely dried. When applying each coat, hold the can about 12 to 16 inches from the surface. Check the label for specific distances.

Above all, don't try to spray just one or two heavy coats. The paint will run and drip and you'll have to start over. This means stripping off the newly applied paint, or whatever you've messed up, and starting on a new one.

The photo below shows the progress in applying multiple coats to wicker, which is hard to paint because of all the crevices. Each coat covers a little more than the previous one. The light-coat approach virtually guarantees a successful spray painting job on all kinds of materials.

Finishing Up

There's nothing worse than a used spray can that won't spray. If you encounter that problem, see page 150. The way to avoid the problem is to clean the spray tip properly after each use.

When you have finished a job, twist and pull straight up on the spray tip to remove it from the paint can. Either stick it onto the long, thin spray tube that comes with a can of WD-40 lubricant, or put it on the can in place of the WD-40 spray tip (below). Squirt a couple of short blasts of lubricant through, then replace the tip on its own can and you'll be ready to shake and spray for the next job whenever it comes along.

PAINT CAN SPRAY TIP

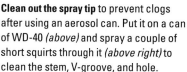

Clean out the spray tip to prevent clogs after using an aerosol can. Put it on a can of WD-40 *(above)* and spray a couple of short squirts through it *(above right)* to clean the stem, V-groove, and hole.

Build up multiple coats; they are the key to spray-painting success. Each coat, left to right, covers better than the previous one—a total of four to make this wicker look good.

Coping with Clogged Aerosol Tips

One of the most frustrating aspects of using aerosol spray paint is when the tip clogs. When this happens, try the following tricks one after the other until the paint sprays freely.

Rotate the tip back and forth about half a turn (*below*). The paint sometimes collects around the stem inside the can. This twisting motion often breaks the intake V-groove in the stem free of the collected mass so the paint flows smoothly through the tip again.

If rotating the spray tip doesn't work, pull the tip off and clean out the V-groove in the bottom end of the stem (*below*). The groove is small, so you'll need a narrow metal object like the blade of an X-Acto knife to clean it. Be careful when you put the spray tip back onto the can. Make sure the spray direction arrow on the tip is pointing away from you, and that you don't push the tip in too far. You could paint yourself and everything around you.

Don't use a needle to clean out the tip's spray hole (orifice). You'll enlarge it and too much paint will come out, making it impossible to apply a light, even coat. If the tip is really clogged or if the paint comes out in irregular spurts and globs, remove the tip and soak it in a small container of mineral spirits (*below*). Let it soak for 20 to 30 minutes and then wipe off the loosened paint. Squirt some WD-40 through the tip (see Finishing Up, page 149), then put it back on the paint can and go to work.

Twist the tip back and forth about a half turn if it clogs. Paint sometimes plugs the tip of the stem inside the can; twisting may break it free.

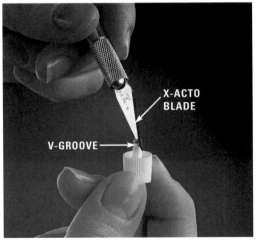

Clean out the V-groove at the base of the stem with a sharp blade such as an X-Acto knife. The groove must be clean for the paint to spray properly.

X-ACTO BLADE

V-GROOVE

MINERAL SPIRITS

Soak coated or clogged spray tips in mineral spirits for 20 to 30 minutes to loosen dried paint. Then wipe them clean. Never clean the tip hole with a needle.

Spray-Painting Equipment

When a project calls for more than spray-can painting, you can rent or buy suitable equipment. Here are the best choices.

Airless Sprayers

This efficient, multipurpose sprayer *(below)* is either gas or electric powered. Most models have a draw tube or hose that you place in a large container of paint, usually a 5-gallon bucket. Others have their own paint container.

Paint is drawn through the tube, then pushed through a supply hose to the spray gun, where it comes out in a fine spray at pressures ranging from 1,200 to 3,000 pounds per square inch (psi). Airless sprayers cover large areas in a short amount of time with good paint efficiency (little loss to the air).

An electric-powered airless sprayer suitable for small- or medium-size projects is quite affordable. For a big painting job, such as a house, rent a commercial-size unit.

Conventional Air Sprayer

This is often called a "cup and gun" sprayer because the spray gun and paint reservoir cup are one unit *(below)*. To operate this sprayer, you need an air compressor (see pages 162–164).

A conventional sprayer atomizes paint at high air pressures of 35 to 80 psi with moderate airflow. But with this method there's considerable overspray—paint that doesn't hit the target.

Conventional air spraying equipment is largely used in stationary settings, such as production line work. Professional painters often use a cup-and-gun sprayer, but most rental stores don't carry these.

High-volume, Low-pressure (HVLP) Sprayers

An HVLP sprayer *(below)* is classified as a finishing painting tool and is generally used wherever you wouldn't use an airless sprayer. It looks like a conventional sprayer, because it uses a one-piece spray gun and paint reservoir cup. However, it uses less than 10 psi of pressure to apply the paint. This extremely low pressure means greater control, with more paint on your project and less overspray. Anyone who has ever spray painted will appreciate that feature.

An HVLP sprayer is portable, affordable, and versatile. You can adjust the nozzle for spray patterns from 1/2 inch to 12 inches wide; it is powered by a standard 15-amp electrical circuit; and you can spray most types of materials, including latex, oil-based, or clear paints and finishes.

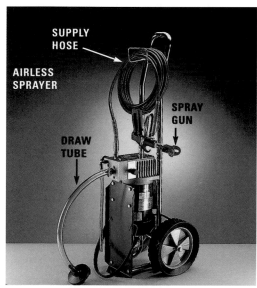

Airless sprayers apply paint quickly, at great pressure—1,200 to 3,000 psi. They're best for painting large surfaces. This kind is readily available at rental outlets.

Conventional "cup and gun" sprayers require an air compressor. They are sold at many full-service hardware stores and home centers.

HVLP sprayers are the latest in sprayer technology. They deliver paint at very low pressure, under 10 psi, which provides excellent control and little overspray.

Spraying Techniques

Whether you're a first-time spray painter or an old hand, there are some spray-painting techniques that will help you do a first-rate job every time. Here and on the next two pages they are shown and described using a hand-held spray gun, but the techniques apply to most aerosol can spraying as well.

Spray Patterns and Arm Movement

To get an idea of what the spray pattern should look like, picture how you mow your lawn. Each pass of the lawn mower's wheels slightly overlaps the previous pass. That's how to apply spray paint *(right)*. There's no need to overlap very much. If you do, you'll end up with an unattractive paint buildup.

The most common mistake when spraying is moving your arm in an "arcing" motion. Instead, keep your arm and body parallel to the surface you're painting. Move your arm and body in a straight line and bend your wrist as necessary to keep the sprayer at right angles to the surface, as illustrated. This technique keeps the sprayer at the same distance from the surface, usually 6 to 8 inches, throughout the arm stroke. If you don't bend your wrist, the coverage will be thinner at the ends of the stroke and thicker in the middle. That's definitely not what you want.

Also, begin the arm motion before you pull the trigger or push the button, and continue your arm motion after releasing the trigger or button. If you don't, you'll have heavy spots of paint where you start and stop.

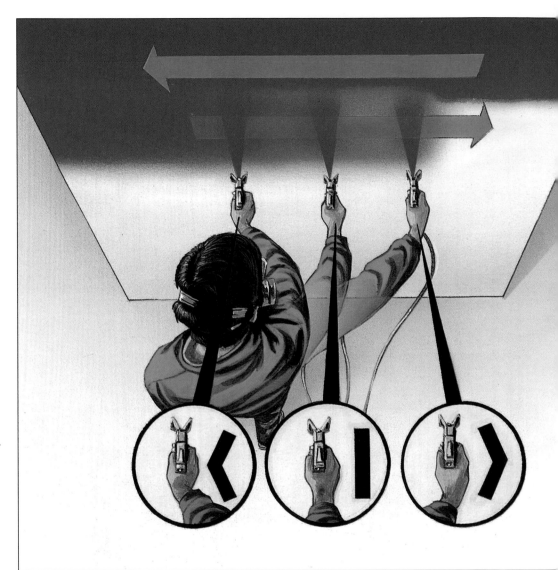

Bend your wrist as you move your arm to apply paint evenly. Slightly overlap each pass of the spray gun to get even coverage. Spray continuously in each direction.

Painting Outside and Inside Corners

An outside corner is one that points toward you; an inside corner is like the inside of a V. Spraying paint evenly on both sides of either corner without getting too much where they join together is not difficult if you use these techniques.

Outside Corner

The best way to spray an outside corner *(below left)* is to face the corner, holding the gun about 6 to 8 inches away from the edge. Move the spray gun in a back-and-forth motion using the arm and wrist movement described on the opposite page.

Inside Corner

To get even, smooth coverage on an inside corner, stand with the gun aimed directly into the V of the corner. This will put your body to the left of the corner if you are right-handed, or on the other side if you are left-handed. Turn the spray gun 90° (on its side) so that the spray pattern fans out horizontally *(below)*. Then move the gun vertically down and up in the corner.

Stand directly facing the edge of the outside corner. Move the spray gun back and forth, bending your wrist as your arm moves. This allows the paint to evenly cover the edge and both wall surfaces.

Face the inside corner and turn the gun or adjust the spray nozzle so the spray pattern is horizontal. Move the gun vertically when spraying. This technique eliminates a heavy buildup of paint in the corner.

Spraying Lap Siding and Rough Surfaces

If you've ever painted lap siding with a brush or paint pad, you know how difficult it is to coat all the edges and surfaces. But it's important that you do so. An unsealed bottom edge of wood or composite lap siding is the number-one cause of premature siding failure.

Spraying lap siding is a three-step process. Here's how to ensure coverage on all areas.

▶ Hold the spray gun horizontally and spray up and under the bottom edge of each course (row) of siding *(Photo 1)*. You can do a number of courses before you move to the next spraying step.

▶ Next, holding the gun vertically, spray a light coat slightly downward *(Photo 2)*.

▶ Now, keeping the gun vertical, spray each course straight on *(Photo 3)*. Use the arm movement and spraying technique that we described on page 152.

It is often necessary to spray rough surfaces, such as textured siding, from both an upward and a downward angle.

Professional painting contractors recommend back-rolling or back-brushing—going over the freshly applied paint with a roller or brush—to force the paint into the pores of the surface. Do this immediately after spraying an area. It's a good job for a helper, as long as he or she doesn't get overeager and reach in before you've stopped spraying.

SPRAYING LAP SIDING AND ROUGH SURFACES

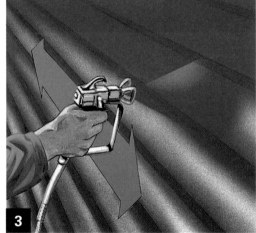

Angle the spray gun upward so that the first application covers the underside of each row. The bottom edge of lap siding must be sealed to keep out moisture.

Hold the spray gun at a downward angle to apply paint on the second pass. This angle ensures that paint covers the face of each row where it meets the bottom edge.

Spray the final coat straight onto the surface. Move your arm and wrist as described on page 152. Make sure the entire flat surface of the siding is coated.

Tips for Success

Whether you're using a spray can or a spray gun, inside or outside, follow these general rules.

Painting Inside

▶ Work in a well-ventilated area, even if you're wearing a respirator. Paint fumes can build up in an enclosed area and be ignited by a spark or flame.

▶ Whenever possible, build a spray booth of cardboard or plastic sheeting to contain any overspray. It will really make a difference at clean-up time.

▶ Practice spraying on a scrap piece of cardboard or wood to get a feel for the spray gun or aerosol can. This also helps you determine how fast to move the spray apparatus and how far away to be so that you can apply light, even coats.

Painting Outside

▶ If it's windy, don't paint. Even a light wind, as little as 3 to 5 mph, will blow the overspray around you and you'll paint your car, kids, or worse, your neighbor's house, car, or hedge.

▶ Cover all shrubs, lights, window glass—anything you don't want the paint on. This preparation time is what most people view as the biggest drawback to spraying. But the time you spend actually painting is usually half that of brushing or rolling—and that's plenty of incentive to spray.

▶ If you have a multistory home on a hilly lot, you may not want to spray. You can use a ladder for the upper parts of a one-story house, but it's best to spray taller houses from a scaffold—and hilly areas and scaffolding just don't mix.

Spray-Painting Tricks

Here are some useful tricks and shortcuts that professionals use.

▶ Mask gutters, windows, and trim before spray painting the side of a house. Do these sections with a brush afterward, painting clean edges right up to the sprayed areas.

▶ When spray painting a flat surface such as a tabletop, begin on the side nearest you and work toward the opposite side. Hold the can at a slight angle, to send the overspray ahead of you. Starting at the near side, you cover the overspray as you progress across the surface.

Working in the other direction, the overspray would leave a pebbly surface on the areas already painted.

▶ To paint just a drawer front, leave it in the cabinet. Mask the cabinet around the drawer, then pull the drawer out about 1/2 inch. This way you can paint the edges without getting paint inside the drawer. When dry, remove the drawer and masking to paint the cabinet case.

▶ To catch drips from an airless sprayer, wrap a rag around it like a bandanna just below the nozzle. That will keep your floor and clothes clean.

▶ Masking off a small area neatly is sometimes difficult, and masking tape leaves sharp ridges when pulled up. To avoid that, cut a 1-inch hole in the center of a piece of cardboard. Hold the cardboard a few inches from the spot to be painted, and spray through the hole with the nozzle 1 inch from the hole. This will confine the spray without leaving ridges.

Safety and Dangers

A respirator (photo, page 148) should be your number-one safety item. Make sure the respirator is approved by the National Institute for Occupational Safety and Health and certified for use with the material you're spraying. You'll find NIOSH-approved paint respirators at most home centers and paint stores. For more information, see Protect Your Breathing, pages 16–17.

Eye protection is also important. Goggles offer the best protection because of their wrap-around design. See Protect Your Eyesight, pages 12–13.

The best clothing to wear is things you won't mind throwing away. Or buy a pair of disposable coveralls. They're lightweight and inexpensive, usually under $10. A painter's cap, sometimes a giveaway item at paint stores, or other head covering is a good idea. If you have long hair, tie it up and cover it.

Gloves are not as necessary as when painting with brushes or rollers, but you may want to wear them. Disposable plastic gloves are both inexpensive and convenient to use. A light coating of skin cream or baby oil on exposed skin surfaces makes any traces of paint easy to wash off.

Finally, when it's time to dispose of an empty aerosol can, never throw it into a trash compactor, incinerator, or fire. It could explode and cause serious injury. Check with your local recycling center. Some centers will take aerosol cans.

Heat Guns

Stripping paint, loosening bolts, softening glue, thawing ice, or drying anything—you get them all, and more, with a heat gun.

FLARE NOZZLE

SCRAPER

When you're finally sick and tired of the smell and mess chemical paint strippers create; when you swear you've gouged a window frame for the last time trying to chip and scrape out old, hard glazing compound; when you've ruined the edge of a good chisel and scraped your knuckles trying to take up resilient floor tiles; when a pipe is frozen, a bolt is stuck, drywall compound and paint are drying too slowly; when any number of DIY problems and frustrations have you at the brink of shouting "Enough!"—that's when you are more than ready for a heat gun.

A heat gun—also known as a hot air gun or electric paint stripper—consists of a high-temperature heating element and a blower in a pistol-grip housing that takes nozzles of various shapes. It blows a continuous, intense blast of very hot air wherever you aim it. A simple model may have only one temperature setting and a single blower speed. More versatile models have High and Low temperature settings, a No Heat setting (for cooling), and two blower speeds.

Almost all heat guns come with a manual containing a few pages of how-to-use information, and many more pages of CAUTIONS! and WARNINGS! These indicate a tool that can be an incredible workhorse if used correctly, but one that can spell disaster if used in the wrong way. Obviously, you have to be careful, but with proper use and care a heat gun will help you work faster and more effectively—and perform tasks no other tool can. Safe paint stripping is discussed on the opposite page. Other uses for a heat gun are explained on page 158.

Stripping Paint

Removing paint and varnish is where a heat gun stars. It strips paint and other finishes from furniture, siding, doors, trim and molding so well that it is sold in the paint section of home centers.

To strip paint, hold the nozzle 1 to 2 inches from the surface and move the heat gun back and forth until the paint softens; often it will bubble or blister. Scrape the softened paint while it's still hot. Once you establish a rhythm, you'll be able to soften the paint ahead of your scraper and continuously move across the piece.

For the best results, use a paint scraper of the right size and shape. Use a sharp-edged scraping knife 3 to 4 inches wide to remove paint from broad surfaces, and a 1- or 2-inch blade on narrower areas. Use contoured scrapers (opposite page) to strip the rounded or irregular surfaces of such things as chair legs, stair rail balusters, and crown molding.

Use a heat deflector to protect breakable material such as window glass (below) from the direct blast of superheated air.

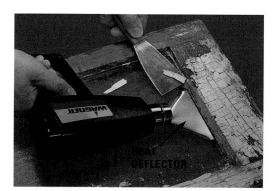

Protect glass with a heat deflector when using a heat gun to soften glazing compound or strip the paint from a window sash.

Keep your scraper clean and sharp. A coffee can or metal drywall compound tray is ideal for scraping residue off the scraper.

Multiple coats of paint may require two or more passes to remove. Be especially careful when stripping down to bare wood. Scorch marks are difficult to remove. Don't expect a heat gun to remove stain or coats of paint that have penetrated into the grain of the wood. In that situation, do as much as possible with the gun, but finish the job with sandpaper, or chemical means such as a wood bleach.

Cautions and Warnings

Don't be casual about using a heat gun. It is a high-temperature (up to 1700° F) air blaster that can produce a second-degree burn in seconds or set fire to wood, paper, curtains, and fumes. It can also release poisonous fumes from lead paint.

Fire

Treat a heat gun with the same care and respect you do an open flame. To prevent fires, keep the gun moving! When stripping paint, direct the blast at the material only long enough to soften the paint. Remember that the material behind the surface being stripped can also catch fire. When aimed continuously at one spot, the gun can blow enough hot air through cracks in woodwork to set dust or flammable material smoldering, where it can break into flame even hours after you've done the work. Have a fire extinguisher nearby and keep a watchful eye and nose. Keep scrapers free of paint. Built-up residue is flammable. Turn the gun off

whenever you put it down, even if only for a moment or two, and watch where you put the metal nozzle—it stays really hot for about 20 minutes after use. When you turn off the gun, set it on end or on something noncombustible.

Lead Paint

Paint manufactured before 1977 may contain lead, and any manufactured prior to 1950 almost surely contains lead. Ingesting lead paint chips or dust is hazardous, and so is breathing in lead-paint fumes. Either test your paint with a lead-testing kit from a hardware store or play it safe and assume it contains lead.

To avoid lead paint hazards, wear an approved dual filter (dust and fume) respirator mask (see pages 16–17). Paper masks are NOT adequate. Surround the work area and cover the floor or ground with plastic sheeting to contain paint chips. Don't eat, drink, or smoke in the work area—or beyond—until you've washed your hands. Finally, don't heat paint so long, or at such a high temperature, that it produces hazardous fumes. Many experts consider 700° F to be the highest heat gun setting you should use.

Contact your local Pollution Control Agency or Environmental Protection Agency before you start. Find out the proper procedure for disposing of the lead paint waste, the drop cloths, your clothes, and the water used to mop the room when you're done. Many communities have hazardous household waste collection sites.

And, of course, read the tool's instruction manual for further safety precautions.

Other Uses for a Heat Gun

In addition to stripping paint, you can use a heat gun for a variety of difficult tasks:

Thawing a frozen water pipe. Identify the frozen area by touch, then move a stream of hot air all along it, not just in one spot. Free up a frozen car door lock with the heat gun, but be careful: Don't burn the paint!

Shrinking plastics. Use the hot air to apply shrink tubing to wires, or to tighten plastic window films.

Loosening stuck bolts and screws. Try heat alone on a fastener in wood, or penetrating oil followed by heat for a fastener in metal *(below)*.

Loosen stuck bolts with oil and heat. Apply penetrating oil to the joint, give the oil time to work, then heat.

Softening adhesives. Removing damaged resilient tiles is easy with a heat gun *(below)*. First heat the entire surface of the tile to make it flexible and begin to soften the adhesive beneath.

Then concentrate the blast at one edge or corner so you can work a stiff putty knife underneath. When you have an edge raised, direct the hot air under the tile to soften the adhesive more and continue working the tile loose with the knife.

Use a similar technique to remove old laminates, window labels—be careful not to overheat and crack the glass—and even bumper stickers.

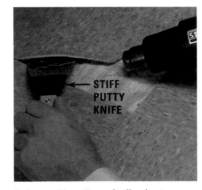

← STIFF PUTTY KNIFE

Soften resilient tile and adhesive to remove floor coverings. Lift a corner of tile and direct the hot air under it.

Drying paint or drywall compound *(below)*. Use hot air to speed up small repairs of this sort. To avoid scorching or blistering, use the low-temperature setting, hold the gun at a greater distance than for stripping paint, and keep it moving over the area.

DRYWALL COMPOUND

Reduce the drying time of drywall compound and paint in repaired areas.

Heat Gun Accessories

The most popular accessories for a heat gun are nozzle attachments. The basic nozzle shape is round. A reducing nozzle will concentrate heat in a small area; a flare nozzle will spread the heat over a wider area. Either or both will give you greater control for many jobs.

A myriad of other heat gun accessories can do everything from cutting Styrofoam sheeting to welding plastic tubing. There is even an attachment that holds special plastic welding rods for joining and repairing plastics. Look for such items in equipment catalogs and at full-service hardware stores and home centers, and ask what other heat gun devices they have. You might find just the thing for your next project.

Bench Grinders

Sharp tools can be used safely and precisely; dull tools slip, bounce, gouge, and cut sloppily. A bench grinder can keep edges sharp; it can clean and buff, too.

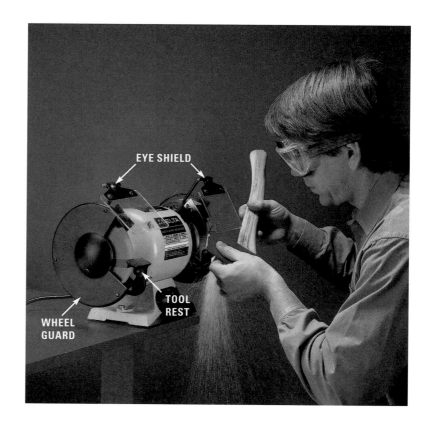

EYE SHIELD

TOOL REST

WHEEL GUARD

A bench grinder is essentially a maintenance tool, because it excels at sharpening, shaping, scraping, cleaning, and polishing metal, plastic, and, to a lesser degree, wood. It's a "must have" tool for carpenters, cabinetmakers, welders, people who work with cars, motorcycles, or engines, and many other professionals. When serious do-it-yourselfers get one, they soon discover its value and put it to good—and frequent—use. That's because sharp, clean tools cut fast and precisely, and because they give the user the greatest control and safety in doing cutting jobs.

Bench grinders are categorized by the diameter of the grinding wheel they use. They cost anywhere from about $50 for a 5-inch basic model to five or six times that for a heavy duty 8- or 10-inch model. The larger the size, the more powerful the motor required to spin the grinding wheel and overcome friction when a tool is pushed against it. A 6-inch, 1/4-hp model can handle most homeowners' tasks. A manual sharpening stone, either an oil stone or a water stone, is also needed for final touch-up.

Well-designed grinders mount two wheels or other accessories, one on each end of the horizontal motor shaft, for versatility and balanced operation. Just like sandpaper, grinding wheels are graded coarse, medium, fine, or extra-fine. Coarse wheels cut the quickest but leave a rougher edge. Most people mount a medium or coarse stone on one shaft of their grinder for rough work and a fine stone or wire-brush wheel on the other for final sharpening or cleaning tasks. Each wheel should have a guard with a spark deflector at the top edge, a tool rest, and an eye shield.

Sharpening with a Grinder

Its aggressiveness makes a bench grinder ideal for sharpening lawn mower blades, hedge trimmers, axes, and other hefty tools. For finer sharpening, such as kitchen knives or scissors, you're better off using a file or whetstone. Bench grinders can overheat and destroy such delicate tools. For tools in between—spade drill bits, chisels, and plane blades—you can use a grinding wheel, but use a fine stone and work carefully.

A grinder wheel rotates downward *(below)*. To sharpen a tool or blade, you hold it with the edge pointing upward, against the rotation of the wheel. Before starting the grinder, first adjust the tool rest so it is just 1/8 inch from the wheel and allows you to hold the tool so its cutting edge contacts the grinding wheel

at its original angle. Then, with the grinder still turned off, practice moving the tool left and right, running the entire length of the edge across the wheel while maintaining the proper angle.

When you have the feel of what you are going to do, put on eye protection and turn on the grinder while standing to one side. Let the grinder operate for a minute to throw off any bits of material that might work loose from its surface. Then make one light pass and examine the tool to see if you're matching its existing angle. A good way to do this is to first darken the cutting edge with a marker, then make the pass. Uneven removal of the dark mark *(below)* indicates irregular sharpening.

Make a series of light passes, rather than a few heavy-handed ones, to correct any unevenness and get the edge really sharp. Check your progress frequently. The better you can see, the better your results, so shine a light directly on the tool rest and examine your work with a magnifying glass. When you need to remove a lot of metal, dip the tip of the tool into water frequently to cool it. If a straw-colored or bluish halo appears near the edge of the tool, you're grinding too hard or too long and overheating the metal; you risk ruining the temper or hardness of the tool.

When the edge has been sharpened, remove any burrs from the back side with a sharpening stone *(below)*. Rub small tools on the surface of the stone; run the stone or a fine metal file along the back of a long or large blade.

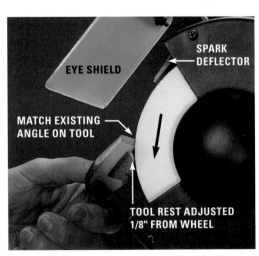

EYE SHIELD

SPARK DEFLECTOR

MATCH EXISTING ANGLE ON TOOL

TOOL REST ADJUSTED 1/8" FROM WHEEL

Position the tool rest 1/8-in. away from the wheel. Adjust it so the tool being sharpened will maintain its original cutting edge and angle.

UNEVEN MARKER REMOVAL INDICATES UNEVEN SHARPENING

LAWN MOWER BLADE

Darken the edge to be sharpened with a marker before making the first pass across the wheel. Marks left after the pass show where sharpening was uneven.

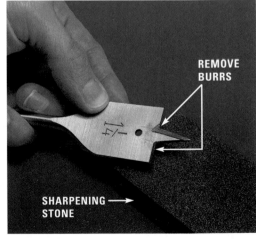

REMOVE BURRS

SHARPENING STONE

Finish sharpening by removing burrs from the back side of the new edge. Run the tool over a sharpening stone, or run the stone over the edge of a large blade.

Dressing the Wheel

A grinding wheel is made up of small, hard grains, or grit, held together by a bonding agent. As a wheel works, those grains become dull and fall off, exposing sharp new ones. If the dull grains don't fall off or if metal particles stick to the wheel, a glazed surface is created. Such wheels cut poorly or not at all.

Dressing a wheel (below) exposes new grains and removes soft metals. A wheel dresser can also be used to flatten the grinding face or "true up" a lopsided grinding wheel.

Hold the dresser on the tool rest, then work it back and forth for 5 to 10 seconds. Serious sharpeners dress the wheel every time they use it.

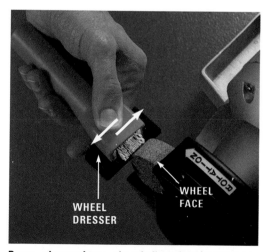

Dress—clean and true—the grinding wheel by moving a wheel dresser back and forth as the wheel spins. This removes clinging metal and dull grit and flattens the face of the wheel.

Other Grinder Uses

Grinding wheels can be used to clean up jagged metal edges, shorten bolts, or smooth welds. Hold small parts with locking pliers for grinding.

A wire wheel (below) makes removing rust or paint fast and easy. Occasionally remove the wheel and reverse its spinning direction so the wires don't get bent too far in one direction and lose their effectiveness. A buffing wheel (bottom), stiff or flexible, is ideal for polishing hardware and other metal objects. You must apply a buffing compound—there are different kinds for different metals—to the wheel.

Remove rust quickly with a wire wheel. Stand to the side to avoid being hit by debris or loose wire strands.

Buff and polish with a buffing wheel. Use the buffing compound meant for the type of metal you're cleaning.

Hollow-grind Sharpening

For the finest edge on a hand tool, hollow-grind it as follows.

Begin by using the tool rest and grind the plane blade or chisel on a grinding wheel to "hollow" the face of the bevel (right top). This will allow you to quickly hone an edge on the tool, since only the leading and trailing edges of the bevel will contact a whetstone.

Hone the bevel on an oil or water whetstone (right middle). Use a short circular motion and even pressure with the front and rear edges of the bevel on the surface of the stone.

Check frequently as you work until the front and back edges of the bevel shine brightly (right bottom).

You can hone the hollow-ground blade four or five times before the entire bevel shines. Then it's time to regrind the blade as above.

Hollow-ground blades are extremely sharp and cut like razors. Never leave them unattended, and protect them with a cardboard or other sheath in your tool kit or drawer.

Air Compressors

Air can pack a wallop, create a blast of sand, or deliver a spray.
Here's how to choose a compressor, and what compressed-air tools can do for you.

Industries, contractors, garages, and many other enterprises use compressed-air tools because they are strong, fast, accurate, and reliable. In addition, it costs far less to run an air compressor than to power tools with electricity.

You can take advantage of these features of air power to make all kinds of home improvement projects shorter and easier. Two are discussed elsewhere in this book: power nailing (pages 129–131), and spray painting (pages 148–155). Several other applications are shown on page 164.

One of the conveniences of compressed-air tools is the quick-disconnect fittings they and the air hoses use *(right)*. Not only are the connectors fast, they lock together so there's no chance of failure, as can happen when the plug pulls out of an electrical extension cord. In addition, unlike using a long extension cord there is little loss of power through a long air hose, even on a run from the ground to the ridge of a roof.

Your first concern is to get a compressor that will meet your needs. You can rent one, but once you appreciate how much air tools can do, you'll probably want to have a compressor of your own. In either case, you need the information on the opposite page to make a choice.

Quick-disconnect fittings make changing tools or adding an extension hose easy. The fittings lock for troublefree use.

Choosing an Air Compressor

Air compressors suitable for DIY use range from compact tankless models to 2-hp large units on wheels *(right)*. Their specifications and uses are given in the chart below. Here's what the figures mean and what to look for.

Air Delivery and Pressure

The column of air a compressor delivers is expressed in standard cubic feet per minute (scfm), at a stated pressure in pounds per square inch (psi). The higher the pressure, the less volume. So you will see the capacity of a machine described as, for example: 4.2/40, 3.7/90. This translates as 4.2 scfm at 40 psi or 3.7 scfm at 90 psi. Because air tools are designed to operate at specific pressures, compressors always have a pressure regulator to adjust the output. All but the very smallest compressors will give adequate pressure for all DIY tools and projects.

Motor Size

Although it is only a rough measure of true air delivery, compressors are often measured by the size of the motor they use. Small compressors are less than 1 hp, medium-sized ones are 1 hp to 1-3/4 hp, and larger ones are 2 hp and up. For almost all home uses, a 1 to 1-1/2 hp compressor with a tank *(see right)* will be fine. The big exception is air tools with motors, like sanders and grinders, which need compressors with at least 2 to 3 hp.

Oilless Operation

Compressors that require oil to lubricate the pistons are obsolete for nonindustrial use; besides, they often leak. Choose only a modern, lubrication-free model.

Tank vs. No Tank

Small compressors, used mainly for inflating tires or balls and similar continuous uses, don't require a tank. But many applications, like air nailing, require relatively small amounts of air at intervals, not continuously. If you are buying a compressor, choose one with a tank.

If you need to carry your compressor around, look carefully at the tank shape and size. Some compressors have a squat, pancake-shaped tank or two small tanks that make it possible to pick up the whole machine with one hand. Large-tank models usually have wheels and a handle to pull them.

Air compressors for DIYers include: (A) a compact 1/2 hp tankless model; (B) a twin-tank 3/4 hp unit that can be carried with one hand; and (C) medium-size, 1-1/2 hp, and (D) large, 2 hp, tank compressors on wheels.

Compressor Specifications and Uses

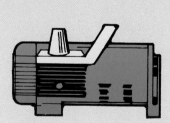

1/2 hp, tankless; 1.5 scfm/90 psi to 2.0 scfm/40 psi

Typical uses:

Household inflation

Blowgun for cleaning

Light spray painting

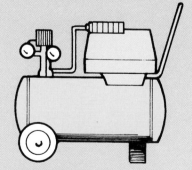

1 hp w/tank; 3.0 scfm/90 psi to 4.0 scfm/40 psi

All uses at left, plus:

Air nailing, stapling

General spray painting

Light sandblasting

Power washing

Driving air wrenches, ratchets

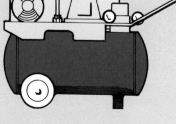

2 hp w/tank; 6.3 scfm/90 psi to 7.8 scfm/40 psi

All uses at left, plus:

High-performance spray finishing

General sandblasting

Intermittent air sanding

Intermittent air grinding

Electrical Needs

If you are looking at 2 hp or larger compressors, check their electrical needs. Some larger motors require a 20-amp, 120-volt circuit or even a 240-volt circuit, which may restrict where you can put the compressor. However, you can use a very long hose to reach the work area without losing much power.

Air Power Applications

Once you have a compressor and hoses, there are tools and accessories you can rent or buy for a wide variety of tasks. In addition to finish nailers, spray guns, and washing wands and nozzles, there are construction nailers *(right)* and staplers, blowers, sandblasters, sanders and grinders, and impact wrenches, to list only some of the choices. Various applications of air power are shown here. There are many more.

Air stapling, like air construction nailing, makes fast work of a repetitive, dreary task. Air staplers are also used to install insulation and electrical cables.

Power cleaning with a blowgun accessory gets into all parts of tools and machinery. It's also the best way to get wood dust off clothing, but only at very low pressure, to avoid injury.

Sandblasting is an effective and economical way to remove paint from masonry and metal. It will destroy the weatherproof surface of brick, however.

Inflating bicycle and mower tires, backyard pools, air mattresses, and other household items are chores that even the smallest air compressors can handle.

Sanding and grinding for auto body and similar work is fast and leaves few scratches, but the air tools for these tasks require a big compressor.

Driving impact tools is a widespread use of air power. An air wrench speeds up operations like removing lug nuts, and easily loosens stubborn nuts.

High-Speed Rotary Tools

In the hand or on a stand, this unique tool is indispensable to carve, engrave, sand, sharpen, drill, clean, and polish small workpieces and tools.

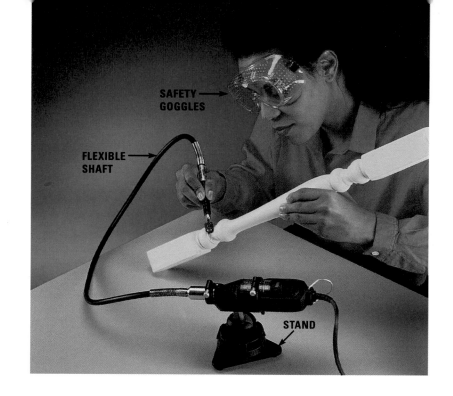

SAFETY GOGGLES

FLEXIBLE SHAFT

STAND

Hobbyists and craftspersons are more likely to know about the versatile high-speed rotary tool than homeowners. But this tool is just the thing for all kinds of intricate tasks that often arise in do-it-yourself projects.

The tool is often called simply a Dremel, the name of the principal manufacturer, or a Moto-Tool, actually the name of just one of several different models. It accepts various accessories in a collet or miniature chuck for direct drive, and a flexible shaft for remote drive and increased versatility. Identical models are manufactured for specific suppliers, such as Sears, but they are Dremels. Ryobi offers a similar tool, and another, by Foredom, is widely used by jewelers and professional craft workers. This tool is far more expensive and cannot be hand-held.

Flexible-shaft operation is shown above, with the motor held in a stand. The shaft is driving a miniature sanding drum *(right),* which can get into curves and tight places hand sanding can't reach. There are drums and disks in several grits for different kinds of sanding tasks.

When accessories are mounted directly in the motor collet, the Moto-Tool can be used in a stand as a stationary tool—for example, for sharpening —or held in the hand. Dremel makes more than 130 different bits, stones, cutters, and grinders for its tools. Hundreds more are offered by other manufacturers; they are fine as long as they are rated for use at speeds up to 30,000 rpm.

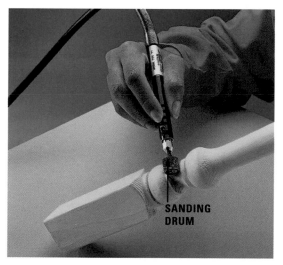

SANDING DRUM

Use miniature accessories, like this sanding drum, to work in awkward, difficult, and otherwise inaccessible spots.

Using a Rotary Tool

The key to success with a Moto-Tool is to let the high speed—30,000 rpm—do the work. Don't force the tool or apply much pressure; instead, make a series of light passes to complete the job. Since many of the bits and disks are small and thin, undue pressure can break or quickly dull them. Work with a light, steady hand.

Always wear safety goggles: If a fragile cut-off wheel breaks at 30,000 rpm, its fragments can cause injury in a flash. Also, take care not to block the air vents in the sides of the tool. They allow air to circulate around the motor to keep it cool.

Here are some applications of this unique tool; there are more illustrated on the opposite page.

Sharpening

Aluminum oxide grinding stones, in a variety of shapes and sizes, make for easy, precision sharpening of small tools such as wire cutters and aviation snips, or tools with strangely shaped cutting blades like curved pruning shears or spurred drill bits. Mount either the dull tool or the Dremel in a table stand *(below left)* or a vise for stability. To avoid burning the edge, sharpen in four- to five-second spurts, and examine the tool edge each time while it is cooling.

Engraving

Use a small-tipped engraving bit *(below)* to mark your name or identification number on wood, metal, and plastic. Try the engraver on scrap metal before

labeling any tools or belongings; the tip tends to wander, but you can control it with practice. For the best control, hold the tip fairly square to the surface that is being marked.

Drilling

The small profile of the Dremel tool allows access to tight spaces where an ordinary drill can't fit, such as inside small boxes and drawers *(below)*. Before drilling metal, use a punch to create a starting dimple for the drill bit. When drilling, adjust a variable-speed tool to its slowest setting. For really difficult spots, use a drill bit in the flexible shaft attachment.

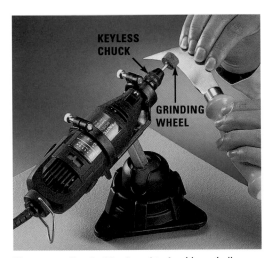

Sharpen small and oddly shaped tools with a grinding wheel accessory. Mounting the Dremel in a stationary position lets you use both hands on the tool being sharpened.

Engrave your name or an identification number on tools, bikes, and other belongings. There are engraving tips for different materials, such as plastic and wood.

Drill in spots where a full-sized tool can't reach. Use the slowest speed on a variable-speed rotary tool, and use the flexible shaft where even the Dremel won't fit.

Additional Applications

The variety of accessories and attachments for a Moto-Tool make it useful for literally hundreds of tasks. Like the flexible shaft, a keyless chuck increases the tool's versatility and makes changing bits quick and easy. You can get router bits, a router table, and even a chain saw sharpener. Some other accessories and their uses are shown below.

Grinding

There is a great variety of shapes of grinding stones for the Dremel tool, in grits from coarse to fine. In addition to sharpening, you can use them to enlarge and shape holes in metal *(below),* remove burrs from cut tubing, round the edges of plastics, and even smooth the edges of chipped glass or ceramics.

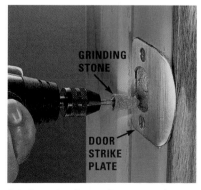

Grind openings in metal parts to make them larger or change their shapes. You can also use grinding stones to remove rivet heads and burrs on metal.

Cutting

Cut-off wheels can be used in all sorts of places even mini-hacksaws can't reach, and they cut much faster. Use a wheel to cut a slot for a screwdriver in the head of a bolt that a wrench can't grip *(below),* or cut new flats on the side of the head so a smaller wrench will fit. Emery and heavy-duty fiberglass-reinforced wheels can also cut through rusted nuts and screws, or through metal tubing. For accuracy, hold the tool firmly with both hands while cutting or grinding.

Cut metal, plastic, and other materials with a cut-off wheel. You can cut slots, square up flat surfaces, sharpen corners. Use a wheel appropriate to the material.

Cleaning and Polishing

Use a wire brush wheel for removing rust and paint from metals and other hard materials. When they are clean, put a polishing wheel in the Dremel and make them shine *(below).* Apply polishing compound to metal, then buff.

You can polish softer materials also, but don't use too much speed or pressure. Variable-speed Dremel tools operate over a range of 5,000 to 30,000 rpm. Use the low speed when polishing plastics, lacquered surfaces, or other materials that might melt if the tool were operated at a fast speed.

Clean and polish objects quickly with a rotary tool. Use a wire brush wheel to clean metal, buffing attachments for polishing. Use low speeds on soft materials.

Wet/Dry Vacuums

Water here, sawdust there, broken glass and leaves everywhere —get it all up fast with a wet/dry vacuum, the workhorse cleanup tool for workshop, basement, and garage.

SQUEEGEE NOZZLE

WATER ON FLOOR

A wet/dry vacuum is a far cry from the shop vacuums of only a decade ago. Today's machines will pick up liquids, dry materials, and combinations of the two without complaint. No do-it-yourself homeowner should be without one. A good basic model, available at any home center or hardware store, costs under $100.

Vacuums are rated by canister (tank) capacity and motor horsepower. An 8- to 16-gallon tank with a 1.5 to 2.5 peak hp motor is usually adequate. Be sure your vacuum has wheels or a wheeled dolly; they're available for all units. Some models require you to remove a paper filter or make some other minor conversion when vacuuming fluids, but these changeovers usually take less than a minute.

Some Limitations

A wet-dry vacuum can clean up almost anything, but keep in mind:

▶ Never use a vacuum to clean up combustible fluids like gasoline, lighter fluid, or kerosene. Sparks from the motor could cause an explosion. And never vacuum up hot coals.

▶ Don't try to pick up lead paint dust, asbestos, fertilizers, or hazardous materials. Very fine particles can pass through the filters and back into the air, creating an even greater hazard.

▶ Always wear hearing protection—the powerful motor sounds like a jet taking off—and safety goggles or glasses. Use a particle mask too, especially when cleaning up fine dust.

▶ Empty the tank and change or clean the filters as recommended.

Vacuum Accessories

A good first accessory is a rack to store all the attachments right on the vacuum. The most useful attachments include:

Wet nozzles and squeegees. These have a flexible rubber lip for picking up liquids or drying floors (above).

Crevice tools. These tapered tubes are ideal for removing debris from hard-to-reach areas: stairways, heat ducts, and the nooks and crannies in furniture, before refinishing.

Extension handles or wands. Usually available in 2- to 4-foot lengths, these make it easy to clean ceiling fans, reach cobwebs in corners, or work without bending over. All other attachments will fit on the end of the wand extension.

Putting It to Work

Almost anywhere, a wet/dry vacuum excels at dealing with accidents such as broken jars *(below)* and spills of all sorts. If you need to save metal parts from the mess on the floor, go over it with a magnet, or use the magnet in the debris sucked into the tank.

In the workshop, use the vacuum as a point-of-use dust collector. The dust port of a miter box or radial arm saw can usually be connected directly to the standard hose of your vacuum. Some portable tools—routers and belt sanders in particular—provide for direct linkage to a vacuum hose; use a smaller, flexible hose so it doesn't kink.

For other tools, build a simple portable dust intake box *(below)*. Place it near a tool to draw away sawdust and give you a place to shove larger chips where they'll be sucked away.

Collect wood chips and sawdust in a 3 x 6-in. collection box with a wide base for clamping anywhere. Bevel the front edge to avoid blocking dust flow.

Outside, in addition to sucking up dirt and debris many wet/dry vacuums can be used as blowers. Some models have twist-off heads for portability *(below)*; others must be used intact. They're great as leaf blowers, creating gusts of over 100 mph. With the right extensions you can use them to clean out gutters while you stand on the ground.

Around the house, the extra power of a wet/dry vacuum makes all kinds of cleanup easy. You can also use it to retrieve things from clogged drains. And many models have accessories that convert them into carpet shampooers.

For remodeling projects, the vacuum can be your best friend in keeping dust and debris under control. Don't try to take up a roomful of fine dust; that can clog the filters. Sweep up the bulk first with a broom. But do rig up your vacuum to collect drywall dust as you work *(below)*; it will save a lot of effort later.

Clean up glass, hardware, wood chips, and other large objects from accidents or work with a large size utility nozzle and a 2-1/2 in. hose.

Blow leaves and debris from walks and driveways. Removable power heads can be fitted with extension wands for use as portable blowers.

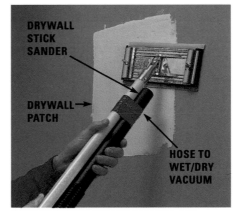

Keep dust to a minimum when repairing and remodeling. Tape the vacuum hose to a drywall sanding stick to remove dust as it's created.

Workplaces & Spaces

Woodworking Bench

Support your woodworking skills with this versatile professional bench. You can build it to your own personal specifications for less than half the cost of buying an equivalent bench.

Sawhorses

You need sawhorses for construction, painting, making temporary tables, and much more. Here's a design for adjustable-height horses, and another for fold-up horses; build either, or both, and make your work easier.

179

Fold-up Workbench

If your workshop shares basement or garage space, this clever bench is what you need for both work surface and tool storage. It's quick, easy, and inexpensive to build.

182

Workshop Improvements

Good work comes from a good workplace. Here are practical ways to improve the organization, heating, ventilation, dust collection, light, and power of your workshop.

184

Woodworking Bench

High-quality work requires excellent facilities as well as craftsmanship. This bench will make it easy to use your woodworking skills to their utmost.

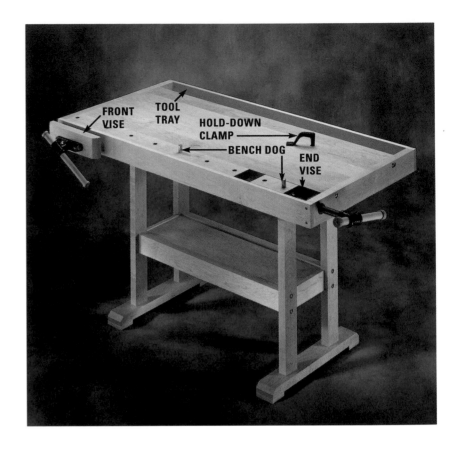

FRONT VISE
TOOL TRAY
HOLD-DOWN CLAMP
BENCH DOG
END VISE

A beautiful and functional workbench is every woodworker's dream. This bench is built almost entirely of solid maple, which is dense, heavy, and strong, making it the perfect wood for the abuse a workbench gets. (If you need something simpler, see Fold-up Workbench, pages 182–183.)

The bench has two vises. The front vise is used to hold workpieces against the front face of the bench. The end vise with its bench dogs is used to hold workpieces from 3 to 53 inches long on top of the bench. There is also a hold-down clamp for securing workpieces directly on the bench

top. It's a black metal clamp that you tap into a hole in the top to hold workpieces tight. The clamp's leg has a slight curve so it grips the sides of the hole as you drive it in. To release it, just tap on its side. It's a good idea to wait before making a hole for the hold-down until you've used the bench a while so you'll know the best place for the clamp.

A tool tray at the back of the bench serves two purposes. It allows for expansion and contraction of the solid top within the wooden frame that surrounds

it. It's also handy for keeping your smaller tools at hand, but below the work surface. A shelf below provides additional storage space for materials or small tools.

You'll need a fair amount of woodworking experience to build this workbench. It takes about 50 hours to construct, and costs about $450—half of what a comparable ready-made bench might cost.

Getting Ready

You need to assemble the parts, materials, and tools itemized in the lists at the right. The vises, vise handles, round solid-brass bench dogs, and hold-down clamp in the Materials List can be purchased individually through a number of woodworking suppliers, but they are also available as a mail-order kit (see note with the list). If your vises come in different colors, spray-paint them to match. You can buy the rest of the hardware called for in the list at your local hardware store.

When you buy wood for the bench, get good-quality maple. Be selective: Don't buy pieces with face checks. If there are end checks, cut them off.

Gather all the tools listed in the Tool List as well as your basic carpentry and layout tools. The pieces for the bench top are jointed with wooden splines set in grooves. The grooves are cut with a 1/4-inch wide x 3/8-inch-deep slot-cutting router bit. If it is hard to find one, you can get it from the supplier of the vise hardware kit (see Materials List note).

Plans and measurements for the workbench are given on the next two pages. A work-surface height of 36 inches is suggested. That seems best for people 5 feet 8 inches to 5 feet 10 inches tall, but you should determine the height that is best for you. Just make the legs longer or shorter to suit your comfort level.

Materials List

Item	Quantity
2x6 x 8' maple	8 pieces
1x6 x 8' maple	4 pieces
3/4" x 10" x 34-1/4" maple plywood	1 piece
3/8" dia. x 2" dowel pins	8
Vise Hardware Kit*	1
1/4" wide x 3/8" deep slot-cutting router bit	1
1/4" x 3-1/2" lag screws	8
1/4" x 3" lag screws	20
1/4" x 2-1/2" lag screws	8
1/4" x 1-1/2" lag screws	4
1/4" x 1-1/2" hex head bolts with locknuts	2
1/4" flat washers	44
No. 14 x 1-1/4" flathead wood screws	6
No. 10 x 2-1/2" panhead screws	8
No. 10 x 1-1/2" panhead screws and washers	5
No. 6 x 1-5/8" drywall screws	5
No. 6 x 1-1/4" drywall screws	38
No. 6 x 1" drywall screws	4
Danish oil finish	1 pint

* Available from Hartville Tool (800) 345-2396. The TFH Vise Hardware Kit includes one front vise with wooden handle, one end vise screw with threaded guide, end guide, and wooden handle; two 3/4" dia. x 4" solid brass bench dogs; and one 8" long x 4" reach bench hold-down clamp. The slot-cutting router bit is also available.

Tool List

Table saw with miter gauge
Router with:
    1/2" radius round-over bit
    1/4" wide x 3/8" deep slot-cutting bit
Circular saw with carbide-tip blade
7/16" socket and ratchet
Cordless or electric drill
No. 2 Phillips screwdriver
No. 3 Phillips screwdriver
Drill bits:
    1/16" twist bit
    7/64" twist bit
    5/32" twist bit
    3/16" twist bit
    1/4" twist bit
    3/8" brad point bit
    1/2" spade or power bore bit
    3/4" spade or power bore bit
    1-1/4" spade or power bore bit
    1-5/8" hole saw
    Countersink bit
Belt sander
Orbital sander
Clamps:
    Five 30" long pipe clamps
    Six 6" long bar clamps
1/2" chisel
Paint scraper
Thickness planer—optional
Jointer—optional
Drill press—optional

Woodworking Bench Assembly Plans

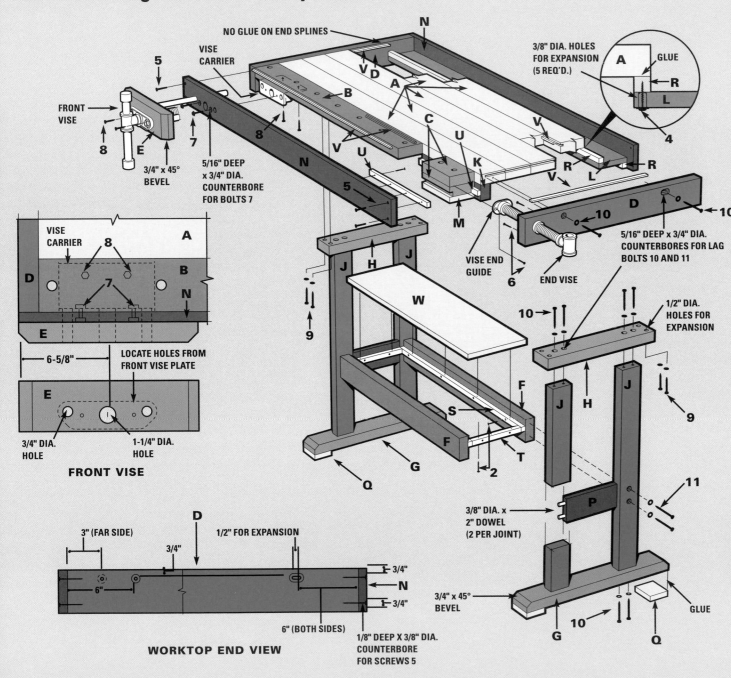

NO GLUE ON END SPLINES

N

VISE CARRIER

5

3/8" DIA. HOLES FOR EXPANSION (5 REQ'D.)

A — GLUE

R

L

4

V D

D A

B

FRONT VISE

8

E

8

7

8

3/4" x 45° BEVEL

5/16" DEEP x 3/4" DIA. COUNTERBORE FOR BOLTS 7

N

V

U

C

U

K

V

V

R

L

R

D

10

5

M

10

5/16" DEEP x 3/4" DIA. COUNTERBORES FOR LAG BOLTS 10 AND 11

VISE CARRIER

A

D

B

8

N

7

E

E

6-5/8"

LOCATE HOLES FROM FRONT VISE PLATE

3/4" DIA. HOLE

1-1/4" DIA. HOLE

FRONT VISE

VISE END GUIDE

6

END VISE

J

H

J

W

F

S

F

Q

G

9

9

10

10

J

J

H

1/2" DIA. HOLES FOR EXPANSION

9

T

2

11

P

3/8" DIA. x 2" DOWEL (2 PER JOINT)

3/4" x 45° BEVEL

G

10

Q

GLUE

WORKTOP END VIEW

D

3" (FAR SIDE)

1/2" FOR EXPANSION

3/4"

3/4"

6"

N

3/4"

6" (BOTH SIDES)

1/8" DEEP X 3/8" DIA. COUNTERBORE FOR SCREWS 5

1. 1" drywall screw
2. 1-1/4" drywall screw
3. 1-5/8" drywall screw
4. No. 10 x 1-1/2" panhead screw and washer
5. No. 10 x 2" panhead screw
6. No. 14 x 1-1/4" flathead screw
7. 1/4-20 x 1-1/2" bolt, nut, and washer
8. 1/4 x 1-1/2" lag screw and washer
9. 1/4 x 2-1/2" lag screw and washer
10. 1/4 x 3" lag screw and washer
11. 1/4 x 3-1/2" lag screw and washer

Assembly Plan Details

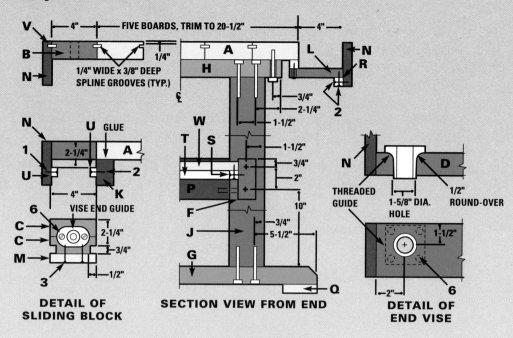

FIVE BOARDS, TRIM TO 20-1/2"

4" · 4"

V
B
N
1/4"
H
A
L
N
R

1/4" WIDE x 3/8" DEEP
SPLINE GROOVES (TYP.)

N
U GLUE
1
2-1/4"
A
U
2
K
6
C
C
M
3

VISE END GUIDE

**DETAIL OF
SLIDING BLOCK**

4"
2-1/4"
3/4"
1/2"

W
T
S
P
F
J
G
Q

3/4"
2-1/4"
1-1/2"
1-1/2"
3/4"
2"
10"
3/4"
5-1/2"

SECTION VIEW FROM END

N
THREADED
GUIDE
1-5/8" DIA.
HOLE
D
1/2"
ROUND-OVER

1-1/2"
2"
6

**DETAIL OF
END VISE**

Cutting List

Key	Pcs.	Size and Description
A	5	1-1/2" x 4-1/8" x 58" maple top*
B	1	1-1/2" x 4" x 43" maple (dog track)*
C	2	1-1/2" x 3-15/16" x 7" maple (end vise sliding block)
D	2	1-1/2" x 3-3/4" x 28-1/2" maple (top ends)
E	1	1-1/2" x 3-3/4" x 13-1/4" maple (front vise face)
F	2	1-1/2" x 3-1/2" x 34-1/4" maple (stretchers)
G	2	1-1/2" x 3-1/2" x 24" maple (bases)
H	2	1-1/2" x 3-1/2" x 17-1/2" maple (top supports)
J	4	1-1/2" x 3" x 30-3/4" maple (legs)
K	1	1-1/2" x 2-1/4" x 15" maple (end vise support)
L	1	3/4" x 4-3/4" x 57" maple (tool tray)
M	1	3/4" x 3-15/16" x 7" maple (sliding block bottom)
N	2	3/4" x 3-3/4" x 60" maple (top, front, and back)
P	2	3/4" x 3-1/2" x 8-1/2" maple (shelf ends)
Q	4	3/4" x 3-1/2" x 3" maple (feet)
R	2	3/4" x 3/4" x 57" maple (tool tray cleats)
S	2	3/4" x 3/4" x 34-1/4" maple (shelf cleats)
T	2	3/4" x 3/4" x 8-1/2" maple (shelf cleats)
U	2	1/2" x 23/32" x 15" maple (sliding block tracks)
V	7	1/4" x 11/16" x 59" maple (splines)*
W	1	3/4" x 10" x 34-1/4" maple plywood (shelf)

* Cut to finished sizes during assembly;
see the step-by-step instructions

Woodworking Bench Measurements

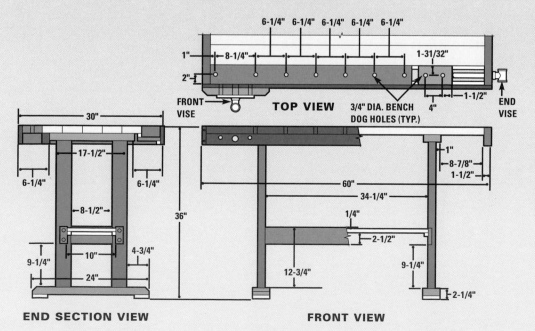

6-1/4" 6-1/4" 6-1/4" 6-1/4" 6-1/4"
1"
8-1/4"
1-31/32"
2"
1-1/2"
FRONT
VISE
TOP VIEW
3/4" DIA. BENCH
DOG HOLES (TYP.)
4"
END
VISE

30"
17-1/2"
6-1/4" 6-1/4"
8-1/2"
9-1/4"
10"
24"
4-3/4"
36"

1"
8-7/8"
1-1/2"
1/4"
2-1/2"
12-3/4"
9-1/4"
2-1/4"

60"
34-1/4"

END SECTION VIEW   **FRONT VIEW**

Building the Bench

Make all measurements with care and cut with accuracy. One of the best adages in woodworking is, "Measure twice and cut once." When you assemble the pieces, don't rush or cut corners; a little extra time in construction will ensure years of additional use of the bench. Here's what to do, step by step.

WORKING TIP

When assembling the top, it's easier to glue the pieces two at a time rather than all at once.

First Steps

▶ Cut all the pieces A through W to the dimensions given in the Cutting List on page 175.

▶ Rout the spline grooves (for pieces V) on the edges of the top pieces (A) *(below)*. Do not rout the outside edge of the board that faces the tool tray at the rear of the bench. Also: Do not rout the outside edge of the

Rout the spline grooves in the top pieces. The splines are used to align the boards when they're glued and clamped together. They also strengthen the joints.

front board that joins with the dog track (B) at this time. Glue, spline, and clamp the top pieces together.

▶ Cut the width of the glued-up top to 20-1/2 inches; you'll add the dog track (B) for the end vise to one side, and the tool tray to the other side later. Trim and square the vise end of the top *(below)*.

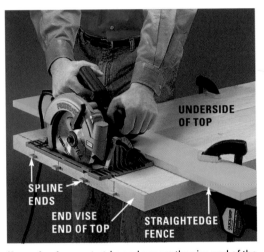

Use a circular saw to trim and square the vise end of the top. Guide the saw against a fence, and cut from the underside to eliminate tear-out on the top side.

Assemble the End Vise Dog Track

▶ Trim and square the vise end of the dog track (B). Lay out the bench dog holes in the dog track relative to the trimmed end, then drill the holes.

▶ Rout the spline groove in the front edge of the top and back edge of the dog track. Stop the spline groove 1/4 in. from the end so the joint is hidden when the pieces are assembled. Glue, spline, and clamp the dog track to the top. Make sure the vise end of the dog track is aligned 15 inches away from the trimmed end of the top.

▶ Trim and square the front vise side of the top and dog track (A and B), cutting it to its finished length of 57 inches at the same time.

▶ Glue and clamp the end vise support (K) and one of the tool tray cleats (R) in place on the underside of the top.

▶ Glue and clamp the two end vise sliding block pieces (C) together. When the glue is dry, lay out and drill the bench dog holes. Use a table saw to cut the rabbets on the bottom of the block.

Drill Assembly Screw Holes

▶ Lay out and drill the lag screw and assembly screw holes in pieces D, G, H, J, L, M, N, R, S, T, and U. The elongated lag screw holes in the top ends (D) let the top expand and contract without splitting.

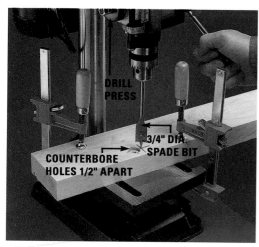

Drill counterbored holes for the elongated screw holes first. Chisel away the wood between the holes, then drill 1/4-in. holes and use a file to finish opening the elongated slots.

Begin Vise Assembly

▶ Lay out the hole for the end vise threaded guide in the outside of part D. Drill this hole with a 1-5/8 inch hole saw. Rout the inside edge of the hole with a 1/2-inch diameter round-over router bit. Hammer the threaded guide into its hole, drill screw pilot holes, and insert screws in the holes.

▶ Rout the remaining spline grooves in the ends of the assembled top, the inside faces of the top ends (D), the front edge of the dog track (B), and the inside face of the top front (N) as shown in the Woodworking Bench Assembly Plans (page 174).

▶ Align and screw, without gluing, the sliding block tracks (U) to the end vise support (K) and top front (N). Clamp the pieces together to keep them from shifting as you insert the screws.

▶ Glue, spline, align, and clamp the top front (N) to the dog track (B). Finish-sand the exposed rear insides of the top ends (D), the top of the tool tray (L), and the inside of the top back (N), and the tool tray side of the top (A and R). Spline and screw—do not glue—the top ends (D) to the ends of the top. Screw the tool tray cleat (R) to the top back. Screw the top front and top back (N) to the ends of the top ends (D). Screw the tool tray in place.

▶ Turn the top upside down and mark the holes for the front vise *(right top)*. Remove the carrier, mark the centers of the circles you just drew, and drill 1/16-inch holes from the back of the top front (N) through to the front. Now drill the holes for the vise rod, vise screw, and bolts through from the front. Also drill pilot holes for the vise carrier lag screws that go into the top.

▶ Align and clamp the front vise face (E) to the top front. Mark the vise rod and vise screw holes in the front vise face *(right bottom)*, then drill the holes.

Align the front vise carrier between the last two bench dog holes. Use it as a guide to mark the holes for the vise rods, vise screw, bolts, and lag screws.

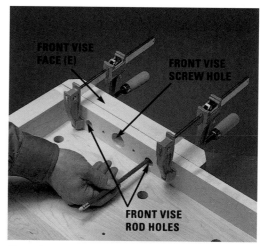

Clamp the front vise face in position and mark through the holes drilled in the top front for the vise rods and screw. Unclamp the vise face and drill the holes.

Assemble Legs and Shelf

▶ Lay out and drill the dowel pin holes in the legs (J) and ends of the shelf ends (P). Finish-sand the shelf ends and the insides of the legs, then glue, dowel, and clamp the pieces together. Glue and clamp the feet (Q) to the bottoms of the bases (G).

▶ Cut bevels on the ends of the bases and front vise face (E) using a table saw and miter gauge. Finish-sand, then assemble all the base pieces. Ease the sharp edges with sandpaper. Don't glue any of the screwed-together base joints. This allows you to easily repair the base in the future.

▶ Bolt and lag-screw the front vise carrier in place. Set the top on the base, align them, and lag screw them together. Slide the front vise face (E) over the front vise rods and the screw, and thread the front vise onto its carrier. Align the front vise face with the top front (N) and drill the lag screw pilot holes.

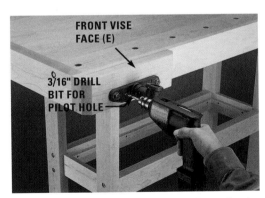

FRONT VISE FACE (E)

3/16" DRILL BIT FOR PILOT HOLE

Drill lag screw pilot holes in the front vise face using the vise to hold the pieces in alignment as you drill. Use the vise the same way later, when you insert the lag screws.

Complete End Vise Assembly

▶ Place the end vise sliding block on its tracks. Thread the end vise screw into its threaded guide. Place the vise end guide over the end of the vise screw and tighten the screw to hold the guide against the end of the sliding block. Now mark the screw hole locations *(below)*. Remove the sliding block, mount the vise end guide, and reset the sliding block on its tracks. Attach the sliding block bottom (M) *(below right)*. Then drill the two bench dog holes in the top of the sliding block.

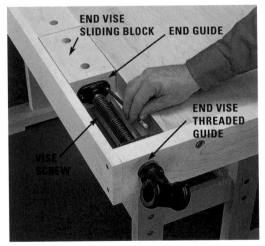

END VISE SLIDING BLOCK   END GUIDE

END VISE THREADED GUIDE

VISE SCREW

Mark screw holes for the vise end guide in the back end of the end vise sliding block. Use the vise screw to hold the pieces in place as you mark them.

Finish the Bench

▶ Drill the screw holes through the vise handle ends. Remove the end vise sliding block and all the rest of the vise hardware. Finish-sand the top and any other parts that haven't been done yet. Ease any remaining sharp edges.

▶ You just want to seal the maple, so apply only one coat of Danish oil to all the wood surfaces. Make sure to do the underside of the top too. You can apply more finish in the future if the maple starts to look really dry. Reassemble the vises and you're ready to start your next project.

VISE SCREW

SLIDING BLOCK TRACK

SLIDING BLOCK BOTTOM

Align and clamp the sliding block bottom to the underside of the sliding block. Drill pilot holes and drive the screws that fasten it in place.

Sawhorses

Sawhorses are workhorses for construction, painting, making a temporary table, and much more. Here are two versatile, easy-to-build designs.

Every workshop needs sawhorses, and the two kinds shown here are especially useful. Instructions for making them are on pages 180–181. The folding sawhorse shown in the photo is very strong, yet extremely lightweight. When you're done using it, just loosen two wing nuts, pivot two braces, and fold the legs so you can store it easily.

The adjustable sawhorse in the background of the photo is the ultimate design. The adjustable support can be raised as much as 20 inches to give a convenient working height, or to create a scaffold: simply lay 2x10 planks (not longer than 12 feet) across the tops of two sawhorses. Both ends of this sawhorse have notches to hold a standard entry door while you work on it. The built-up construction method makes this sawhorse sturdy but very lightweight.

Building a Folding Sawhorse

Study the plans below, gather the materials and tools, and go to work. The following instructions are for one sawhorse; to build two horses, cut two of each part.

▶ Cut three long top piece 1x2s to length.

▶ Cut the pivoting leg braces to size, drill the 5/16-inch hole, cut a 45° angle on one end, and round the other end. Attach the corner bracket to the angled end.

▶ Line up the three top piece 1x2s and the pivoting leg braces. Then cut the two 1x2 end pieces to size and attach to the three top pieces with drywall screws.

▶ Cut the 1x4 top to size and attach with drywall screws.

▶ Cut and attach the 2x2 legs with carriage bolts. Note the 20° angle at the top end where the bolt goes through.

▶ Drill the holes for the carriage bolts and bolt on the pivoting leg braces.

▶ Hold each 2x2 leg cross brace in position against the legs, mark the angles, then cut them, lapping the ends halfway.

▶ Hold the 2x2 leg cross braces in position again, rotate each pivoting leg brace into position, and mark and drill 3/16-inch holes for the brace bracket.

▶ Attach the fixed braces to the legs, then attach the pivoting braces.

Folding Sawhorse Assembly Plans

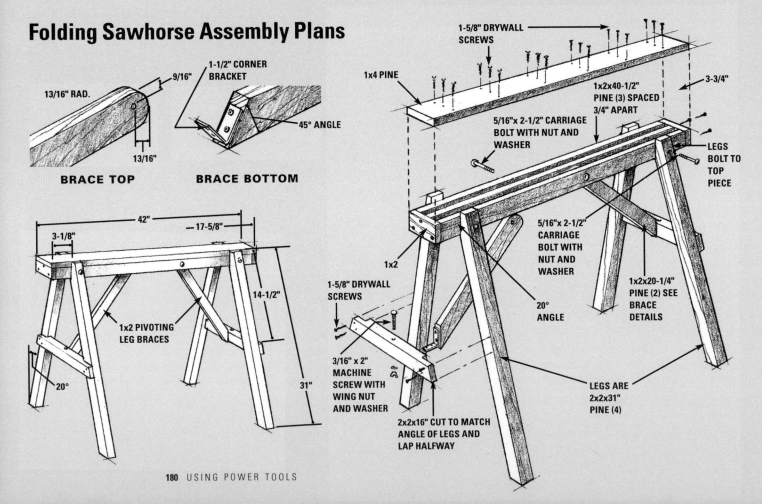

13/16" RAD.
9/16"
1-1/2" CORNER BRACKET
13/16"
BRACE TOP
45° ANGLE
BRACE BOTTOM

1-5/8" DRYWALL SCREWS
1x4 PINE
1x2x40-1/2" PINE (3) SPACED 3/4" APART
3-3/4"
5/16"x 2-1/2" CARRIAGE BOLT WITH NUT AND WASHER
LEGS BOLT TO TOP PIECE

42"
3-1/8"
17-5/8"
14-1/2"
1x2 PIVOTING LEG BRACES
20°
31"
1x2
1-5/8" DRYWALL SCREWS
3/16" x 2" MACHINE SCREW WITH WING NUT AND WASHER
2x2x16" CUT TO MATCH ANGLE OF LEGS AND LAP HALFWAY
5/16"x 2-1/2" CARRIAGE BOLT WITH NUT AND WASHER
20° ANGLE
1x2x20-1/4" PINE (2) SEE BRACE DETAILS
LEGS ARE 2x2x31" PINE (4)

Materials List

To build two sawhorses:

27 linear ft. of 2x2 pine

30 linear ft. of 1x2 pine

7 linear ft. of 1x4 pine

Four 1-1/2 in. corner braces (steel)

Four 3/16 x 2-in. machine screws and wing nuts

Twelve 5/16 x 2-1/2 in. carriage bolts and nuts

1-1/4 in. and 1-5/8 in. drywall screws

Building an Adjustable Sawhorse

This sawhorse is so versatile you may well want more than two for a project such as remodeling an entire room. One pair can be used to support materials for work, another pair to provide an adjustable worktable, and a third pair as a scaffold. The directions here are for one sawhorse.

▶ Cut and assemble the 2x4 lumber for the adjustable support. The notches for the vertical supports are 3/4 inch deep; cut them by making repeat cuts with a circular saw.

▶ Tack-nail a top 2x2 to the edge of a worktable, then nail a 2x4 alongside it to hold it in place. Measure 1/2 inch in from the edge of the 2x2, draw a line, then cut a 20° bevel with a circular saw (adjust the saw's sole plate), following this line. Cut two pieces this way.

▶ Rip a 2x4 in half to get the 1-5/8 inch center pieces.

▶ Lay the parts from the preceding two steps on a flat surface, position the adjustable support to align them, then assemble the top portion with 2-1/2 inch drywall screws. Note that the 2x2s with the 20° cut are oriented wide side down.

▶ Cut the 1x4 legs and attach.

▶ Cut the 1x4 leg braces and attach.

▶ Cut the 1/2-inch plywood to match each end and attach.

▶ Cut the lower 2x2 guides to length and attach to the plywood ends. Do not omit these; they add rigidity as well as guide the adjustable support.

▶ Slide the adjustable support into place. Add short 1x2 or scrap lumber guides across the 2x2 guides, on the outsides of the adjustable support's two legs.

▶ Finally, mark and drill a series of centered 1/2-inch holes through the support legs for 3/8-inch bolts. Use wing nuts on the bolts so they can't work out of the holes as you use the sawhorse.

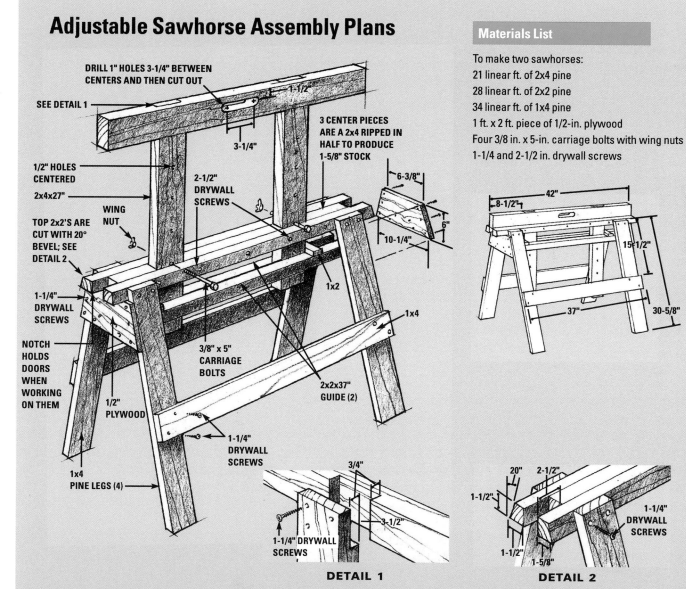

Adjustable Sawhorse Assembly Plans

DRILL 1" HOLES 3-1/4" BETWEEN CENTERS AND THEN CUT OUT

SEE DETAIL 1

1-1/2"

3-1/4"

1/2" HOLES CENTERED

2x4x27"

WING NUT

TOP 2x2'S ARE CUT WITH 20° BEVEL; SEE DETAIL 2

2-1/2" DRYWALL SCREWS

3 CENTER PIECES ARE A 2x4 RIPPED IN HALF TO PRODUCE 1-5/8" STOCK

6-3/8"

6"

10-1/4"

1x2

1-1/4" DRYWALL SCREWS

NOTCH HOLDS DOORS WHEN WORKING ON THEM

1/2" PLYWOOD

3/8" x 5" CARRIAGE BOLTS

2x2x37" GUIDE (2)

1x4

1-1/4" DRYWALL SCREWS

1x4 PINE LEGS (4)

Materials List

To make two sawhorses:
21 linear ft. of 2x4 pine
28 linear ft. of 2x2 pine
34 linear ft. of 1x4 pine
1 ft. x 2 ft. piece of 1/2-in. plywood
Four 3/8 in. x 5-in. carriage bolts with wing nuts
1-1/4 and 2-1/2 in. drywall screws

8-1/2"   42"

15-1/2"

37"   30-5/8"

DETAIL 1

3/4"

1-1/4" DRYWALL SCREWS

3-1/2"

DETAIL 2

20"   2-1/2"

1-1/2"

1-1/4" DRYWALL SCREWS

1-1/2"

1-5/8"

Fold-up Workbench

Quick and easy to build, this clever workbench gives you both work surface and tool storage. It's the ultimate space saver.

You may be one of the majority of do-it-yourselfers who don't need a professional woodworking bench (see pages 172–178) but do need a place to work on occasional projects and to store tools. If so, this fold-up/fold-out workbench may be just what you need, especially if you work where space is limited and must be shared, as in a garage, basement, or utility room.

Construction is straightforward and simple—anyone can build this workbench, even if they've never built anything before. The bench is essentially a box with a 2x2 frame that attaches to wall studs, and a drop-down front with hinged legs.

The only tools necessary are a saw and a drill. All lumber is inexpensive and standard sizes, and you should be able to buy both the perforated hardboard (Peg-Board) and plywood or particleboard bench top already cut to the correct size. All hardware listed is readily available and inexpensive.

The total estimated cost, if you have to buy everything shown, will be about $60–$75. The entire project should take only three to four hours. Just follow the plans and step-by-step instructions on the opposite page.

Building the Fold-up Workbench

Gather the materials in the list at right. For lumber, the total linear length listed includes an allowance for some waste when cutting. Proceed as follows:

▶ Build the frame from 1x2s and the sheet of Peg-Board. Estimate how high you want the workbench surface to be and add about 22 inches to that figure. Mount the frame with its top at that distance from the floor, using 3-inch drywall screws.

▶ Build the box unit from 1x10s as shown, using drywall screws. It fits over the wall frame. Mount it to the frame with screws.

▶ Assemble the workbench frame (the drop-down box front) from three 1x4s using 1-1/4 inch drywall screws. Then attach the plywood bench top.

▶ Cut two legs to the working height you estimated in Step 1. Then attach the two 2x4 hinge brace pieces to the workbench. They are on the outside of the bench top when it is folded up. Use one T-hinge per leg, with the strap portion on the leg and the "T" on the hinge brace.

▶ Position the workbench against the box unit assembled in Step 2, square things up, and attach it to the box with T-hinges. The long portion of the T-hinge goes on the box frame. Check to see that everything works freely, without binding.

▶ Shelves for the box are optional and can be positioned to best suit your needs. The plans show two shelf areas, as well as an open pegboard for hooks. To make a shelf easily adjustable, use four large screw eyes as shelf supports.

Fold-up Workbench Assembly Plans

Materials List

Wall Frame
12 linear ft. of 1x2 pine
2-ft. x 4-ft. piece of 1/8-in. Peg-Board

Box Frame
12 linear ft. of 1x12 pine

Bench Top Frame and Worktop
16 linear ft. of 1x4 pine for the bench top frame and hinge bracing
2-ft. x 4-ft. piece of 1/2-in.-thick plywood or particleboard, for the workbench top

Folding Legs
8 linear ft. of 2x4 lumber cut to the length that suits you best as determined in Step 1

Inside Shelving (optional)
6 linear ft. of 1x8 pine

Hardware
1-1/4 in. drywall screws
Four 3-in. drywall screws
Four 6-in. T-hinges
1/4-in. x 1-in. lag bolts with 1/4-in. washers
Swiveling safety hasp to secure/lock workbench in closed position
Right- and left-hand folding braces for the legs

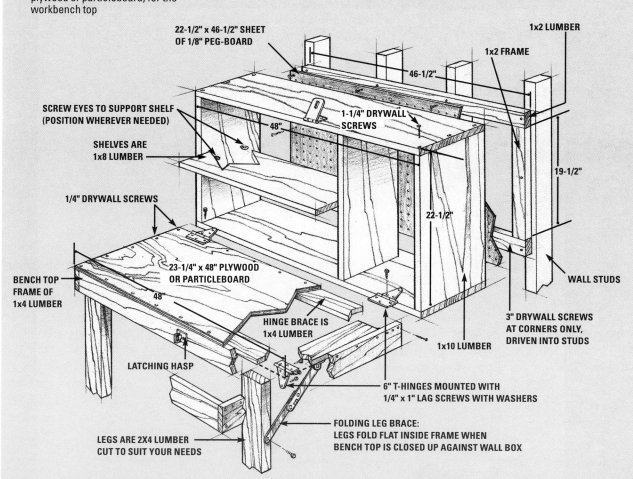

Workshop Improvements

The place where you work can affect the results you get as much as the tools you use. Here are ideas to make your workshop a better, easier, and safer place to work.

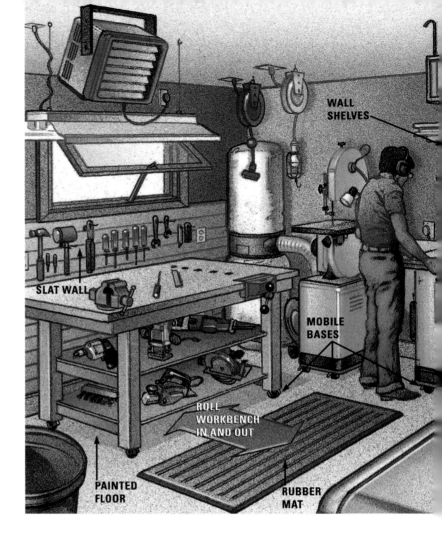

WALL SHELVES

SLAT WALL

MOBILE BASES

ROLL WORKBENCH IN AND OUT

PAINTED FLOOR

RUBBER MAT

Almost all home workshops are located in the garage or basement, where they either interfere with the primary use of the area, or vice versa. That doesn't have to be the case. There are several steps you can take to make your workshop easy and convenient to work in alongside your car, yard equipment, laundry, or recreation room.

The following pages explain how to achieve this peaceful coexistence by making improvements in four aspects of your workshop—organization, floors, heat and air, and light and power. You probably won't want or need to use all the ideas discussed, but using just two or three will make your shop a more comfortable, more pleasant place to work.

Workshop Organization

The old adage "A place for everything…" is especially appropriate for a workshop that shares space in a garage or basement—your tools have to be kept out of the way for their own protection and so they don't interfere with other activities. Besides, you can work more efficiently when you know where your tools and materials are. Here are some of the organizational ideas illustrated on the opposite page.

▶ Put up shelves to store both tools and materials. Hang them from the walls so that you have room for floor-standing equipment underneath. Make shelves with triangular supports screwed to wall studs, or use standard-and-bracket systems sold at home centers. To prevent small items from falling onto a work surface or tool below, fasten shelf planks together, cover them with 1/8-inch hardboard, or use plywood. Space brackets no more than 32 inches apart to hold long pieces of lumber, to avoid sagging and warping during storage.

▶ Use grooved "slat wall" panels to hang small tools on the wall. A slat wall is used for displays in shoe stores and other shops. You can often pick one up free when stores are remodeling or buy it from specialty lumberyards in 4 x 8-foot sheets. You can hang hooks, get shelving brackets that fit into the horizontal grooves, or use 1/4-inch Peg-Board hardware, which fits neatly between the slats. An inexpensive alternative to the slat wall is sheets of Peg-Board.

▶ Put stationary tools like table saws, band saws, and radial arm saws on mobile bases. These low-slung dollies fit under the bases of heavy tools to help you move them easily into working position or back to their storage spots when a job is over. They have locking wheels for stability and are made in several sizes. Your best source is a stationary tool retailer or a mail order tool supply company.

▶ Make your workbench mobile by putting heavy-duty locking casters under the legs. That way you can move the bench away from the wall to work on all sides, then stow it again without difficulty.

Workshop Floors

The floor of your shop is as much a work surface as the top of the workbench or the table on a stationary tool. Here are two ways to improve it.

▶ Make the floor a light color to reflect light for better working vision and to help you spot small items that roll off the workbench. And make the floor surface smooth for easy cleaning. Cover a wooden floor with plywood or underlayment panels and light-colored resilient sheet flooring or tiles. Paint a concrete floor white or another light color. To do the job right, scrub the floor with a nonsudsing cleaner like TSP-90 or Soilax, and wash it with a diluted muriatic acid solution before rolling on the paint. Use a paint specifically intended for concrete, and follow any special instructions on the label.

▶ Put floor mats in work areas. Hours of standing on a hard floor can leave you with aching legs. Floor mats make a big difference at the end of a long work session. Soft rubber mats about 3/8 inch thick are available in many sizes at most home centers. Get one for each area where you spend a lot of time standing.

Roll-down Workshop Walls

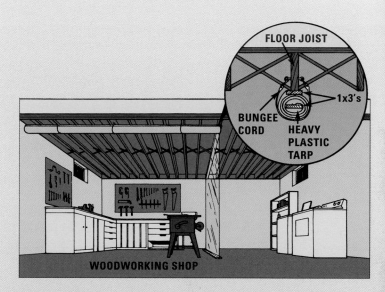

A major problem with a workshop in a garage or basement is that sawdust, wood chips, and other shop debris infiltrate everywhere. Putting up partitions restricts the size of the individual areas and flexible use of the overall space. Installing a high-efficiency dust collector (page 186) may be impossible for reasons of space or cost. In any case, here's a simple way to wall off a work area.

Buy large plastic tarps—8 x 16 ft. is a standard size; they are usually blue in color. Also, for each tarp buy two lengths of 1x3, two elastic shock or bungee cords, and four screw eyes.

Staple a 1x3 to each long edge of a tarp and screw one 1x3 to the ceiling. Install screw eyes on either side near each end. Roll up the tarp around the bottom 1x3 and suspend it by hooking bungee cords into the screw eyes. Now you have roll-down walls for when you sand, saw, or do other dusty work, and roll-up walls when you need a larger work area.

Workshop Heat and Air

A comfortable working temperature and clean, dustfree air are two important factors in making a better workplace. Consider the following improvements for your workshop, illustrated here:

▶ Install insulation in a garage workshop if you live in a cold climate; it will be money well spent. You can't keep your mind on working safely when you are cold and uncomfortable. Insulate the walls and ceiling throughout the garage, not just in the workshop area, with fiberglass batts or rolls. Put up a vapor barrier of plastic, then finish with drywall or paneling to protect the insulation and keep out dust.

▶ Use a heater for comfort in cold weather, and for overnight gluing projects or finishes that must dry at a moderate temperature for several hours. Install an electric heater with a built-in thermostat and a switch to shut it off when the shop is unoccupied. An electric heater is much safer to use than a gas model, although it is more expensive to operate. The flame of a gas heater is a potential danger in sawdust-laden air, and especially in a garage, where there may also be oil and gasoline fumes.

▶ Install a dehumidifier if the climate is humid during part of the year, especially if you have a basement workshop. Removing moisture from the air will provide working comfort, and will help protect tools and hardware from rust.

▶ Put in a dust collector. Sawdust on the floor is unsafe, and dust floating in the air is unhealthy to breathe. A collector like the model shown can remove up to 90 percent of the dust in a shop right from the source. With a little ingenuity and some help from tool suppliers, you can outfit almost any woodworking tool with a dust collection system. Get a dust collector with wheels that you can move from tool to tool, along with some hoses and hoods to fit your stationary power tools.

▶ Install an overhead air filter to remove whatever flying sawdust a dust collector doesn't get. This kind of unit has an exhaust motor that pulls in air from the shop, filters it, and returns it to the shop. Don't run a dust collector or air filter if you're using solvent-based finishes in the shop. They can be explosive if fumes collect in the area. Ventilate the shop with an open window or door when you use such finishes.

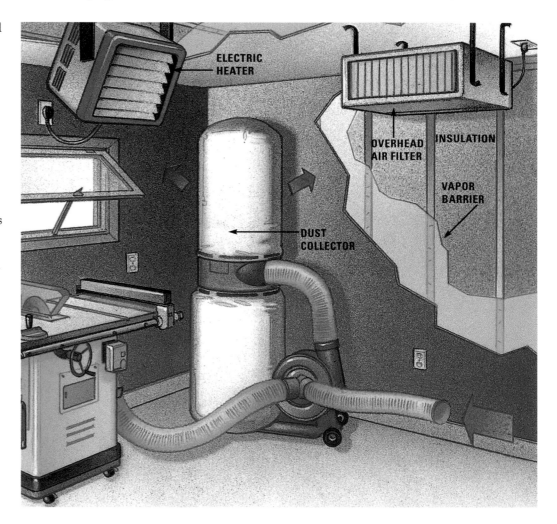

ELECTRIC HEATER

OVERHEAD AIR FILTER

INSULATION

VAPOR BARRIER

DUST COLLECTOR

Workshop Light and Power

A single, one-bulb light fixture hanging in the middle of a garage or basement area may keep you from bumping into things, but it is hardly adequate for doing any work. You need general lighting for the shop, and task lighting for individual tools and work areas. You also need enough outlets of proper capacity to run your power tools safely.

▶ Use fluorescent light fixtures to light the shop. They spread more illumination over a larger area than a plain incandescent bulb hanging in the middle of the shop. Fluorescent work lights are available at home centers. Get several and position one or more over the area where you work most often.

▶ Provide task lighting directly where you need it for a particular job. A great specific-area fixture is a magnetic base lamp that sticks right to a stationary tool, like the one on the band saw at the right. You can also get the same type of light in a clamp-on style for nonferrous surfaces.

▶ Get portable task lighting with a reel cord lamp, which can be pulled out up to 50 feet to throw light into nooks and crannies. It's also handy when you need to stick a light under the hood of the car. A quick tug on the cord, and it winds up and out of the way.

▶ Consider beefing up the power supply to your shop. Some large stationary tools like table saws and radial arm saws have motors that run on 240 volts instead of the regular 120 household voltage. General-purpose, 120-volt receptacles in a garage or basement require GFI (ground fault interrupt) protection while 240-volt receptacles do not. You should add a GFI-protected 120-volt circuit for extra receptacles where you need them, so you won't have extension cords wrapping around your ankles. You may also need a separate 240-volt line for an electric heater. If you're not experienced in electrical work, don't take chances. Call a licensed electrician to do the work or guide you through the project.

▶ Install an overhead reel extension cord above a workbench to get the cord for hand power tools up and out of the way. You can also use it to get power to the middle of the shop where no fixed receptacles are located. Get a reel extension cord at hardware stores and home centers.

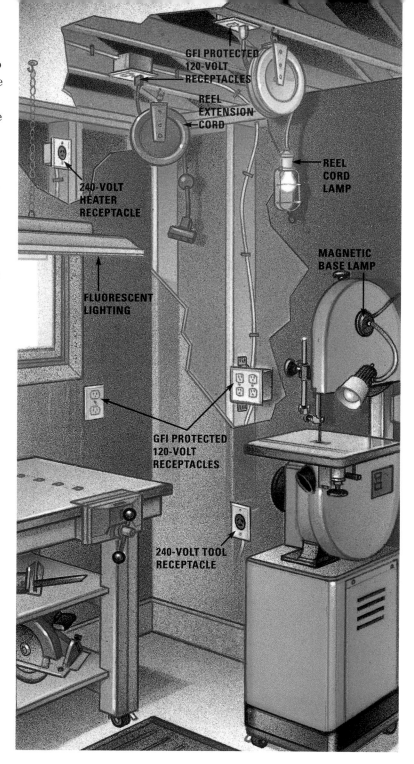

GFI PROTECTED 120-VOLT RECEPTACLES

REEL EXTENSION CORD

REEL CORD LAMP

240-VOLT HEATER RECEPTACLE

MAGNETIC BASE LAMP

FLUORESCENT LIGHTING

GFI PROTECTED 120-VOLT RECEPTACLES

240-VOLT TOOL RECEPTACLE

Acknowledgments:

Ron Chamberlain, Ken Collier, John Emmons, Bill Faber, David Farr, Hope Fay, Roxie Filipkowski, Jon Frost, M. Bernadette Goering, Barb Herrmann, Al Hildenbrand, Shelley Jacobsen, Duane Johnson, Bruce Kieffer, Bob Kinghorn, Mike Krivit, Phil Leisenheimer, Gerry Lofland, Craig Lossing, Done Mannes, Bill O'Connell, Doug Oudekerk, Deborah Palmen, Don Prestly, Dave Radtke, Art Rooze, Mike Smith, Dan Stoffel, Eugene Thompson, Mark Thompson, Bob Ungar, Alice Wagner, Bruce Wiebe, Gregg Weigand, Mac Wentz, Michaela Wentz, Gordy Wilkinson, Marcia Williston, Donna Wyttenbach, Bill Zuehlke.

This book was produced by Roundtable Press, Inc.,
for the Reader's Digest Association
in cooperation with *The Family Handyman* magazine.

If you have any questions or comments, please feel free to write us at:

The Family Handyman
7900 International Drive
Suite 950
Minneapolis, MN 55425

Measuring the Metric Way

for Using PowerTools

Use these guides and tables to convert between English and metric measuring systems.

Fasteners

Nails are sold by penny size or penny weight (expressed by the letter d).
Length is designated by the penny size. Some common lengths are:

2d	25 mm/1 in.
6d	51 mm/2 in.
10d	76 mm/3 in.
20d	102 mm/4 in.
40d	127 mm/5 in.
60d	152 mm/6 in.

Below are metric and imperial equivalents of some common bolts:

10 mm	⅜ in.
12 mm	½ in.
16 mm	⅝ in.
20 mm	¾ in.
25 mm	1 in.
50 mm	2 in.
65 mm	2½ in.
70 mm	2¾ in.

Calculating Concrete Requirements

Multiply length by width to get the slab area in square meters. Then read across, under whichever of three thicknesses you prefer, to see how many cubic meters of concrete you will need.

Area in Square Meters (m²)	Thickness in Millimeters		
(length x width)	100	130	150
	Volume in Cubic Meters (m³)		
5	0.50	0.65	0.75
10	1.00	1.30	1.50
20	2.00	2.60	3.00
30	3.00	3.90	4.50
40	4.00	5.20	6.00
50	5.00	6.50	7.50

If a greater volume of concrete is required, multiply by the
appropriate number. To lay a 100-millimeter thick patio in an area
6 meters wide and 10 meters long, for example, estimate as follows:
6 meters x 10 meters = 60 meters square = area.
Using the chart above, simply double the concrete quantity for
a 30-meter square, 100-millimeter thick slab (2 x 3 m3 = 6 m3)
or add the quantities for 10 m2 and 50 m2 (1 m3 + 5 m3 = 6 m3).